Bodies of Thought

Bodies of Thought

Embodiment, Identity and Modernity

Ian Burkitt

SAGE Publications
London • Thousand Oaks • New Delhi

© Ian Burkitt 1999

First published 1999

SAGE Publications Ltd
6 Bonhill Street
London EC2A 4PU

SAGE Publications Inc.
2455 Teller Road
Thousand Oaks, California 91320

SAGE Publications India Pvt Ltd
32, M-Block Market
Greater Kailash – I
New Delhi 110 048

British Library Cataloguing in Publication data

A catalogue record for this book is available from
the British Library

ISBN 0 8039 8848 6
ISBN 0 8039 8849 4 (pbk)

**Library of Congress catalog card number
99–073803**

Typeset by Photoprint, Torquay, Devon
Printed in Great Britain by The Cromwell Press Ltd,
Trowbridge, Wiltshire

For Kathleen, Caroline and Marjorie

Contents

Acknowledgements

I would like to thank all those who have provided help and inspiration during the long gestation of this book. A number of friends and colleagues commented on sections of the manuscript in its various drafts or, in some cases, on all of it. I have benefited from the advice and encouragement of Brian Burkitt, Richard Cleminson, Kenneth J. Gergen, Ercument Gundogdu, Liz Harlow, Jennifer Mackenzie, Joan Pujol and Chris Shilling. A joint research project with Charles Husband, Jenny Mackenzie and Alison Torn at Bradford University rekindled my enthusiasm to finish the book, and I thank them for the many interesting discussions on related topics. Students in a Capstone seminar at Swarthmore College, Pennsylvania, discussed an early paper outlining my ideas for the book and passed comments that made me rethink aspects of my approach to embodiment. Ken and Mary Gergen were warm and friendly hosts during my short stay there. Alan Scott, Arvick Baghramian and Brian and Beryl Burkitt listened to my tales of woe about writer's block and helped more than they probably know. Karen Phillips, my editor at Sage, has shown great patience and, as always, given helpful advice and encouragement. Despite such support, I bear full responsibility for what is written in this book and thus for any failings within it.

A version of Chapter 6 was first published as 'Social relationships and emotions', in *Sociology*, vol. 31, no. 1 (1997), pp. 37–55, and I thank the editors for their kind permission to reprint it here. In different places throughout the book I have drawn on parts of a published article, 'Bodies of knowledge: beyond Cartesian views of persons, selves and mind', in *Journal for the Theory of Social Behaviour*, vol. 28, no. 1 (1998), pp. 63–82.

Introduction

And if the body were not the soul, what is the soul?

Walt Whitman, *I Sing the Body Electric*

It is often thought today that the human person, the nucleus of the self which is considered to be the soul, is something that can be regarded as separate from the body. When we think of what composes the self we tend to feel as though we are made of a non-fleshy essence which is somehow distinct from our bodily casing, as in the old saying that the body is the temple of the soul. The seventeenth-century French philosopher, René Descartes was so certain that his own essence as a person was distinct from his physical presence as a body that he claimed he was what he was despite his body and could still exist without it. Such certainty is radically challenged in the short extract from Walt Whitman's poem, *I Sing the Body Electric*, quoted above. Whitman asks another question: if we subtract the body from the person (or soul) then what is left? If the body is not the person, then what is a person?

While it is not my argument in this book that the person can be reduced to his or her body, I nevertheless claim that it would be impossible to contemplate being a person without one's body. How could we ever have become, or how could we remain, a person with our own sense of identity if we were not a bodily presence capable of movement and sound, able to attract the attention of others who could then focus upon us as a distinct being made of flesh and blood? The answer, surely, is that we couldn't. The person is centred on his or her body. While this may seem like a blindingly obvious thing to say, the body has until recently been an almost invisible object for the social and psychological sciences, which have preferred on the whole to concentrate upon the realm of rational action and the mind rather than upon the body. It was only through the work of Bryan Turner (1984, 1992) that the issue of the body began to be recognized in mainstream social science. Perhaps the body has been excluded from the social sciences for so long because it tended to be thought of as unruly and unpredictable, the seat of the emotions and passions, things which cannot be calculated or represented in any regular way. Thus a study could never be made of the body, only of the more regular and lawful processes of the mind and the activities which it inspires. I disagree with this view and hope to present the case here that it would be impossible for us to think without our bodies. Rather than suggesting we can neatly divide the mind from the body, it is my view that we are bodies of thought, a view which I will expound throughout this book.

At the same time, though, it is impossible to reduce us as persons purely to our bodily presence. It is clear that we can think of ourselves – and regularly do so – as distinct from our bodies, as in the case of the anorexic who still thinks of herself or himself as fat when he or she only weighs five stones. Body and self-image may not correspond to the actual appearance of the embodied person. For me, such anomalies occur because our body image, our sense of being a person, is partly a symbolic construction which never corresponds exactly to the physical body. However, as Turner (1992) pointed out, it is also common for individuals who have undergone surgery which has radically altered their physical features also to feel that their self-image has changed as well. There is obviously a complex process going on around the body, in which the body itself can create a symbolic image and under-standing of itself, yet changes in the body can also radically alter its symbol-ization. The way in which we sense our body in the world seems to be just as important in creating meaning as cultural meaning is itself in shaping the image of our body. In this sense I am arguing here for a multi-dimensional approach to the body and the person which conceives of human beings as complexes composed of both the material and the symbolic. In fact, I argue more generally that all human life must be seen in this way rather than as divided between the material and the representational.

Because of these views I have some differences with approaches in the social sciences that are generally grouped under the banner of 'social con-structionism'. This is because one of the things that tends to unite these approaches is their adherence to a linguistic or discursive understanding of the construction of self and body. All we can speak of and locate is within the boundaries of the discourse we are using, and this, in turn, constructs the objects and essences – the 'real' things and identities – that we take to be the pregiven factors which make up our world. I am unhappy with discursive constructionism because it has difficulties in dealing with human embodi-ment and also, therefore, with the multi-dimensional way in which we experience reality. For me, we are not just located in the world symbolically; nor do we experience reality purely through the text: instead, we are located in relations that transform the natural and social worlds in which we live. It is within networks of interdependence that we can affect the actions of other people and also change the face of reality.

This means that embodied persons are not simply constructs, but are *productive bodies* capable of activities that change the nature of their lives. Through acquiring various capacities it is possible for human actors to alter dramatically their natural habitats and also change their social scenarios. Humans are also *communicative bodies* with the power to symbolize through gestures, metaphors and speech. We are locked in relations of communica-tion with one another and, through the discourses or speech genres of our culture, give expression to the conditions of our lives. As with the power of production, communication can bring about change and can allow people to challenge the prevailing ideas of their day. In both these ways all individuals become *powerful bodies*, with abilities and capacities that can radically alter the conditions of life. We are also *thinking bodies* because the powers of agency and communication involve thinking, something that does not simply occur 'inside' the body, for it is inseparable from social activity and speech. However, relations of power – which I define in subsequent chapters – involve more than the infusion of human bodies with various powers; they also constitute attempts to restrain and curtail bodily powers through regulations around the formation and exercise of capacities and agency. Relations of power also extend into production and communication (in fact, these three forms of relations must not be viewed as separate and discrete), silencing certain voices, directing the forces of production and attempting to censor or at least to direct thought.

In the light of these considerations, I hope the metaphor of the productive body will be an enabling one, presenting our corporeal presence as not just trapped within relations of power but as possessing the capacities to change them. I am not, then, in this work, recreating the notion of a pre-social, irrational, emotional body that must be contained and disciplined by a rational and orderly society. Instead, the body and the emotions are seen as having pattern and form because they are part of social relations. These relations, which re-form the body, may not correspond to the prevailing relations of power in society more generally, in which case the body and its habits may appear opposed to the social order. Yet this does not mean that it is irrational or pre-social. The body has been formed over much longer time-scales than those of contemporary society, while it is also part of local relationships and associations, which may cause friction between the body and the attempts of the wider society to regulate it. In this clash, powerful and dominant social forces do not always win.

I am, then, interested in the evolution of the human body but understand this to be always interrelated with socio-historical relations. The social and the biological are understood to be inseparable processes in which social relations have selected certain attributes in human beings that then become ingrained through biological inheritance. However, despite these overlapping and reciprocal processes, recent history and philosophy in the Western world have tended to emphasize dualism, such as between the body and the mind, the material and the insubstantial, the emotional and the rational. Yet it is my view that we do not operate as dualistic beings in everyday life and this means that other forces are coming to the fore which are currently beginning to unravel such dualisms. All these themes are threaded through the book in the following way.

In Chapter 1, I engage in a prolegomenon to bodies of thought, in which I develop a number of introductory thoughts and themes that frame my general argument throughout the book. Here, I outline the Cartesian view of mind, body, knowledge and objects, developing a critique of this position. In place of the Cartesian dualistic vision, I begin to form a notion of the thinking body located in time and space, particularly in the overlapping time dimensions of bio-history, socio-history and everyday life. Threaded through this are the concepts of the productive body, the communicative body and the powerful body, located in relations that transform reality, relations of communication and relations of power. I conclude the chapter by focusing on what I believe to be the multi-dimensional nature of human experience, created by an active body located in various levels of time and space, as well as in the symbolic dimension.

Having set the scene of this study in the prolegomenon, Chapter 2 concentrates on the development of the embodied mind and forms of knowledge in bio-history. Using the work of Bateson and Leontyev, the central concept developed is of life as a relation within the unit of survival, which is the ecological system itself. The thinking body evolves within the spaces and times of its various ecological niches as it is placed in relations of transformation, communication and power. I will argue that central to the formation of the thinking body is the invention and use of artifacts by human groups, an invention which means that the unit for the transmission of culture is no longer the gene, but the artifact developed and used to transform nature. Artifacts are prosthetic extensions of the body and their use makes possible new ways of knowing the world, along with re-formed bodies with new capacities. The general conclusion of the chapter is that mind is immanent in the ecology of human beings as they survive in and develop the means to transform their environment. The mind cannot be separated from the body or from the ecology in which we are corporeally embedded. Alongside this general theme, the chapter also contains an enquiry into the evolution of relations of power and the various attempts to centre theories of power in the human body.

Chapter 3 picks up the theme of relations of power as they have developed in the West since the sixteenth century, and how such relations have divided human beings between experiences of the body and those which are felt to centre on a disembodied mind. I begin with the example of the 'grotesque body', which was an experience available to the people of the Middle Ages of the body as an open system related to all the people and things in its world. The period that followed ushered in the experience of the closed body, which is one that conceals as much as it reveals. This experience of the closed body emerged along with changing power relations in the West, with the collapse of the old religious authorities and the rise of secular powers and normative forms of regulation. However, I disagree with Foucault, for whom the normative forms of regulation were located mainly in institutions that work to reform the body through practices organized by various discourses. For me, this misses the important realm of the everyday relations of power, in which individuals regulate one another's behaviour within their interactions. It is here, in the daily forms of normative control, that the emergence of the closed body is to be located, as much as in the institutional practices of correction and reformation. Centred on this closed body, sealed off from others and from 'external' nature, there emerge the dualisms of the modern world: the division between mind and body, self and others, the subject and the object. The self is increasingly related, in truly Cartesian fashion, to 'cognitive apprehension' (Mellor and Shilling, 1997), centred on mental processes and also on vision, while the other bodily senses are called into doubt. However, I also suggest that modernity opens up spaces in which people can resist normative controls, and that the relations between humans are not just relations of power but also relations of communication and relations which transform the real. It is in this nexus that we become embodied beings, and at the end of the chapter I claim that we could not be persons or selves without bodies, even though personhood cannot be reduced to the body.

Some of the current critiques of Cartesian dualism are considered in Chapter 4, especially the challenge located in social constructionism and the way in which it contrasts itself with the residual rationalism to be found in realism. However, in my view, while social constructionism is successful in challenging the historical constructs of the isolated, rational cogito, and in exposing its universal ambitions, it is less successful when it analyses the relation between the human and the non-human and the relations that transform the real. Because constructionism has so firmly located itself in the 'linguistic turn' of the social sciences, there is a tendency towards discursive reductionism and for the continuation of a form of Cartesian doubt in terms of the gap between our discursive constructs and materiality. In creating an alternative to discursive reductionism, I pursue the multi-dimensional approach and argue that knowledge is located primarily in the experiences of the active body, which is part of time and space, such experiences becoming extended and elaborated in the symbolic dimension. Thus, the symbolic/ artifactual realm and the bodily/material domain are always interwoven as dimensions of experience, which constantly inform one another in a two-way process that cannot be flattened out on to a single plane.

Many of these themes are continued in my consideration of feminist theories of the body in Chapter 5, reflecting how such theorizing sought to tackle the divisions of Cartesianism, while simultaneously pointing out the gendered nature of this division. It is men who have traditionally been associated with the 'mind', and the rational, disembodied element of modern forms of power and government. Women have been relegated to the irrational and the emotional; such a perception of femininity is one element in the establishment and preservation of male domination. I then consider some feminists who have challenged this domination both in theory and in practice, seeking in the process to reconsider issues of embodiment. While I critique the work of constructionist thinkers, such as Judith Butler, for their almost total concentration on the linguistic sphere, there is much in the work of Moira Gatens, Emily Martin and Iris Marion Young to support the thesis of this book. In general, the feminist writings I use to advance the argument are those which suggest that the body cannot be understood simply as the materialization of prior discursive and normative controls, but that it is the source of our collective experiences and a site for opposition to established power relations and ideological hegemonies. This does not place the female body outside culture as the primitive source of resistance to modern forms of power; instead, the daily, embodied associations can become sites of resistance to dominant power relations as well as being channels for their operation. The gendered body, then, is at the centre of material and cultural contestations.

Issues relating to the body within feminism also raise the topic of emotions for the social sciences, which have previously ignored the affects, as they were understood to be intimately connected with the body – and therefore the biological – as opposed to the cognitive and cultural. Even today, there are claims that the emotions can only be understood as linguistic or cognitive categories, for we cannot identify bodily feelings as particular emotions unless we have a name or a category for them. In Chapter 6 I try to get away from the notion of emotions as bodily processes identified by a separate cognitive mechanism, and also from the purely discursive view of emotions as linguistically constructed. Again, I wish to combine the constructed and the experiential components of emotions, suggesting that this can best be done by taking a relational view of the emotions: that is, understanding them as aspects of the relations between humans and between humans and their world, rather than as individual processes that arise physiologically or through linguistic presentations. I also suggest that emotions are best understood as complexes, that within the relational nexus emotions arise as phenomena that are acted out, possessing a physical and a discursive component. Emotions need to be understood as complexes that arise as bodily actions within relations of power and guided by moral precepts.

In the final chapter I explore the particularly modern experience of embodiment in space and time and how it is affected by the flexible accumulation practices of contemporary capitalism, as well as by the new information and media technologies. My view is that, while the issue of a particularly postmodern experience is dubious, certain features of modern Western societies have been heightened in the late twentieth century, which increased the dualistic experience of the division between body and mind, yet began to undermine it. On the one hand, new information and communication technologies provided the means for more disembodied relationships between individuals; while, on the other hand, the feelings of fragmentation so common in these relationships, and in the impact of powerful modern institutions, initiated a trend towards a desire for wholeness and the integrity of the body and the person. The modern experience of both fragmentation and wholeness underlies the emergent emphasis on relations, which provides us with new possibilities in social life and a new basis for the social sciences.

1 Prolegomenon to Bodies of Thought

In the Western world individuals have grown accustomed to a way of understanding themselves which divides their existence between the mind and the body. The classic statement of this dualism was made by Descartes in the seventeenth century when he equated human being with the rational mind which gave us clarity of thought and free will, placing us near to the divine: in contradistinction, the body is an automaton – a physical machine indistinguishable from the bodies of other animals. Many versions of this 'Cartesian dualism' have survived into the twentieth century, although perhaps shorn of its religious overtones; nevertheless, they survive in the contemporary social sciences and, most notably, in the cognitivism that is so popular in psychology. However, in this book I want to challenge this concentration on the mind when it comes to the study of humans and their behaviour, and instead will re-focus this study on social relations, activity and human embodiment. This means I wish to undermine the division between mind and body and to suggest that, instead, thought is an embodied, social activity. By the same token, I do not want to preserve the idea of the body as a machine whose operation is fixed in place by biological processes; rather, I want to explore the body as a social and natural construction, as a malleable organism which is open to re-formation through its location within networks of historically variable social relations. What will be explored here is the notion that the body is made active by social relations because it is brought into being and mobilized by its positioning in the interweaving networks of human interdependence. As Shilling (1993: 199) says, 'the body is not only affected by social relations but forms a basis for and enters into the construction of social relations.' From this basis, I will develop an outlook similar to Hirst and Woolley (1982), who argue that social relations have a decisive influence on human attributes, which cannot be characterized as either natural or social because they are both at the same time – human attributes are socio-natural. I also share their view that social relations do not form one interconnected whole, but may be fragmentary and disparate (Hirst and Woolley, 1982: 24). This means that bodily dispositions and capacities will not be uniform or even within cultures, and in any group we will find people of different characters, skills, beliefs or abilities, due largely to the varied influence of social relations upon them.

Throughout this book, then, I will develop and use notions of the productive, communicative, powerful, thinking body (Ilyenkov, 1977), metaphors which I hope will be enabling and which present our corporeal presence as not just trapped and constrained within social relations, but as possessing the capacities to change such relations and also to transform different aspects of the physical world. The transformation of the material world in which we live has been achieved through the creation of artifacts which we use to re-work the conditions of our existence and, as such, are prosthetic extensions of the body. Indeed, my argument will be that we cannot separate the thoughtful activity that has previously been attributed to some inner realm of 'the mind' from the social and material contexts in which such activity takes place, including the means by which activity is accomplished. This position involves rejecting the Cartesian idea of the existence of two fundamentally different realms or substances, mind and matter, and replacing this notion with the assumption that there is one, complex reality. In order to develop this idea, I will use Elias's (1987a) metaphor of a five-dimensional reality, which includes a symbolic dimension that is part of, but irreducible to, the other dimensions of space and time. I argue that this helps to lead us out of the division of mind and matter that is to be found in Cartesianism and its modern forms.

However, Cartesian dualism is real in the sense that there is, in the contemporary Western world, a historical experience of being divided between mind and body, thought and emotion, which is lived by certain people in particular times and places. In this book I will explore some of the historical roots of this experience and trace it back to the social relations and power configurations that have shaped and sustained it. Yet this is only one aspect of Western tradition and historical experience; there are others, some that I will explore throughout this book, which emphasize the unity of mind and body rather than their dislocation. But to say that Cartesian dualism is an influential strand of historical experience means that we need to deal with it in a little more depth here before exploring alternative views throughout the rest of the book. It also means that we need to explore how such contradictory philosophical traditions, and the experiences that initiated them and still sustain them, can exist together within the same culture, pulling us in different directions.

The Cartesian View of Mind and Body, Knowledge and Objects

René Descartes gave the clearest expression, in philosophical terms, of an experience of which people in the seventeenth century were becoming increas-ingly more aware: that they existed as persons or minds which were somehow distinct from their bodies, or at least they could not be reduced to any aspect of their body. According to Descartes, people experience and understand themselves in two different ways: first, as bodies occupying a specific location in space and time, and, secondly, as persons or selves who are associated with the processes of thinking. Descartes claimed that, if we stop and reflect upon it, we cannot associate ourselves with any aspect of our own bodies, for if many of the attributes of our physical presence were to disappear we would still continue to exist as a self. We could still think of ourselves as the same person as we were before, even though our bodies may have changed, or certain of their characteristics have been lost. This is why as we grow older we may not associate ourselves with the age that we really are, feeling ourselves younger than our outward appearance; or why someone who has lost limbs or who is paralysed may feel that his or her personality has not changed. Who we are is not associated with our bodies, but with our thought processes. Indeed, if a person is medically considered to be 'brain dead' or in a 'persistent vegetative state' after an accident or illness, many people believe that they should not be kept physically alive, for once a person can no longer think of his or her own existence, can no longer act or is incapable of free will, then the person has really 'died' and his or her body is no more than a living carcass. Here we see a clear example of how a person is associated with his or her thought processes and not with his or her bodily existence.

However, while the body in such a personless state is a good illustration of Descartes's idea, it should not be taken as proof that the idea is correct, certainly not for those people who are conscious and mobile. In these cases it does not necessarily apply that the person associates only with his or her thinking, nor that thought is somehow disassociated from a body which exists only as an unthinking thing – as a machine. As Descartes puts it:

> therefore, from the mere fact that I know with certainty that I exist, and that I do not observe that any other thing belongs necessarily to my nature or essence except that I am a thinking thing, I rightly conclude that my essence consists in this alone, that I am a thinking thing, or a substance whose whole essence or nature consists in thinking. And although perhaps (or rather as I shall shortly say, certainly,) I have a body to which I am very closely united, nevertheless, because, on the one hand, I have a clear and distinct idea of myself in so far as I am only a thinking and unextended thing, and because, on the other hand I have a distinct idea of the body in so far as it is only an extended thing but which does not think, it is certain that I, that is to say my mind, by which I am what I am, is entirely and truly distinct from my body, and may exist without it. (Descartes, 1640/1968: 156)

This is an extremely radical and, in my view, very wrong idea of the body. While Descartes does admit that we are united with our bodies, he does not examine this unison in any way: instead, he maintains that because we have the *idea* that we exist purely in thought or spirit, then this is the basis for the sense of self – the inner being we refer to when we speak of 'I'. In short, what Descartes does not pursue is the connection between embodiment and thought, nor does he question the notion that the sense of self can only emerge from the inner process of thinking. However, if we pursue the connection between mind and body we find that being embodied and located in the extended world of time and space is not only a necessary precondition for thought, it is, rather, its very basis. That Descartes conceptualizes this not to be the case stems from his view of the human mind and its role in the creation of knowledge.

Descartes claims that we cannot know our own selves through our bodies or through any bodily sensations, nor can we know anything about the external world of objects in this fashion. We cannot know that the different parts of our world are discrete and separate entities or objects purely through sensation, just as we cannot know that we are really associated with our bodies. Sensation cannot be the guarantor of knowledge because the senses can be fooled and are thus unreliable. What we know of the world is not based on the information gathered by touch, sight, smell or sound, but how this is classified and worked on by the intellect. It is the mind that defines the different objects of the world and creates ideas about their nature and their differences. Nothing can be known with certainty unless the mind creates ideas of the objective world, which are clear and distinct. Descartes, then, was asking in his philosophy whether any perception, consciousness or knowledge about the world could be regarded with any certainty. Do we possess any knowledge that, under certain circumstances, cannot be doubted? In the search for this certainty of knowledge, Descartes tested everything that we normally take as tacitly given by subjecting it to doubt, questioning everything that ordinarily would be regarded as certain. His doubting took him to the very extremes of uncertainty, rejecting even the notion that God would never allow humankind to deceive themselves totally about the true nature of the world. A truth can only be claimed as such after it has stood the test of doubt.

> I shall suppose, therefore, that there is, not a true God, who is the sovereign source of truth, but some evil demon, no less cunning and deceiving than power- ful, who has used all his artifice to deceive me. I will suppose that the heavens, the air, the earth, colours, shapes, sounds and all external things we see, are only illusions and deceptions which he uses to take me in. I will consider myself as having no hands, eyes, flesh, blood or senses, but as believing wrongly that I have all these things. I shall cling obstinately to this notion; and if, by this means, it is not in my power to arrive at the knowledge of any truth, at the very least it is in my power to suspend my judgement. (Descartes, 1640/1968: 100)

However, there is one thing that Descartes concludes he cannot doubt and, thus, only one thing that is certain. 'I had persuaded myself that there was nothing at all in the world: no sky, no earth, no minds or bodies; was I not, therefore, also persuaded that I did not exist? No indeed; I existed without doubt, by the fact that I was persuaded, or indeed by the mere fact that I thought at all' (Descartes, 1640/1968: 103). The ability to think, then, is what gives Descartes the certainty of his own existence and for him to say, 'I think therefore I am' is the only thing that cannot be doubted.

As I said earlier, Descartes did believe that the mind and body were united, to such an extent that we do not view things which happen to our bodies in a passive and disinterested way. Descartes explains this in his *Sixth*

Meditation by way of an analogy: we do not look at our bodies in the same way as a captain views his ship, so that if some damage occurs to it he sees it with his eyes and notes what has occurred. If damage occurs to our bodies we do not just note this, we *feel* it. The mind records this occurrence as if *it* has been injured, so that the relationship we have with our bodies is an intimate and necessary one. Similarly, when we experience dryness of the throat the mind will tell us that we are thirsty and need to drink: however, it is not the bodily sensation which we call thirst, but the ideas that are stimulated in the mind. It is ideas such as these that we associate with ourselves and which create the notion of our own body with its different needs and sensations. These will only be clear to the extent that the mind has clear ideas about what these needs and sensations are related to. It is still the mind, then, as distinct from the body, that makes possible the sense of self and which generates ideas about the nature of objects in the world, seeking in itself the essence of truth. The body can be considered as a reactive machine whose dispositions are set by its own organic nature, whereas the mind is the element that introduces to humankind free will, imagination and truth-seeking.

More than this, though, Descartes's mechanical metaphor applies not only to the human body but also to all material objects in the universe and their interrelationships. Taking mathematical reasoning as the only science that had so far been able to arrive at any proofs, Descartes contemplated a perfectly geometrical universe wherein all bodies were aligned in symmetrical and regular constellation. It was through mathematical reasoning that Descartes felt secure enough to arrive at the conception of objects or 'things' whose existence was beyond doubt, and which were objectively located in the realms of time and space. Such reasoning allowed him mentally to divide the world into its constituent parts, the various things or individuals which compose it, 'beginning with the simplest objects and the easiest to know, in order to climb gradually, as by degrees, as far as the knowledge of the most complex, and even supposing some order among those objects which do not precede each other naturally' (Descartes, 1640/1968: 41). Here we see clearly the Cartesian method, which is to begin with the smallest indivisible individual entity and to build, through reason, one's knowledge of larger complexes by working up to a picture of the whole as constituted by its individual parts. Such objects are ontologically prior to the whole, which in turn can only be understood as the sum of its parts. As Harvey (1993: 29) says, 'relations between entities are, furthermore, clearly separable from the entities themselves. The study of relations is then a study of the contingent ways in which entities (e.g. billiard balls or people) collide.' The method I employ in this book is directly opposed to this Cartesian method, beginning with relations between bodies and individuals within an ecosystem. Furthermore, time and space is not to be conceived of as externally given and absolute, but is itself immanent in the socio-natural system and, as such, is variable and multi-layered.

What is Wrong with Cartesian Dualism?

While I think Descartes is right to claim that the person or self does not entirely reside within the body and cannot be identified with any of its parts, I believe he is wrong to set up a duality between body and mind on this basis. Although they cannot be reduced to one another, what we call 'mind' only exists because we have bodies that give us the potential to be active and animate within the world, exploring, touching, seeing, hearing, wondering, explaining; and we can only become persons and selves because we are located bodily at a particular place in space and time, in relation to other people and things around us. Furthermore, it is not necessarily the 'mind' that brings us understanding of the world and of ourselves, so that none of these things would exist without some spiritual essence that we can label the 'mind'. Rather, I want to suggest throughout this book, using the work of a diverse range of social scientists, that there is no such 'thing' as the 'mind' considered as something complete and contained within itself: that is, as an entity or essence separate from the (non-mechanical) body and its spatially and temporally located practices. Rather, the 'mind' is an effect of bodily action in the world and of becoming a person from the recognition of one's position in a diverse network of social relations.

I am also opposed, then, to the Cartesian method that begins with individuals or things and works up to studying the higher levels of relatedness. In Cartesianism, even at higher levels of relations, bodies remain discrete in themselves, so although they may affect each other's movements in time and space, they cannot affect each other's pre-given individual identity. The view I am putting forward here fundamentally challenges this, for, in terms of human individuals, embodied persons become identified within the multiple relations in which they are located and which, as agents, they change through their mutual interactions. Put in the language of parts and wholes, this means that, in the dialectical view of Levins and Lewontin (1985: 3):

> Parts and wholes evolve in consequence of their relationship, and the relationship itself evolves. These are the properties of things that we call dialectical: that one thing cannot exist without the other, that one acquires its properties from its relation to the other, that the properties of both evolve as a consequence of their interpenetration.

In this dialectical view, things are assumed from the beginning to be heterogeneous at every level, but this heterogeneity does not mean that they are constituted by fixed, natural identities or essences. People and things have their own individual identities, making the system heterogeneous, and yet these identities develop within the system of interrelationships, so that it becomes difficult to draw exact boundaries between identities. For example, in a nation-state, people will share similar values, beliefs, lifestyles, work and leisure activities, and so identify as part of a community and its practices. But where does that identity reside: in the individuals, their neighbourhood, local community or region, or in the national boundaries as a whole?

It would be impossible to identify the cut-off point between these analytic-ally distinct forms of human association. This also means that none of these 'entities' is discrete and so the identities within them are heterogeneous: for example, a Muslim living in Britain may have different sets of identifica-tions – with things that are British and also with values and beliefs from Muslim culture. Even at the level of the nation-state, this 'system' leaks into others and makes it impossible to draw boundaries. Thus, there are no 'basic' individuals or entities, for all 'things' can be decomposed into smaller units which are themselves systems with internal relations. Without the notion of fixed and given individuals with which we can begin an enquiry in absolute certainty, we must focus on the series of interrelated systems in which parts make wholes and wholes make parts, and neither can be seen as having ontological priority.

This view also has drastic implications for Descartes's view of time and space as given, unchanging dimensions. I don't think that I could put this better than Harvey (1993: 31):

> Space and time are neither absolute nor external processes but are contingent and contained within them. There are multiple spaces and times (and space–times) implicated in different physical, biological and social processes. The latter all *produce . . .* their own forms of space and time. Processes do not operate *in* but *actively construct* space and time and in so doing define distinctive *scales* for their development.

This ties in with the notion that there are no basic units which we can analyse as pre-given entities, for what constitutes the scale of space and time within one particular ecological niche will be dependent upon all the relations within it, and will be very different from an ecosystem of a different scale. Furthermore, deciding what constitutes the scale of any ecosystem is difficult because, as with human associations, they blend into one another so that different objects or species may be members or inhabitants of more than one niche. I want to remain sensitive to such issues in considering the thinking bodies of humans acting in different dimensions of time and space. This is extremely important for any consideration of contemporary societies because, as Giddens (1990, 1991) illustrates, modernity disembeds humans from the traditional experiences of space and time, reconstituting them at both global and local levels. I will explore these issues further in Chapter 7. For now, the main point I am making is that, unlike Descartes, I believe that the mind is only present in the various socio-natural systems and space–time contexts inhabited by individuals.

Thinking Bodies in Time and Space

Thoughtful human activity has then to be located within the socio-natural world that we all inhabit as embodied beings. As Elias has said, there are 'three basic co-ordinates of human life: the shaping and positioning of the individual within the social structure, the social structure itself and the relation of social human beings to events in the non-human world' (Elias, 1991a: 97). Following Foucault (1982), I believe that we can think of these basic co-ordinates, or relations, as relations of communication, relations of power and relations that transform the real. In terms of relations that transform the real, we can say that this describes the relation of social groups and the social individuals within them to the non-human world, or, put in a different fashion, to the material objects and events that occur in the environment and our attempts to change or influence them. It also relates to the artifacts that are devised to bring about this transformation and the way in which the use of these impact on the human body, creating new abilities, capacities, skills and identities. Relations of communication describe the positioning of the individual within the interdependencies of the social group and the reflection of that position back to the individual using the socially created system of symbols, signs and language, thus giving the place of the individual a meaning within the group and adding to the development of the person's self-identity. Finally, relations of power describe the formation of the social structure, including the inequalities that have arisen between individuals in their positioning within the structure. They also refer to the actions of people on the actions of others, designed either to maintain existing power relations or to challenge them, and the means or resources that individuals or groups use in such power struggles (such as means of production, means of violence or coercion, or symbolic and ideological means). However, just as the main co-ordinates of human life cannot be separated from each other, nor can the relations that define them. That is to say, we may make abstract distinctions between them for analytical purposes but in practice these three relations all coexist and reinforce (or undermine) one another. Foucault (1982: 217–18) makes the point in the following way:

> Power relations, relationships of communication, objective capacities should not therefore be confused. This is not to say that there is a question of three separate domains. Nor that there is on one hand the field of things, of perfected technique, work, and the transformation of the real; on the other that of signs, communication, reciprocity, and the production of meaning; finally that of the domination of the means of constraint, of inequality and the action of men upon other men. It is a question of three types of relationships which in fact always overlap one another, support one another reciprocally, and use each other mutually as a means to an end.

This reinforces what was said earlier about the fragmentary nature of social relations: they are not to be conceptualized as a unitary and homogeneous whole, but rather as existing as an unstable and fragile series of human interconnections which must constantly be reproduced. The three types of relations talked of above do not neatly dovetail into each other; rather, they need to support one another in some kind of unplanned and unco-ordinated reciprocity to produce an identifiable social structure or configuration of relations. The human body is located within these relations and draws its various powers and capacities from them – its varying degrees of ability to transform the environment, its skills of communication and the power to affect the actions of others and to determine its own field of activity. From this positioning of the body in relations there is also created the identity of the person, along with his or her abilities and capacities, knowledge and beliefs, none of which can be separated from the creation of the 'mind'. Indeed, far from the mind being something distinct from the body located in space and time, as Descartes thought, the mind can be reconceptualized as an emergent effect of a body active within the social, historical and biological dimensions of space and time.

This point is stressed here because the way in which Descartes conceives of time and space is of two interlocking yet 'flat' dimensions: that is to say, they are described as neutral dimensions which appear to have no textured or multi-levelled quality to them, other than that bestowed on them by the mind. But if we see bodies connected to space and time, not only by the mind but by the three mutually supporting relations described above, then time and space are no longer independent and unchanging phenomena, there for contemplation by a mind which in all other respects is abstract from them. Instead, space and time are multi-levelled and constituted as such by the various forms of relations. In fleshing out this idea, I will loosely follow the different levels of time devised by Braudel (1973, 1977), who suggested that history may be conceptualized as consisting of three interlocking time-scales. The time of longest duration, *histoire de la longue durée*, is constituted by the pace of biological, geo-physical and climatic changes, which move at a slow pace and require the perspective of centuries to grasp the meta-morphoses they undergo. Next is the intermediate range, the time of *con-jonctures*, which includes the pace of change in social structures, economies, political institutions and cultures. This intermediate level can change at a much more rapid rate than the structures of longest duration, yet, in the lifetime of most generations, they remain relatively stable. The shortest time-span is that of *micro-history*, which is the fast-moving pace of change in the everyday lives of individuals, where events can happen at a rate that is sometimes hard to grasp, so that life appears to be ephemeral.

However, for my purposes here, and taking into account what has already been said, I want to readapt this scheme as follows, keeping the idea of three overlapping levels of time and space. In the scheme set out below, *bio-history* represents the time of longest duration, while *socio-historical relations and practices* is equivalent to intermediate time, and *everyday life* is of the same order as micro-history.

Bio-history

This is a term which comes from the work of Foucault and refers to 'the pressures through which the movements of life and the processes of history interfere with one another' (1979: 143). However, beyond this very bald statement, Foucault does not have much to say about bio-history, preferring instead to pursue the concept of bio-power. For my purposes here, this notion of bio-history is a vital one because, in terms of the relations between life and history, the body is the very axis of this relation. Also, bio-history would encapsulate what Braudel calls *la longue durée*, referring to how the human body has evolved in relation to both environmental conditions, on the one hand, such as changes in climate and terrain, and, on the other hand, in relation to historical developments such as the use of tools and language. Indeed, I want to suggest that life itself can only be regarded as a relation, because no form of life – human or non-human – can exist without the conditions that sustain it and, in turn, a form of life also becomes a condition which supports another life form. When Foucault talked above about the movements of life, this is what such a concept can mean: that life is a relation that can only be sustained as an ecology, as a series of interrelationships between different life forms, and between these life forms and the environment. If there are changes in one of these life forms, or in any aspect of the environment, then this has consequences for all the others and the whole ecology of life may change. Ecological conditions are, then, in a continual process of change and within this envelope life is a series of relations. It is within these conditions that the human body is formed and slowly changes. As Benton (1991: 21) says:

> social practices are spatially and temporally extended. But to recognize this is also to recognize that social relations take as their terms not just persons, or social institutions, but also physical objects, spatial 'envelopes', land, material substances and other living things, which are, likewise, space–time embedded. The properties – including the relational properties – of these non-human elements in contexts of human social forms and practices, must enter essentially into any adequate account of societies as 'levels'.

So the role of bio-history must always be taken into account in any attempt to understand social relations and human embodiment. The body is shaped within this bio-history but that does not mean that it is a fixed and determined machine whose actions are pre-set. This is because bio-history is always interrelated with socio-historical relations, which are one of the main co-ordinates that mediate between the human and the non-human and, as such, are a major influence on the socio-natural development of the body. If bio-history is the way in which the relations of life and the relations of history are intertwined and influence one another, then social history has had a profound effect on human evolution. Benton claims that forms of social organization and social practices affect the survival chances and reproductive success of certain individuals, in which case:

> Both a capacity for and a dependence upon social life is built into our very anatomical and physiological constitution, and into our developmental rhythms: 'premature' birth, extended infantile dependency, the neurological basis for linguistic capacities, the anatomy of the vocal organs and many other features attest to this. In so far as these biological features are to be regarded as

'adaptations' produced by selection then the environment which did the 'select-ing' was at least in part a social context. (Benton, 1991: 23)

This illustrates the duality of human nature: the body is shaped within bio-history to become open to various cultural processes, yet this can only occur within limits. The body is malleable but not infinitely so. This means that while the human body can only develop into a recognizable person within culture, adopting many aspects of the practices, beliefs and values contained in social relations, it cannot respond to every social demand. A body can be worked too hard, placed under too much stress, and the person may not be able to control some of the functions of his or her body in a way that would suit social codes. The inappropriate sounds or smells of the body in a public place, or blushing at a misdemeanour when one wants to appear cool and sophisticated, are just some of the innumerable perils of being a body in Western culture. In this sense I agree with Mellor and Shilling's (1997) concept of the 're-formed body', which claims that the human body is not *formed* anew in each generation and shaped exactly according to the social influences of the moment; however, the body is open to *re-formation* at the point where bio-history and social history meet.

Socio-historical Relations and Practices

Human beings have always existed in social relations and communities of practice. I talked earlier about the three co-ordinates of human life and the three types of interconnected relations central to them: relations that trans-form the real, relations of communication and relations of power. It is at this level of time and space that we find historically specific social relations and communities of practice exerting their influence on the human body. If I am arguing here that in bio-history there is no fundamental split between the body and the mind, then I need to explain how the experience of Cartesian dualism arose and why it has made sense to so many different generations. How did the feeling and the idea arise of a body located in space and time being separate from a mind that was a substance in itself, but an immaterial, non-temporal and non-spatial substance?

Interestingly, both Foucault and Elias trace this back to the changes in the power structures of society in the seventeenth century. If they are correct – and I believe them to be so – then the notion of humans as divided between body and mind, thought and emotion, is one that has its origin in the power relations of Western Europe during this particular period. For Foucault, the changes in power relations centre on a transformation from a sovereign power over life and death – a power which reserved the right to take life, often in an arbitrary fashion, and whose symbol was the sword – to a modern form of power which deals in the right to live and the administration of life itself. This is a pastoral form of power that pledges itself to preserve life and to care for it, but can also take life if the survival of the population is threatened (Foucault, 1979, 1982). Even war is waged in the name of life, so that life is taken only to preserve a higher or worthier form of it. Foucault claims that, beginning in the seventeenth century, the power over life – or, as he also refers to it, *bio-power* – evolved in two basic forms which are linked by a series of intermediary relations, constituting two poles of development:

> One of these poles – the first to be formed, it seems – centred on the body as a machine: its disciplining, the optimization of its capabilities, the extortion of its forces, the parallel increase of its usefulness and its docility, its integration into systems of efficient and economic controls, all this was ensured by the procedures of power that characterized the *disciplines: an anatomo-politics of the human body.* The second, formed somewhat later, focused on the species body, the body imbued with the mechanics of life and serving as the basis of the biological processes: propagation, births and mortality, the level of health, life expectancy and longevity, with all the conditions that can cause these to vary. Their super-vision was effected through an entire series of interventions and *regulatory controls: a bio-politics of the population.* (Foucault, 1979: 139)

So, here we find Foucault showing how the life of the population is drawn into the machinery of politics and how, for the very first time, bio-history becomes the subject of social control and planning: there is an attempt to make life itself bend to the political designs of the forces of power relations. Interestingly, at the first pole that Foucault identifies, he talks of the body as becoming a focus for relations of power and, in the process, being turned into a machine through the forces of regulation and discipline. He has charted the actual mechanisms of this disciplining over a number of publications, including the sites at which this occurs, such as mad houses, asylums and prisons, but these works are now so well known I do not intend to summarize them here (see Foucault, 1967, 1977). What interests me is the notion of this disciplining turning the body into a machine and its links to Descartes's notion of the body as an automaton. But Descartes was not the subject of this institutionalized form of discipline (although many others belonging to the lower classes were during this period), so what was the source of his feelings of the body as a machine and the similar feelings of others like him?

First of all we must remember that Foucault came to realize that the power exerted over the individual and his or her body is not just about social forms of regulation, but is also to do with self-regulation. While Foucault dealt with this in terms of the ancient civilizations (Foucault, 1986a, 1988), he did not detail the powers of self-regulation in Western Europe from the seven-teenth century onwards. However, this has been done by Elias (1991a) who has made many comments on the emergence of the Cartesian experience. For Elias, Descartes's philosophy was the product of a time in which there was a decline in the authority of the church and a waning of the religious understanding of the world, corresponding with the rise of secular authorities and styles of knowledge. In religious orders, sensuousness was both tolerated and, in some religions, encouraged, with the sensuous experience of the world interpreted through holy writings or by holy men. Without such authorities to interpret sensate experience, individuals such as Descartes had to begin to interpret the senses through the power of reason. This transition from an authoritarian to an autonomous mode of thinking led people to examine themselves more carefully and to view their bodily sensations and emotions as objects that were to be scrutinized, categorized, regulated, controlled and tested by doubt. Here, then, are the origins of the experience in which the body becomes the object of a mind that is felt to be separate from it. Indeed, for Descartes, the only divinity that appeared to be left in the world was in the very process of human thought, which seemed to be able to float free of this earthly and bodily existence and yet was, in actuality, the very product of a specific, historically embodied life.

Not only did this lead to the experience of a separation of body and mind, it also led to the division between an embodied knowledge of the world as it exists in space and time, and the thought processes which are able to understand its order. If the 'I' – the process of thought – is only contingently linked to the body, how can sensation ever provide the mind with adequate data on which to think? How can the body be a reliable extension into the world of time and space in order to connect the mind to it and allow reason to settle on the truth? The problem is that it can't, hence Descartes's ultimate fall-back position, which is the necessity of doubt. But now the mind is not only divided from the body, it is also separated from the 'external' world of space and time, trapped for the duration of its mortal existence in its bodily casing. Thus thought becomes regarded as like a 'thing', an intangible organ separated from the other organs of the body. This is the origin of the problem in our linguistic and conceptual tools through which we tend to equate the mind with the functioning of the brain, and yet it makes as much sense to say that thought has its seat in the brain as it does to say that 'speech has its seat in the throat and mouth, or walking in the legs' (Elias, 1991a: 114).

In the change from overt social control to more covert forms of regulation, including the movement to increased levels of self-regulation, there is another effect which reinforced the Cartesian experience; that is, the increasing pressure on individuals to govern their own impulses and emotions, leading to an intensification of the feeling that the self, or 'I', is trapped in a bodily shell. Without overt physical force or religious teachings to control or to guide the actions of individuals and regulate their relations to others, it was now left to the individual's own techniques of self-regulation to modulate his or her responses to the behaviour of others. Social situations in the modern world and 'civilized' codes of conduct demand that we no longer respond impulsively towards others and that our conduct is always considered in terms of how it will affect those we interact with. This sets up an invisible barrier between ourselves and others, one that is felt to merge with the visible boundaries of the body, the controlling 'I' trapped within its confines. Indeed, defence mechanisms towards others, and our own emotional responses to them, have been described as like a bodily armour (Reich, 1950). This bodily armour is felt to be a 'presented self' or a 'false self', displayed to others yet hiding the 'real' 'I' inside. Because this often leads to

feelings of individual isolation and alienation from others, it is hard for
people to remember that this feeling of self-entrapment stems from changing
modes of social relations, which imposed more self-restraint on feeling.

It is in these socio-historical relations, then, that we find the emergence of
the idea of humans as divided between body and mind, separated from
others and divided within themselves by socially instituted disciplines and
regulations which are, in part, self-imposed. However, within everyday life,
people do not always operate or think in a Cartesian manner, despite the
forces at work upon them. This is because we are located in everyday
relations as embodied beings, with connections to other people, and with our
own experiences that cannot be neatly compartmentalized. In daily experiences, when we think and feel our way through various activities without
any discernible distinction between the two processes, and when we constantly realize our relations to the others with whom we are interdependent,
then something of this experience cuts across the forces of dualism.

Everyday Life and Communication

Within socio-historical relations we can always discern patterns of everyday
life in which individuals are located in joint practices and face-to-face interaction. It is within this context that our understanding of space and time is
constructed through everyday activities, and we assume a personal identity
through our bodily location in various overlapping networks of relations.
While this book is not specifically focused on the everyday world, it constantly
relates to it, especially in terms of the issues of communication and experience. It is argued that, in modernity, socio-historical power relations are not
all encompassing and there are many spaces opened up for the creation of
informal ideologies and the elaboration of personal experience in relations
of communication. Although the notion of experience is recognized as a
problematic one, I nevertheless regard it as useful for the social sciences as
it expresses something of the way we are positioned as individuals within
social relations, both with regard to other people and towards things. This
active, bodily relation to the world gives each one of us a sense of personal
experience, and while this cannot be separated in any naïve way from the
wider cultural forms of understanding, nevertheless we each have a specific
'take' on the world constructed from our own embodied location in culture
and social relations. Furthermore, as I take up some of Merleau-Ponty's
(1962) ideas about the construction of experience through the active body,
this provides us with a useful basis on which to develop notions of resistance
within the social sciences. The body is not only constrained by relations of
power, but finds within them spaces of resistance in which it can formulate,
with others in a similar position, its own personal viewpoint on the forms of
government that seek to shape it. This is most clearly illustrated in Chapter
5, with the example of how the experience women have of their bodies is
both influenced by dominant medical ideologies, and at the same time forms

a point at which opposition to those ideologies can emerge with the construction of alternative notions of embodiment and bodily processes. Thus the body and its experience are understood as multi-dimensional: active, communicative bodies located in space and time are seen as the source of the symbolic understanding of the world, yet this is also influenced by already-established ideologies which seek to define both symbolic and material existence. However, because the symbolic is not the only dimension in which experience is constituted, and there are many spatial and temporal points in which relations of communication are conducted, it is always possible for people jointly to create alternative forms of understanding.

The Five Dimensions of Experience

So far, I have tried to show that knowledge and thought cannot be understood as separate from human embodiment in the various levels of space and time. Furthermore, this embodiment is not a static location in an absolutely fixed space and time, as humans are active and mobile in the various levels of their socio-natural environments. Perhaps Elias (1991b) has best illustrated this by noting how, in abstract contemplation, we tend to ponder on the question of language, reason and knowledge as if these nouns referred to separate realms of existence. However, if we change these words from the substantival to the verbal form, what emerges are not three separate entities but three interrelated human activities – to speak, to think, to know. Put in this way, we are no longer detached observers contemplating an external world; we are active beings engaged with each other and with the social and ecological systems of which we are a part. Because of this, as Elias points out, the subject (thinker) and object (the thought of) are not separate; they are fused in the many social activities we engage in. Symbols, knowledge and thinking are based within this world – within our spaces and times – so that they do not form in isolation of their objects. That is to say, knowledge and thinking are never divorced from the objects of the world located in moments of time or points of space. To elaborate on this idea, Elias uses the metaphor of 'five dimensions' of human life in which three dimensions are the dimensions of space (breadth, depth and height), a fourth is the dimension of time, and the fifth dimension is the symbolic (which includes language and other signs).

The reason why I like this explanation, cast in terms of dimensions, is that using it allows us to think of different dimensions of human life which are distinct and cannot be reduced to each other, yet at the same time cannot in any way be separated. To illustrate this, just think of a three-dimensional image like a hologram: we are aware of the three dimensions, the experience of breadth, depth and height in the image, yet no one can say where any one of these dimensions begins or ends, nor can we identify a point where one dimension begins to merge into the others. So it is with space and time, for Einstein demonstrated how these two dimensions are inextricably linked even though they are experienced as distinct. The same is also true for the symbol dimension and its blending with space and time. Take, for example, the symbolization of time, with which we are all familiar in terms of the various cultural markers we use to measure time – the seconds, minutes and hours of a clock, or the days, months and years of the calendar. Although these are purely symbolic markers, they are not unconnected to the dimensions of space and time in the human ecological niche, such as the orbit of the earth, the dawning of the day and the onset of night, and the change in seasons which affects climate and environment. Also, at this particular point in the intersection of bio- and socio-history, we are all aware of the general rate at which human bodies in the ecosystem age and eventually die, and in symbolic terms we can generally expect to last a little over the biblical three score years and ten. The way in which we think about the duration of our lives, then, is composed of spatial, temporal and symbolic markers and it becomes impossible to separate these out from one another. Could anyone say where the dimension of the symbolic measurement of time ended and some 'pure' dimension of time 'in itself' began? I think not, nor do I believe it would be fruitful to try because life is irreducibly multi-dimensional and this is the hub of my analysis.

While I think that the notion of five dimensions has many exciting possibilities, I do have some disagreements with Elias in terms of the specifics of his argument. As I shall outline in various chapters here, I don't think that symbols alone can characterize what is unique about the patterns of human relations, action and thought: instead, I suggest that it is the creation and development of artifacts which mark out what is distinctive about human life as compared to that of other animals, and such artifacts include language, tools and other instruments or inventions. Language is not, then, the only mode for the transmission of knowledge, which provides the 'lift-off' point from genetic and biological forms of behavioural transmission. The bio-history of human culture has diverse roots. Also, we must be aware that Elias is not very sensitive to the multi-levelled experiences of space and time, and we must be careful not to fall back into a Cartesian conception of these dimensions. These quibbles aside, the notion of the five dimensions of experience will be used throughout this book.

Conclusion

In this prolegomenon, I have attempted to draw with some rather broad strokes the general problematic and framework within which this book has been composed. I hope that this sets the scene for the following chapters where many of these themes and problems are drawn out in greater detail and my own ideas and syntheses are elaborated. The next chapter is particularly concerned with the evolution of the body within bio-history, while Chapter 3 focuses on the relation between socio-history and bio-history in terms of the way in which the body has been re-formed in the Western world since the Middle Ages. In one way or another, the following chapters all turn on this relationship between bio-history and socio-history in which the body is the axis: this runs through the debates about social constructionism, the feminist writings on the body, the emotions, and the body as it is constituted in modernity. All chapters build on the theme of embodiment as a focus of restraint, regulation and dualism, yet the body is also understood as having a powerful potential which makes possible the transformation of current realities. It is in this spirit that we turn to notions of embodiment, the artifact and power.

2 The Ecology of Bodies of Thought

In this chapter I will discuss the effects of what Foucault (1979) called 'bio-history' upon the human body and the way in which it is enmeshed in social relations and practices, leading to the development of culture, knowledge and thinking. Remember that Foucault defined bio-history as 'the pressures through which the movements of life and the processes of history interfere with one another' (1979: 143), but did not pursue the nature of this inter-connection. What is being suggested here, though, is a very fruitful idea: that the processes of biological life can never be separated from the processes of history and, at various levels, the two interact and affect one another. In terms of human life, the body is at the crux of this interrelationship between biology and history and has evolved as we know it today – including its capacity for knowing and thinking – because of this relationship and the factors that mediate it. The view I will present here is of life as a series of interconnected relations, each of which affects and changes the others. These relations, including the relations within and between animal species, and between the various species and the environment, are what we refer to as the ecological conditions of life. It is only within these conditions as they interact with human history that we can properly understand the formation of the human body. Furthermore, knowing and thinking also develops in this context so that, in opposition to Descartes's ideas, we have to understand how what we refer to as the 'mind' developed as one of the capacities of an ecologically situated body – that is, a body located in the various levels of space and time. We cannot, therefore, refer to the body and the mind as if the two were separate, and should instead, following Ilyenkov (1977), refer to the 'thinking body'.

The Evolution of the Thinking Body

In most neo-Darwinian theories of evolution it is proposed that the main purpose in human life – in fact, in all animal life – is for the individual to pass on his or her genes, and so the focus of attention has been on the indi-vidual and the family line. It can be argued that this is a view of biological evolution that mirrors exactly the world-view of Western capitalist societies, with their emphasis on individuals and the competition between them, rather than on more co-operative forms of association and relationship. Indeed, as Harvey (1993) shows, there are two metaphors at the heart of Darwin's *The*

Origin of Species, the first being the metaphor of stock-breeding practices in which the artificial, or 'domestic selection', procedures used by farmers breeding their animals was transposed on to nature as a process of 'natural selection'; the second metaphor, taken from Malthus's *Essay on the Principle of Population*, sought to explain how natural selection worked: organisms struggle for survival in a world where resources are in short supply and must successfully compete for these resources in order to keep themselves and their offspring alive, thus ensuring the reproduction of those best fit for this competition. In employing this metaphor, Darwin actually went beyond Malthus and developed alongside this view of natural selection a theory of 'sexual selection', appropriating the Victorian view of gender relations in which males were regarded as in competition with each other to acquire females, 'both by being more attractive to them in courtship displays and by physically excluding competing suitors' (Levins and Lewontin, 1985: 32). The mechanisms of natural selection and sexual selection taken together were used by Darwin to explain the survival and reproduction of certain species and populations, along with the individual variations within them.

However, what I am suggesting here is that we should abandon the metaphors of stock-breeding and the economic market when studying the evolution of bodies, replacing them with the view that *life is the relationship between organic bodies and between bodies and the ecological system.* Furthermore, this is not just a one-way relation, with the ecological system selecting, supporting and sustaining bodies, but a two-way interrelation in which bodies act on the ecological system in order to select and change aspects of it. Bateson (1973: 309) has reflected on this two-way process when he says that evolution is not just the adaptation of organisms to the con-ditions of life, but is about 'the relationship between animals and environ-ment. It is the ecology which survives and evolves.' It is not the individual, then, which is the unit of survival in the evolution of life, it is the ecology and the relationships within it that must be preserved. As Bateson (1973: 459) says when talking of Darwin's theory of survival:

> Darwin proposed a theory of natural selection and evolution in which the unit of survival was either the family line or the species or sub-species or something of the sort. But today it is obvious that this is not the unit of survival in the real biological world. The unit of survival is organism plus environment.

Similar views are echoed strongly in the work of A.N. Leontyev, who claims that 'we are compelled, both theoretically and factually, to regard life first and foremost as an interaction between an organism and its environ-ment' (1981: 10). However, as far as human beings are concerned, it is not just the interaction between organism and environment that defines our being, for these 'movements' of life are also interrelated with, and affected by, our history as social and cultural groups. This means, as Benton (1991) claims, that social practices are spatially and temporally extended, so that the ecological envelope of land, soil, objects, climate and weather always affects social history. At the same time, though, social organization itself affects the processes of life in two different ways: first, social formations can change the ecological balance by utilizing and transforming aspects of the environment; secondly, social relations and practices re-form the human body by selecting certain attributes and developing bodily capacities which, if they are sustained over a long duration, can become biologically rooted and transmitted. Hence the idea developed by many biologists that, in humans, instinct has become weakened so that individuals are open to learning from their culture (Buytendijk, 1974; Futuyama, 1995). As Levins and Lewontin (1985: 65) say, 'In human evolution the usual relationship between organism and environment has become virtually reversed in adaptation. Cultural invention has replaced genetic change as the effective source of variation. Consciousness allows people to analyze and make deliberate alterations, so adaptation of environment to organism has become the dominant mode.'

In this section, I will develop these themes to explore the ways in which the development of culture has affected the biological evolution of the human body – the thinking body – especially through the creation of artifacts that are designed by humans to change the environment in order to meet their needs. Ilyenkov (1977) used the term 'artifact' to refer to an object created within human culture in which activity is embodied. That is to say, the artifact has been fashioned for some use within social practices and therefore embodies and transmits that activity. Such artifacts can be tools used to transform the geo-physical environment in labour practices, or they can be signs that affect the actions of other individuals in communicative practices, which can also be used to affect one's own actions (Mead, 1934; Vygotsky, 1987). In both these instances the development of artifacts re-forms human embodiment because, in the case of artifacts which transform the real, the body forms new capacities with the creation and use of these artifacts. Equally, with the development of signs, the body becomes a signifying body, whether as a painter, scribe or speaker, and all these changes to embodiment result in the emergence of a thinking body. The formation of such capacities involves techniques of the body developed in social practice, some of which may become biologically ingrained, a process I will examine later in this chapter.

For now, suffice it to say that I am interested in the way the body has been re-formed in relations that transform the real, relations of communication and relations of power. I have attempted to present here some of the possible ways in which the body has been affected by relations of transformation and communication, and will present more detail to this argument later in this chapter. But what of relations of power? Are they the result of these other relations or are they separate, with their own roots in human evolution?

Evolution and Relations of Power

In the literature on sociobiology – or, nowadays, 'evolutionary psychology' or 'evolutionary biology', as many authors prefer – power in human groups is often studied in the light of aggressive conflicts in other animal species which take place around competition for mates or territory (Ardrey, 1966; Badcock, 1991; Lorenz, 1963). Those who are more successful in the various forms of violent competition are those more likely to be successful at finding mates and reproducing, referring back to the neo-Darwinian notion that the basic motive of the organism is to pass on its genes. Aggression is thus seen as biological necessity, rooted in the genetic make-up of the species, giving rise to power structures in all animal societies, including human society. While human males may no longer physically fight each other for dominance of females or over territory, their aggressive tendencies are channelled into other forms of competition – economic, political, sporting – in which the fittest win out.

I do not want to spend time on evolutionary psychology and its critique for an extensive critical literature already exists. Needless to say, the approach can be criticized for taking present-day values and projecting them back into our evolutionary past, thus naturalizing them and making them seem unchangeable. Evolutionary biologists are still unconsciously using Darwin's stock-breeding and Malthusian metaphors, failing to recognize them as metaphors drawn from farming techniques and nineteenth-century political economy, and instead falsely believing them to be mechanisms present in life itself, controlling evolutionary processes. The masculine values and attitudes of such stories are not hard to spot either, with males being pictured as dominant sexual predators and females as sexually passive and nurturing. That all of human (male) aggression is often explained by sociobiologists purely in terms of individual instinct can also be criticized for ignoring the causes of modern military conflicts in the alliances and oppositions of nation-states, in ideological, religious or political oppositions, and the economics of industry, trade and the arms race. All this makes evolutionary biology look a little bit too simplistic as an explanation for contemporary social life.

However, the main reason I recount this here is that, through Nietzsche's use of the Greek notion of the '*agon*', a similar 'fiction of emergence' appears in the work of Foucault (Smith, 1994), whose notion of bio-history is central to this project. Not that Foucault bases his story of human power and aggression on the model of sexual selection, but rather he grounds it in Nietzsche's own neo-Darwinian idea of the will to power and to knowledge. Before exploring this issue, let me say that Foucault realized there were two forms of power: one is the power 'exerted over things [which] gives the ability to modify, use, consume, or destroy them – a power which stems from aptitudes directly inherent in the body or relayed by external instruments. Let us say that here it is a question of "capacity" ' (1982: 217). The other form of power is that which exists between people in human societies, and what characterizes this power 'is that it brings into play relations between individuals (or between groups)' (Foucault, 1982: 217). However, what can Foucault mean by this – that there is a power that brings into play such relations? What is the 'it' which could do such a thing?

This becomes more puzzling when one considers Foucault's view that power is not a 'thing' which one can gain, hold and lose; rather, power is a *relation* or, more accurately, an interlocking series of relations which produce a configuration or global strategy of power, one which is neither designed nor controlled by any person or group. This, then, does not explain why Foucault should think there was some 'thing' that brought into play relations of power. Instead, I will argue here that *power is the effect of a mutually supporting or conflicting alignment of social relations* rather than an 'it' which brings them into play (something Foucault clearly indicates in other parts of his work, as does Elias in his writings; see Burkitt, 1993). However, perhaps a clue to what Foucault means when he talks of the power relation as though 'it' had some agency of its own lies in his references to the ceaseless struggles and confrontations that transform or strengthen relations of power (1979: 92). These ceaseless struggles and confrontations are traced back to the human will because, for Foucault, at the very heart of the power relationship there lies the recalcitrance of the human will which acts as a permanent provocation to others. Thus, 'Rather than speaking of an essential freedom, it would be better to speak of an "agonism" – of a relationship which is at the same time reciprocal incitation and struggle; less of a face-to-face confrontation which paralyzes both sides than a permanent provocation' (Foucault, 1982: 222).

The roots of the concept of 'agonism' are to be found in Nietzsche's philosophy, for it was he who first used the term '*agon*', or competition, drawn from his studies of ancient Greek culture (Hollingdale, 1965: 45). This helped Nietzsche formulate the idea of the 'will to power', a natural instinct that he thought led all humans into conflict with one another, creating the desire to dominate and subjugate others. The concept was also partly derived from Darwin's theory of natural selection as a struggle for survival within and among the different species. However, the will to power does not simply result from conflict with others; it also emerges from the inner conflicts within an individual between the different instincts and reactions that govern behaviour. Will emerges when one impulse becomes the strongest and can command the others. In the past, we have often mistaken this act of willing for a metaphysical or spiritual quality inherent in being human, such as Descartes's notion of conscious free will associated with the 'I', or cogito. Instead, Nietzsche (1973) claims that consciousness of self and the will only emerges through the desire for power, which occurs when one instinct has gained mastery and begins to command the others.

As far as human society is concerned, in the midst of this sea of struggles between the wills and instincts of different individuals, social order can only be attained when a particular social group has gained mastery over others and can impose their commands and moral regulations on the struggling masses. As Nietzsche says, 'In all willing it is absolutely a question of commanding and obeying, on the basis . . . of a social structure composed of many "souls" ' (1973: 49). Thus, for Nietzsche, social relations – including relations of power – are not fundamental to human existence; rather, social relations between individuals are created out of incessant conflict through the attempt to master and command the clash of wills and instincts, both collective and individual. However, to maintain social relations and a semblance of order, humans had to repudiate the 'old instincts' of 'wild, free, prowling man', which were 'enmity, cruelty, joy in persecuting, in attack, in change, in destruction' (Nietzsche, 1977: 117). All these instincts had to be turned back against those who possessed them and subjugated under the weight of a guilty, or bad, consciousness: 'man' was made to feel bad about what Nietzsche considered to be some of his truest and noblest feelings. Knowledge is also harnessed to the will to power and has become a means of domination within human societies, subjecting the other diverse drives to its will. Instead of the thirst for knowledge being one of the playful drives, as Nietzsche claims it once was, it now forms a power in itself, a will to knowledge. Such conditions of domination through power and knowledge will only be overthrown when the old and terrible instincts assert themselves again, as Nietzsche believes they will in the supermen – an elite group of free men who integrate these instincts into the rest of their personality and cease to be ashamed of them, creating in the process their own values that answer to no one else.

So, for Nietzsche, agonism springs from the clash of instincts that are involved in every historical instance of struggle, and power and knowledge emerge as wills which attempt to master the instincts and enslave them. Although Nietzsche's view of the emergence of power is slightly different from the sociobiologists', it plays on many of the same themes. Agonism is clearly based on the aggressive instincts which are innate in human males, and the image of the male warrior who will admit these instincts without guilt is a metaphor for the free man that runs throughout Nietzsche's work. Strangely, although a contemporary philosopher like Foucault has never sought to defend Nietzsche's neo-Darwinian leanings, nevertheless he has taken them to the heart of his own concepts of agonism and power.

Like Nietzsche, Foucault wants to use a genealogical method where what is found at any point of emergence is the disparity of things, rather than a single unified origin. Genealogy therefore traces the roots of all seemingly unified identities or relations back to the differences and dissonances from which they emerged. Foucault says that genealogy is not the history of the growth or evolution of a thing, but of 'an unstable assemblage of faults, fissures, and heterogeneous layers that threaten the fragile interior from within or from underneath' (Foucault, 1986b: 82). Furthermore, this flawed union is created in the initial stages of struggle between the disparate elements that will eventually compose its unstable existence. That genealogy sees emergence in terms of multiple points of origin makes sense, but what is extremely problematic is the view of nature and, especially, human nature which is at its core wherein life is seen as perpetual struggle and endless domination. Here, for example, is Foucault's account of emergence, which quotes directly from Nietzsche's *Beyond Good and Evil*:

It is in this sense that the emergence of a species (animal or human) and its solidification are secured 'in an extended battle against conditions which are essentially and constantly unfavourable'. In fact, 'the species must realize itself as a species, as something – characterized by the durability, uniformity, and simplicity of its form – which can prevail in the perpetual struggle against outsiders or the uprising of those it oppresses from within'. On the other hand, individual differences emerge at another stage of the relationship of forces, when the species has become victorious and when it is no longer threatened from outside. In this condition, we find a struggle 'of egoisms turned against each other, each bursting forth in a splintering of forces and a general striving for the sun and the light'. (Foucault, 1986b: 84)

From this we can clearly see Foucault replicating the idea of how an original struggle for survival against an often hostile environment is turned into a struggle between individuals – a struggle against the uprising of the dominated and a struggle between individual egoisms that is repeated at each point of emergence in history. This view, however, tends to clash with the more historical aspects of genealogy which come to the fore in other places in the works of both Foucault and Nietzsche, for this eternal conflict seems to possess the same structure and intensity at each moment of emergence. Indeed, Foucault does not see the confrontation of forces occurring in a historical field that has already been partly constituted by previous power relations, but rather as taking place in a pure distance between opposing forces – in a 'non-place' where 'only a single drama is ever staged', which is 'the endlessly repeated play of dominations' (Foucault, 1986b: 85).

While I want to support the notion of the multiple origins of bio-history and social history, including the way in which the two are inseparable in many ways, I wish to reject the Nietzschean view of the violent origin of human culture and its perpetuation at each new point of emergence. As Smith (1994) has noted, this account of a single drama of violence in the emergence of culture is a 'fiction' that appears not only in Nietzsche and Foucault, but also in Freud's (1930) account of the origin of the incest taboo with the murder of the father in the primal horde and the imprinting of the crime in the human phylogenetic memory. These notions of the origins of culture can be labelled as 'fictions of emergence' (Smith, 1994) because they are stories that can never be referred back to any recorded events in human bio-history. They are stories invented by the respective philosophers to support their own ideas about human nature and contemporary society.

However, having said this, must it not be the case that all accounts of bio-history are fictions, infused with the wishes, values and desires of the story-tellers, for there is no way of verifying any account of culture which takes place long before individual or collective memory? Indeed, many would argue that even recent events, which are recorded in writing, on film or in the oral accounts of those living at the time, are themselves open to many forms of interpretation and rewriting, and, in this sense, are also fictions. On this matter I feel it can be said that, while it is impossible to have a value-free account of human origins, we can, nevertheless, aim for two things: first, we can be aware of how our accounts of bio-history express a desire for a particular form of human life, so that the ideas we create about our origins feed into the human self-image and present us with possibilities for the future; secondly, the accounts of bio-history should relate to the findings of archaeologists and palaeoanthropologists and thus interact with the traces that early human cultures have left us in the remains of their dwellings, their tools, implements, paintings, carvings and their bones. While these things do not prove any particular account of our species' origins, any responsible account must refer to them because, like any artifact, they 'speak' to us, they convey messages and meanings and invite interpretation. Also, a responsible version of bio-history must be aware of the image of humankind it is fostering and how this might support or undermine not just a particular view of the past, but also of the future and the political possibilities open to us.

Given this, I feel the fictions of emergence in Foucault and Nietzsche are irresponsible on all counts. Had they considered the material remnants of early human cultures, they would have found artifacts that invite descriptions of the violence of societies, such as weapons, along with those that speak of a different bio-history – tools, utensils, symbols, carvings, paintings – which say something of the everyday matters of living together, of producing, hunting, cooking, procreating and forging the means of transmitting knowledge from one generation to the next. This is not, as Nietzsche thought, a renunciation of human nature, a repression of the basic instinct for cruelty and domination in the construction of social relations and knowledge; instead, it is the expression of another aspect of bio-history and nature, of the human capacities to produce and communicate and to pass on knowledge to future generations in the form of artifactual (rather than genetic) means of transmission. Collective knowledge need not, therefore, be a means of power and domination, although it can be; rather, it is also part of relations of transformation and communication.

The account of bio-history provided by Foucault and Nietzsche is also irresponsible in fostering a view of human nature that binds us to a violent past and offers no possibility of changing this in the future. Indeed, the story only promises the eternal recurrence of violence and domination, an ultimately conservative outlook offering little hope for more positive political programmes of social change. As Smith points out, in accepting the Nietzschean fiction of emergence, Foucault 'seems to define a human essence based in domination and submission' (Smith, 1994: 47), the problem being that this story could actually become a self-fulfilling prophecy for, if people believe it, they feel it is worthless trying to create anything different and simply accept domination as their fate. In many ways, Foucault is doubly irresponsible in his project, for in claiming that his histories are no more than 'fictions' he aims to absolve himself both of the possible political consequences of his genealogy and of the criticism that it is not based on proper historical research. Instead of a fiction of emergence, I will offer here an

account of bio-history that I feel is more responsible in both a palaeoanthropo-
logical and a political sense.

The Emergence of Culture: 'Memes' or Artifacts?

In his critique of the Nietzschean/Foucaultian fictions of emergence, Smith
(1994) wants to set aside any reliance on the notion of a single violent drama
constantly replayed through history, replacing it with a version of emergence
based on the work of the biologist, Richard Dawkins (1989). Smith believes
that this allows him to re-establish the multiplicity of emergence contained
in the original idea of genealogy, as well as a view of the emergence of
culture and knowledge that rests on the concept of transmission rather than
violent domination and division. In this view, knowledge is not primarily a
means of the internal division of the soul and the external division of the
population, thus becoming intertwined with the will to power; it is regarded,
instead, as an essential factor in the survival chances of the human species.

> Without the violence of emergence, culture does not repress instinct but embays
> it, flooding the areas where it can no longer guarantee survival. In addition, the
> body is no longer scarred by an internal battle between culture and instinct.
> Certainly, history acts on the body, cutting and healing it, but the body is not
> divided against itself. The sacrifice of humanity in a consuming fire for knowl-
> edge, while dramatic, depends on an internal tension where discovery destabilizes
> and disrupts and revelation details the grotesque carnage underlying the masks of
> history. (Smith, 1994: 51)

Without this fiction of emergence, instead of the sudden burst of violence
in which culture was born, Smith suggests an understanding whereby 'if
culture is not a sudden process but a slow deliberative acquisition transmitted inter- and intragenerationally, with the acuity of hindsight we may
conjecture that natural selection favoured those early humans who were
gaining proficiency at extrasomatic transmission of information' (1994: 48).
Instinct and other genetically transmitted forms of behaviour were therefore
proving insufficient to guarantee survival, so alongside the gene other modes
of transmission began to develop. These do not act against the gene and
instinctual behaviour, but complement genetic functions, reshaping them and
taking them over. Following Dawkins (1989), Smith labels the new route of
transmission the 'meme', a single unit of cultural transmission that can
replicate itself under proper conditions. However, despite the fact that Smith
believes the concept of the meme to be useful for breaking the monolithic
image of culture, fragmenting it into its smaller units or replicators, there are
problems with Dawkins's sociobiological version of the development of
culture. While it may be true that culture became a factor in natural selection, how exactly does Dawkins describe the 'meme' and what defines it as
a unit of transmission?

Examples of memes are tunes, ideas, catch-phrases, clothes fashions, ways of making pots or of building arches. Just as genes propagate themselves in the gene pool by leaping from body to body via sperms or eggs, so memes propagate themselves in the meme pool by leaping from brain to brain via a process which, in the broad sense, can be called imitation. (Dawkins, 1989: 192)

However, the main problem in the above account is that, while Dawkins has realized that genetics is not adequate in itself to explain either bio-history or social life, he is still searching for a unit of survival that can be modelled along the same lines as the gene – hence the notion of the meme (which even rhymes with its sister concept). The difficulty with this notion, though, is that while it recognizes the limits of biological and genetic explanations, there is still an unwillingness to give up genetics as a blueprint of cultural evolution. So while the meme may appear to offer the possibility of a truly hybrid account of the different points of emergence of culture, it actually poses the threat of reductionism by drawing all explanations back to analogues of biological and genetic models. Instead of the concept of the meme, I suggest that the artifact is the unit of cultural transmission which affects the thinking body of humans, because, as a prosthetic extension of the body, it makes possible new practices and, through them, creates new capacities. In fact, if you read carefully Dawkins's examples of memes given above, he is actually referring to the various artifacts produced in human culture. I think, though, that he is wrong to suggest that artifacts are only replicators transmitted through imitation, for artifacts are more often than not used as a means of changing both the environment and the actions of others through their employment in relations that transform the real and in relations of communication. This is not a question of 'memes' leaping from brain to brain, but of artifacts employed in the multi-levelled relations of humans and their ecological niches.

Using the concept of the artifact rather than the meme also extends the insights of Smith in other ways, building on the vision of an active rather than a passive subject. Whereas in the fiction of a violent emergence all of humanity becomes divided and most of it dominated, the concept of trans-mission allows people to be seen as active agents. Focusing on the artifact extends this agentive view because, if artifacts are taken to be tools, imple-ments, signs and words, then activity is not just about transmission of information but is also about transformation. It means that we can change some aspect of the world by working on it, or we can change the behaviour of another person by communicating with them. Hence there arises the two forms of power that Foucault talked of: the power exerted over things and that which is exerted by individuals or groups upon one another. Central to both of these is the artifact.

We are beginning to explore here the way in which knowing the world is connected to particular forms of social activity and communication, yet we have not detailed how this creates a thinking body, capable of the type of conscious intervention in the world that is a feature of all humanity.

Bodies of Thought

A further problem in the understanding of bio-history encountered in the work of thinkers like Dawkins is that of atomism. That is to say, like Descartes, such evolutionists believe that the world can be decomposed into its basic individual building blocks and analysed from that point of view (Dawkins, 1986). For Dawkins, the unit of survival is not the various eco-systems as a whole, with all the interrelationships within and between them; rather it is individual genes that manage to survive throughout the generations, making them the 'immortal' units of survival. Individual bodies are just 'survival machines' built by the genes to allow them to reproduce more successfully, and although the 'mind' (which is taken by Dawkins to be synonymous with the brain) has some autonomy in its ability to make rational decisions, this again only serves the long-term purposes of the genes. It is they who have created brains in order to make the body a better survival machine, for it now has the capacity to make intricate decisions on the spur of the moment which, in the long run, increases its chance of survival and the propagation of its genes (Dawkins, 1989). Taking up some of Dawkins's views, Pinker (1998) develops a similarly atomistic theory of brain and mind, claiming that thought and the sensory functions, such as sight, have evolved under the pressure of natural selection and are built from neural elements which perform as information processors. The explanation of mind is atomistic because consciousness and sensory functions are seen as emerging from the particles which compose them, and this also makes the model an individualistic one because, in neo-Darwinian fashion, it is focused on the individual organism and little else 'beyond' it.

Because of the individualism and atomism of these theories of mind, they ignore the evolutionary pressures exerted by the ecosystem on the body and how this plays an important role in shaping the kinds of bodies we have. But it is not simply the pressures of an 'external' environment upon the body which evolves it in certain ways; rather it is the *activity* of the species within its ecosystem that forms the body, including its sensory and neural functions. The unit of survival is the ecology, and the social activity of humans within it creates evolutionary pressures on the body, re-forming its capacities for thinking. Power relations and knowledge do not act against the instincts in bio-history, then, creating a body that turned against itself at the origin of culture. Nor, as Descartes thought, is the ability to think separate from the ability to sense and to feel, the two theorized as distinct processes only externally related, where sensation is the poorer partner which the mind can only treat with total doubt. In this doubt, the mind, certain only of its own existence, must become uncertain of anything existing beyond it, including the body, its senses and the world in which they are embedded.

This view is challenged by Bateson (1973) who sees the human mind as immanent in the unit of survival – organism and environment – so that it is an element of the ecosystem, inextricably related to it. A similar, but more detailed, elaboration of this idea can be found in the work of Gibson (1979), in whose theories the human body and its sensory functions have developed through the active exploration of the environment. Gibson therefore opposes the kind of atomism found in Dawkins and Pinker, where the 'mind' and senses are built from their smaller components, instead presenting the idea that perception is formed as a whole through the animate exploration of the ecosystem by the organisms inhabiting it. Perception is therefore 'direct' in that the relation between organism and environment is an immediate one and is not necessarily mediated by any mental representation of the world. We do not see the world in our 'minds' as a picture because 'the information available in a picture (or indeed any static view) is impoverished, since a picture, by its very nature, lacks the limitless information that becomes available to any perceiver free to move around and explore his or her surroundings' (Costall, 1995: 469). This form of perception is literal rather than schematic and so is a universal mode of perception shared by all human beings, no matter what the cultural influences on their knowing and thinking. Therefore, Gibson (1979) proposed that humans can perceive in two differ-ent ways, literally and schematically, and the former provides the back-ground for the latter. Furthermore, given this, we need two different theories of perception to understand the two modes of perceiving and these need to be complementary. To my knowledge, Gibson never fulfilled this task.

Instead, he went on to develop the concept of 'affordance', which refers to the meaningful interaction between humans and their environment, a relation where objects have properties which invite and sustain certain bodily actions: for example, some objects are edible, some graspable, others pliable or usable for a purpose. Whatever the nature of the object, this is detected by the perceptual system of the body, and objects can take on a meaning because of the role they play in affording human action. Also, action is afforded by cultural as well as natural objects of the environment, and such cultural arti-facts are both natural and social, creating a crossover or hybrid point where nature and culture become inseparable. Costall (1995: 471) has explored this idea in more depth, suggesting that we need to 'socialize' Gibson's affordances: if we consider the world we all inhabit with its multitude of socially created artifacts, we all live in an environment 'transformed by the activity of generations'.

As I said earlier, the term 'artifact' refers to a created object in which human activity is embodied because it has been fashioned for some use within human practices (Ilyenkov, 1977; see also Bakhurst, 1991). For example, a saw or a hammer, invented for a certain purpose, is designed to be used in a particular way so that we all know what a sawing or hammering motion of the body looks like when we are using these tools. Being brought up in the human community, we all learn from the early days of infancy how to use such artifacts, along with the practices, purposes and capacities that accompany their usage. As A.N. Leontyev (1981) has pointed out, artifacts are a 'crystallization' of social activities and these are 'appropriated' whenever we use them. Thus, artifacts support and reproduce types of transformative practices through their use. In the process, people develop 'techniques of the body' through the appropriation of activity from artifacts, which is to say that certain forms of bodily carriage and movement appear, or ways of handling objects and manipulating them, which are culture specific (Costall, 1995; Mauss, 1979). Thus, our way of 'being-in-the-world', of acting, knowing and thinking, is largely dependent on artifacts and how they re-form embodiment.

More than this, Ilyenkov's (1977) point is that such artifacts acquire a significance or meaning because of their central position and mediating role in practice. They are not dumb objects like those found in the natural world; they speak to us and take on a significance because we see reflected in them our own activity and strivings. As extensions of bodily practices and the social contexts in which they function, they have social meaning embedded in them and invite not only use but also interpretation. For Ilyenkov, words are also artifacts because they are physical entities which have human activity embodied in them, thus having meaning due to their use in social practice. Mead (1934) once referred to words and signs having meaning because they are collapsed social acts: that is, the word contains the action it signifies within the network of meaningful interaction, and it can be used to signal this activity – or its possible occurrence – to others. Language only has meaning because of its use within the joint activities of the social group. However, Ilyenkov reverses the argument often run by Mead and the latter-day social constructionists that objects take on a meaning because of their inclusion in symbolic systems, thus giving primacy to signs. Instead, for Ilyenkov, symbols and words are sub-classes of all humanly created meaningful artifacts, rather than the primary base of all meaning. So all artifacts that embody practice are meaningful, and symbols, signs and words are but one element of the humanly created, objective, artifactual world. Moreover, meaning does not just reside in those objects that have been fashioned by humans, for once this process has begun meaning infuses a large part of the environment. Even those objects not created by humans are given a meaning, so that we no longer live in a purely physical environment, but one saturated with meaning in which people can recognize their humanity, purposes and needs in even the most inert, non-human objects.

Given what I am saying here about the importance of the artifact and its central role in mediating activity and thinking, we need to return to the problem that Gibson never solved, which is the relation between embodied perception of the environment and the cultural or artifactual forms of embodied knowledge. How can we distinguish between direct and mediated perception, where one begins and the other ends, so divining their relationship? The fact is that this is impossible because, as I began to argue in Chapter 1, human experience is multi-dimensional and one can never separate out a direct perception of a given reality from one that is mediated (the example I gave was of time). When we look at the world and move around in it, what we perceive is as much a product of our cultural, symbolic artifacts as the result of vision, hearing and touch that have developed in relation to the ecosystem. Looking out of my window now, I am seeing with human eyes evolved for activities in a given ecological niche with colour and stereoscopic vision. I am detecting the falling of light on the land and the shade on the landscape, but I am also seeing houses, roads, a school, fields, trees and moorland. I don't think I can see anything that I cannot also put a name to, so where does my perception end and my knowledge begin? The point of transition between these dimensions – as in the three-dimensional image – is indefinable and so must be conceived as a multi-dimensional experience. We do perceive elements from the socio-natural world in its various times and spaces, but the artifact 'diffracts' (Haraway, 1991) them so they are never perceived directly. The artifactual dimension, with its meaning-giving properties, is always fundamental to conscious perception, blending with the reality it diffracts.

Employing this multi-dimensional perspective helps us to avoid the pitfall of a discursive social constructionism which ultimately tends to reduce all human experience to the symbolic or, if it admits a 'reality' 'outside' language, claims that this is of no importance because we can never have direct knowledge of it. In this view, because we can only know, and speak of what we know, in terms of a language, then the only method open to social science is to analyse linguistic practices in order to understand how the world is constructed. The problem here is the anthropocentrism and lingo-centrism of this view which will not admit, or seeks to deny (Craib, 1997), the influence of the non-human upon the human or the limits set by our own fleshy bodies (Shilling, 1993). This style of social constructionism also preserves Cartesian doubt and an element of dualism, for while it has transcended Descartes's individualism, it keeps intact the radical doubt about the relation of knowing and thinking to any 'objective' world. Physical reality is either bracketed out as unknowable (Edwards et al., 1995) or a split is effected between the physical and the social. Harré (1991a: 352), for example, refers to human life as being lived within two intransigent realities: first, that of physical space and time, containing embodied agents with physical powers; secondly, the social and psychological order in which conversation, or discourse, is the primary human reality. But Harré does not resolve the dichotomies this dualism creates between the physical and the cultural within the ecology – or, as he refers to it following von Uexküll, the *Umwelt* (Harré, 1990) – nor that between direct and indirect perception in his use of Gibson.

Another problem with the constructionist view is that, in preserving the above dualisms, it also replicates the Cartesian split between knowledge and the world, between mind – or, rather, in this case, discourse – and matter. For discursive constructionists, the material world is always deferred in the process of discursive practice, as if that practice were not taking place in an ecosystem which is not itself purely linguistic, with features and objects that are not always the product of human activity; and as if discourse was not itself embodied, the product of a speaking or writing body located at a point in space and a moment in time. A way of overcoming these views and advancing a notion of speaking and mediated thinking located in a material world can be found in the work of A.N. Leontyev (1981). Like Gibson, Leontyev believes that what we call 'mind' – defined more precisely as thinking and consciousness – is a property of matter in motion, of activity and of the increasing complexity in the many relations composing life. In the active interrelation of organism and environment, all life forms develop a 'sensitivity' to the ecology which orients their activities within it. Sensitivity is a product of the active interrelationship of the organism with the ecosystem. This approach is opposed to the Kantian notion of sensitivity, which divided sensation from the formal, logical operation of the mind. Instead, in Leontyev's approach, the origin of the mind does not stem from an inherent mental capacity, but evolves from bodily sensation. Body and mind are united at the very point of origin.

For Leontyev, what distinguishes human consciousness from the more sensate forms of thought found in all animals is that it is a process governed by social laws rather than the purely natural relation between organism and environment. Consciousness is formed as certain species-specific powers, such as capacities for labour and language, become developed and passed on through the generations in external form rather than through the internal mechanisms of genetic inheritance. This dissemination of human knowledge through the generations involves linguistic communication and learning from others within social relations, and also appropriating the practices and skills crystallized in artifacts. Consciousness, then, is a product of these social relations and the artifacts that mediate them. However, conscious thought always retains a sensory basis, even though sensation no longer defines the entire experience of conscious thinking. As I suggested, conscious perception of an object reflects not only its material physicality, its form, colour, mass or material composition, but also its meaning and function – a book, a table or a food (A.N. Leontyev, 1981: 218). Human consciousness is, for Leontyev, multi-dimensional.

The active interrelation of humans and the world, then, is always mediated by relations with other people so that activities are to be regarded as joint endeavours in a socio-physical environment. In particular, our relations to others are mediated by language, while the relation to the non-human world is mediated by other artifacts devised to transform reality through the process of labour. This brings us to the question of the evolution of objective capacities in relations that transform the real and relations of communication.

Embodiment of Relations that Transform the Real and Relations of Communication

It is through the artifact, then, whether this be a symbol or sign or a material object such as a tool or utensil, that the human relation to the world becomes altered and people are able to transmit and accumulate knowledge through an external means, building what we have come to call human culture. I therefore agree with Dobzhansky (cited in Hirst and Woolley, 1982: 19) that culture should be regarded as the entire way of life within a particular group, including the material aspects. So often human culture is defined purely in terms of the development of language, and the evolutionary 'lift off' that is supposed to take us beyond biological evolution is thought to occur with the development of signs and language (Elias, 1991b). What I am arguing here is that the particular form taken by human evolution must be seen as a result of diverse factors: in particular, there is the creation of artifacts which become a means of transforming the real and of communicating, and these develop objective capacities in the humans who use them. But then there are the evolutionary pressures formed by the emergence of these new social relations and the demands that they place on individuals who must have the capacity to live in more complex social organizations. As we will see, sexual selection may have played a role in this.

To begin, though, with artifacts, which have had profound effects on the thinking body of humans and its objective capacities. Until fairly recently, palaeoanthropologists held the view that the human species evolved up to a certain point, under the selective pressure of various environmental factors, where it became possible for humans to develop tools and change their patterns of social organization. In the early 1960s, however, this view was revised with the discovery of tool use among prehuman primates, suggesting that the development and use of tools was not an outcome of human evolution but perhaps the cause of it. As Sherwood Washburn (1960: 63) claimed:

> Now the tools have been found in association with much more primitive creatures, the not-fully bipedal, small-brained near-men, or man-apes. Prior to these finds the prevailing view held that man evolved nearly to his present structural state and then discovered tools and the new ways of life that they made possible. Now it appears that man-apes – creatures able to run but not yet walk on two legs, and with brains no larger than those of apes now living – had already learned to make and to use tools. It follows that the structure of modern man must be the result of the change in the terms of natural selection that came with the tool-using way of life.

It was this tool-using way of life that formed one of the main evolutionary pressures towards bipedalism – walking and running on two legs while the hands are freed for other functions. The hands now become more refined instruments themselves, able to master other skills with greater dexterity and finesse. Equally, the mouth is freed from the function of carrying objects and this is an important factor in the human development of speech (Leakey and Lewin, 1977). All of these things form a chain or a loop of 'positive feedback', so that it is wrong to think in terms of fundamental causal mechanisms about whether changes in the physiology of the body caused tool use or vice versa; instead, it is necessary to think of all these things as interrelated and of mutual influence upon one another. For example, tool use and speech began to be ingrained in human social life and lodged in the fundamental aspects of societal organization, further reinforcing changes to the human body which affected our biological being; in turn, this embedded social and bodily changes even deeper within the human constitution. As Washburn (1960: 69) says:

> English lacks any neat expression for this sort of situation, forcing us to speak of cause and effect as if they were separated, whereas in natural selection cause and effect are interrelated. Selection is based on successful behaviour, and in the man-apes the beginnings of the human way of life depended on both inherited locomotor capacity and on the learned skills of tool-using. The success of the new way of life based on the use of tools changed the selection pressures on many parts of the body, notably the teeth, hands and brain, as well as the pelvis. But it must be remembered that selection was for the whole way of life.

The reduction of the size of teeth is mentioned here because their early function in tearing, carrying and protecting the group is replaced by hand and tool. Equally, the brain evolves under the influence of this changing way of life: the capacities of the brain are not the original cause of the emergence of new abilities, for the brain itself is restructured under the pressure of new forms of social activity, such as relations that transform the real through tool use. For example, the selection pressures that favoured a large thumb, so that the hand can manipulate tools and other objects, led to the development of a large cortical area of the brain to receive sensation from the thumb and to allow for sensitive, powerful and skilful hands (Washburn, 1960: 73). In early human groups, such hands were not only used for the production of tools but also for painting, carving and the marking of early signs that had some symbolic content. It is also clear from the way that early human groups decorated their tools and other artifacts, such as utensils, that they saw them as symbolic as well as functional. Indeed, as Leakey and Lewin (1977: 103) have said, the way in which tools are fashioned, in terms of their shape, style and size, depends on the culture of the group as much as the function of the tool. As Ilyenkov (1977) claimed, tools and signs are not separate things, for both are artifacts produced by the human group and therefore closely linked. It is the use of the artifact, then, that has distinguished human evolution from that of other animals, for while other living creatures have developed tools, these have not become artifacts with a symbolic significance. Language is also an artifact, even in its spoken form, and has a profound influence on the human body. It is strange in this sense to think of the way in which language is often thought of in contemporary Western cultures as an immaterial phenomenon, for language is materially produced by writing or speaking bodies and has material effects. Language is important in the co-ordination of more complex forms of social relations and is also vital in the organiza-tion of the division of labour (A.N. Leontyev, 1981). Forms of social organization that now revolved around artifacts entwined in an evolutionary complex that was both responsible for, and becomes a consequence of, the different features of the human body and its brain (Leakey and Lewin, 1977: 180–1).

Thus, we should not be lured by the explanations of the human way of life given by many neurologists, neuro-psychologists and cognitive scientists, who claim that it is a direct product of the structure of the human brain and the hard-wiring of its cognitive system. This is because 'the reason that the human brain makes the human way of life possible is that it is the result of that way of life. Great masses of the tissue in the human brain are devoted to memory, planning, language and skills, because these are the abilities favoured by the human way of life' (Washburn, 1960: 73). This also means, of course, that we cannot view any particular form of human life as the direct product of our physiological make-up, including the structure of the brain. The human brain *makes possible* the human way of life – tool use, language, memory and other skills – but it *does not determine* that way of life. That is to say, it does not determine the ends towards which tool use will be directed, nor the contents of language and memory, for these things have a different impact on the relations within a group and the pattern of social practices, which vary from group to group. Thus the brain does not produce specific social practices, nor does it structure the contents of knowledge and thought; it makes possible human life in its general form, but not in any specific form. That is down to the artifact, which is now at the centre of human life, replacing the gene as the mode of transmission and change within societies. As a species, humans have evolved to use artifacts and this has influenced the formation of the human body; however, while the blueprint of our bodies is encoded genetically, the artifact has taken over as the transmitter of information at a higher level, mediating the relations of communication between individuals and the relations between the human group and the non-human world. Culture and social relations are so varied because artifacts vary between human groups allowing for the transmission and transformation of various ways of life.

That the artifact has supplanted the gene as the root of transmission of culture can be seen in the 'premature' state of the human body at birth. A human infant is dependent upon those around her or him for feeding, clothing, protection and for education in the use of the artifacts of the culture. Children are supported by adults in their exploration of the environment, assisted in the development of upright walking, and are constantly exposed to the language going on around them. Even when adults do not guide children, their exploration of the artifacts that populate their surroundings is a form of social practice, as the child is learning to manipulate and use the objects that it finds. In terms of language, Borchert and Zihlman (1990) have pointed to the possibility that raising and educating children may have created evolutionary pressures on the human group, and therefore on the human body, in that the teaching of children through language – by the parents and, particularly, the mother – created the drift towards language and reinforced its influence on biology. The possibility of language use becomes ingrained in the human body in the formation of the larynx and vocal chords, the size and shape of the mouth and throat, the flexibility of the tongue and lips, and the enlargement of the cerebral cortex of the brain because the pressure towards the use of language acts directly upon each new generation of human infants in their upbringing.

Once again, though, the problems with some of these accounts of bio-history is that they are the repository of many taken-for-granted values and social roles embedded in our present-day culture which we read back on to the people of prehistory. While I feel that Washburn's work is valuable in showing how culture transforms biology as much as biology influences culture, Haraway (1992) has clearly underlined some of the cultural assumptions of this type of primate study. Washburn's notion that the earliest tools belonged to 'man the hunter' reflect sexist assumptions in which the role of women in culture is completely written out. As feminist accounts of hominid evolution began to develop in the 1970s and 1980s, palaeoanthropologists such as Adrienne Zihlman (see Haraway, 1992) began developing notions of 'woman the gatherer', outlining the role of women in the development of culture through the creation of tools for gathering plants and roots, the invention of slings to carry babies while they worked and, as we have seen, the central role that women must have played in the formation of language through nurturing and educating children. Furthermore, the notion of the strict division of labour between the sexes, thought to be in existence at this originary point of human culture, was challenged with the development of the idea of early humans as gatherers; this meant that the emphasis was more on the sharing of tasks and food among the human group, between men and women, and between adults and children. In this interpretation much more power is given to females as joint creators of tools and language and as major players in the process of sexual selection, choosing partners who were not just the aggressive brutes of sociobiological myth, but displayed other aspects of human behaviour such as intelligence and the social skills needed for co-operation (Taylor, 1997).

However, there is a danger even in these accounts that the role of women in bio-history becomes somewhat homogenized and stereotyped, so that 'the challenge facing those who generated the figure of woman the gatherer is to mutate her further to tell better the heteroglossic stories of sexual difference and difference within sex – while remaining responsible scientifically for constructing and reading the data' (Haraway, 1992: 348). The gendered assumptions and lack of sensitivity towards difference within sex are also clearly drawn out by Taylor's (1997) reading of sex in prehistory, illustrating the way in which human skeletons are categorized rather crudely by archaeologists on the basis of bone size and shape as belonging to males or females, ignoring the possibility that they may be the remains of people of indeterminate sex. In other words, we read back into prehistory our own assumptions about sex, gender and sexuality.

Conclusion

Where are we now after our brief excursion into the study of the evolution of bodies of knowledge and thought? First of all there is mounting evidence that human bodies did not evolve purely under the pressures of 'natural' selection, nor solely from the pressure for gene replication. Rather, nature and culture become indivisible in the biological evolution of the human body, with artifacts taking over from the gene as an important channel for the transmission and transformation of cultural knowledge. Furthermore, artifacts are used to transform the socio-natural contexts of human life and, in the process, they re-form the human body by creating new capacities. Some of these capacities are stored purely at the artifactual level, such as the knowledge of how to use particular tools or the contents of a system of beliefs, but others can be ingrained in the body itself, changing the structure and function of limbs, hands, feet, the nervous system and brain. While these changes to the body allow for certain potentials, such as the creative use of artifacts, they do not determine or structure the actual process of human social practices or the formation of types of knowledge or belief. That is the role of historical relations of power and relations of transformation and communication. Power should not be viewed as already existing at the birth of social relations, a structure of domination, subjugation and cruelty bound to repeat itself at each point of historical emergence, and to which knowledge is but a handmaiden. Rather, power relations are inherent within the changing forms of social relations as a whole and knowledge becomes part of, though not entirely reducible to, these struggles. As much as knowledge is used to divide, separate and dominate a group, it can also be used for sharing, unifying and liberating people. Relations of communication also spread knowledge from generation to generation and this process interacts with power relations in complex, subtle and ambiguous ways, so that we can never say that knowledge is used only to dominate. It still has the capacity to enlighten and inform.

The political advantages of this reading of bio-history is that it does not root bodies of knowledge and thought in aggressive instincts or in the will to power and, as such, it allows us to think of our socio-political futures as open and as yet to be made. The power structures we know today in the industrialized world, with aggressive conflicts occurring over property and territory, ruthless economic competition and exploitation, and the domination of women, races and sexual minorities, may well be a product of the more recent bio-history of humans where, in the farming communities of the Neolithic period, land was declared as private property and protected by physical force, with the growing importance of men as farmers, warriors and stock-breeders (Leakey, 1981; Taylor, 1997). While there is a danger of blaming all the ills of present-day society on our farming ancestors and romanticizing the lifestyles of those in prehistory, about whom we know very little, what such speculations do suggest to us is that power relations and forms of domination are variable and uneven, and we must avoid at all cost the disempowering notions of the eternal recurrence of familiar patterns of domination. Relations of transformation, communication and power are not configured in ways that are unchangeable because the origins and influences on human society and culture are so diverse, unidirectional and non-deterministic. The same also applies to their effects on the body.

3 The Body as Object: from the Grotesque to the Closed Body

If the human body has been re-formed through bio-history in relations of transformation, communication and power, these relations have also had a more recent and dramatic effect upon the body and the way in which people in the Western world have experienced their embodied selves. As I claimed in the Introduction, since the seventeenth century Westerners have begun to feel that they are living a dual existence, divided between the life of the mind and that of the body. The experience of the self has essentially been disembodied and the body cast into a shadowy and troublesome existence. For Descartes, the body was nothing more than an automaton, a fleshy machine with which humans could hardly identify; instead, it was the mind by which we identified ourselves, so that when we refer to 'I' we are speaking of the mental substance or essence of which we are composed and not our flesh and blood. Foucault (1979) associated this trend towards dualism with the emergence of what he called 'bio-power', which is a form of power exerted over the population and over the bodies of individuals, disciplining and regulating them, and turning them into rational and calculable machines. Through bio-power, life is brought into the field of political calculation and manipulation and there develops a bio-politics of the population, fascism being one of the most extreme examples. But such bio-politics was also evident in Malthus and, through his influence on Darwin, in the theories of evolution, which took domestic selection – the human breeding of the best animal stock – as a metaphor for 'natural' selection. Whatever the fashion, in Foucault's view, politics began to intervene in the very reproduction and regulation of life itself. Here, I will only partially agree with Foucault's analysis, believing that it needs supplementing with other analyses of the emergence of the Cartesian subject and the disciplining of the human body, particularly those of Bakhtin and Elias. Mainly, what I will do in this chapter is to sketch the emergence of the modern, Western body, and the configuration of the lines of power relations which cross, intersect and divide it. This is not meant to be an exhaustive historical analysis, but a selective view that illustrates the emergence of Cartesian dualism, a view that is provocative in presenting some possibilities for transcending it. I will begin by presenting a particular image of the medieval, 'grotesque' body and how this became transmuted into the disciplined and concealed modern body.

From the Grotesque to the Modern Body

Bakhtin (1984) has traced images of the medieval body through the writings of François Rabelais (c.1494–1553), especially in his employment of terms from carnival and folk culture. For Bakhtin, the language and imagery employed by Rabelais is the unofficial language of the people – of the carnival and the marketplace, of laughter and ribaldry – and not the serious, official language of the church and feudal culture. The language of the carnival and marketplace consists of humorous abuse, which has a tradition spanning back over the centuries to ancient pagan festivals. Carnival imagery also contains a form of 'grotesque realism', in which the material body appears in exaggerated form, and can be linked to the festive world of giants, monsters, dwarfs and fools. Bakhtin is not claiming that the people of the Middle Ages and the early Renaissance lived out their material, bodily lives in grotesque fashion, but that it was still possible to experience the body and its functions in their more earthy form. People could have an experience of the lived body that was more direct and unmediated – a sensuous involvement with the world where the boundaries between the inside and outside of the body, and the dividing line between the individual and the collective, were not as sharply drawn as they are today. This was possible only in the strictly delimited time of the carnival, yet the sensuous body and its imagery still comprised a very present and real force.

Furthermore, the carnival was not a spectacle to be watched like modern-day processions and public events, but was something all people participated in, irrespective of rank or position, so that the carnival was a great leveller. It represented the world temporarily turned upside-down and inside-out, mocking the pious and serious tone of ecclesiastical teaching and practice and also the chivalrous manners and rituals of the nobility. Carnivals and feasts were also linked to natural, biological or historical time; they were related to breaking points or moments of crisis in the cycle of life or events within society. Celebration and the festive perception of the world are therefore always linked to notions of death and revival, change and renewal. For a time the people enter a utopian realm of unbroken continuity with their ancestors, and experience feelings of community, freedom, equality and abundance. The suspension of social rank and hierarchy during carnival time also added to this feeling and led to a special type of communication, that of marketplace speech and gesture, which was frank and free, permitting no distance and liberating people from the norms of etiquette and decency imposed at other times. According to Bakhtin (1984: 11), then, we find in the carnival a utopian atmosphere where there is 'the sense of the gay relativity of all truths and authorities'.

Rabelais takes from this culture of carnival and folk humour his grotesque images of the material body. In this 'grotesque realism', the image of the body is a positive one; like the carnival itself, the body is not seen as a private possession, but a universal, lived phenomenon, represented in everyone. The material body of the individual is part of the collective, ancestral body of the people. Also, like the carnival, the body has regenerative power; it not only consumes and takes in from the earth, it also reproduces and gives birth. In the grotesque image of the body, emphasis is placed on orifices and protuberances, especially in the lower bodily strata – the bowels, buttocks and genitals – which are linked to the earth and its reproductive power. The earth swallows through the grave, but also gives birth in the form of new life, just as the human body consumes and excretes, takes in and gives life. Grotesque bodies are not closed, but are open to the world, and emphasis is placed on the body parts that stretch out into it, such as the nose, pot belly, phallus, breasts, and those open to it, such as the mouth, genitals and anus, all of which connect us to the earth and to other people. Because clear lines were not drawn between the inside and outside, the human body of the early Renaissance could be an ambiguous body, reflecting at one and the same time life and death, youth and age, reproduction and degeneration, as in Kerch's terracotta figurines of senile pregnant old hags (Bakhtin, 1984: 25). For Bakhtin, it is impossible for us today to understand such figures, just as it is impossible for us to grasp the meaning and the humour of Rabelais's writings, unless we know something of the culture which inspired them and the type of bodily experience which is at its root. In modern society, the emphasis on the lower bodily strata, the images of excrement and birth, of fertilizing and generating, appear vulgar or coarse and the complex meanings within them are lost.

The meaning of bringing someone 'down to earth' also had a more literal sense in the world of the carnival and the marketplace, where tossing dung at passers-by was a ritualistic gesture, and debasing expressions were used such as 'I shit on you' (Bakhtin, 1984: 148). Bringing someone down to earth is associated with images of smearing with mud or excrement and it is linked to the carnivalesque aims of levelling and reducing the social hierarchy. Curses always indicated a downward motion, directed at the legs and the buttocks, and shit was the means of degradation. However, this lowering of those in the higher social echelons, which could also be witnessed in the mock crownings that occurred in carnivals, is also linked to change and renewal. It is not simply an attempt to destroy the existing social order but to generate a new one. To some extent, it is also linked to the regeneration of the existing order, for the carnival spirit is very much limited to its own time, and, when that time is over, social life continues, having been invigorated.

But the main functions of the carnival are to connect the people to the collective and to the earth through participation in festivities and through indulgence in the abundance on offer at the feast, as well as to dispel fears through collective laughter. The person who eats and drinks and develops a big fat belly is associated with the pregnant woman about to give birth: the full stomach is a celebration of life and its abundance and a way of participating by eating oneself into the community (Falk, 1994; Mellor and Shilling, 1997). Human labour ends in the production and enjoyment of food, and humans triumph over the world in devouring it. Eating, drinking and swallowing is a way of taking the world into oneself and then giving out again. Thus, there was also a strong link made between food and speech, as well as with sex and birth; Rabelais, for example, claimed that he only wrote while eating and drinking, and free and frank truths were exchanged at the banquet. Wine liberates from sanctimoniousness and is connected to laughter and merriment, which dispels the fears of the world. Food and wine, then, are seen in philosophical terms as having their own truth, which is a tendency to superabundance, victory and merriment, opposing the serious world of fear and oppression.

Perhaps this is why Rabelais was such a popular author in his day, the period of the early Renaissance in France, where the carnival tradition was still a recognizable genre. And yet, as Bakhtin (1984) shows so clearly, Rabelais was soon to lose his popularity, becoming a much misunderstood writer, as the world which he inhabited slipped away and was replaced by new social and political configurations where people bodily inhabited the world in a very different fashion. During the period of the Renaissance, bodies and objects began to acquire a private, individual nature, one that was closed off to the world and complete within itself. Thus, rather than the open and unfinished body, accent was placed on its sealed and finished nature. Bakhtin refers to this as the 'classical canon' as opposed to the grotesque, in which attention shifts from the body's openings, orifices and protuberances, to its closures – its skin, smooth surfaces, musculature and, in particular, to the face and the eyes. Those parts and aspects of the body which were publicly celebrated in carnival culture became privatized and experienced as sources of shame. Sexual life, giving birth, death, eating and drinking turned into private acts and lost their public, symbolic content. That is, they became what we refer to today as 'body functions', the by-products of the bodily machine, and as such they lost their meaningful place in the cycles and rituals of public life. The body still consumed food and drink and could do so in abundance, but it became the private, greedy body of bourgeois society, whose aim was not so much to be satiated and satisfied, as to hide away, sequester and guiltily indulge. One could say that this body no longer aimed to satisfy need, but followed the dictates of the law of desire (Falk, 1994). Sex, urination and defecation were also bodily acts consigned to specific private areas – chambers or rooms – and regarded as functions one did not speak of in polite society.

Laughter became a matter of private amusement and not the collective force that had the power to dispel the fears and insecurities of natural and social life. The grotesque still lives on today to a small degree in popular culture and comedy theatre, but it is a product for private consumption and has lost its rambunctious and threatening element of full public participation. Pre-romanticism and Romanticism in the eighteenth and nineteenth centuries attempted to revive the grotesque genre, only with a radically transformed meaning; it became the expression of a subjective, individualistic world outlook. Romanticism could be regarded as a backlash against the classicism of the Enlightenment, including the disembodied, rational beings of Descartes's philosophy. Yet the emotive, heroic, tragic figure of Romanticism had about her or him a private chamber character, which was very different from the bodily experience of the collective, indivisible and regenerating grotesque. However, Romanticism created its own figure of the 'interior man', who is deep, complex and has inexhaustible internal resources. Bakhtin refers to this as the *interior infinite* which was unknown in medieval and Renaissance literature (1984: 44), only now elements of the grotesque are reflected in an inner life rather than the public one. Here we find Romanticism's contribution to modernity, in the view of humans with hidden and unfathomable inner depths, like the unconscious 'inner universe' investigated by Freud.

However, as Romanticism died away as a movement in the latter part of the nineteenth century, the overriding influence on contemporary Western societies has been classicism, which has dominated the modernist perspective (Gergen, 1991). Bakhtin claims that the classical canon has predominated since the seventeenth century:

> [which] was marked by the stabilization of the new order of absolute monarchy. A relatively progressive 'universally historic form' was created and expressed in Descartes' rationalist philosophy and in the aesthetics of classicism. Rationalism and classicism clearly reflect the fundamental traits of the new official culture; it differed from the ecclesiastic feudal culture but was also authoritarian and serious, though less dogmatic . . .
>
> In the new official culture there prevails a tendency toward the stability and completion of being, toward one single meaning, one single tone of seriousness. The ambivalence of the grotesque can no longer be admitted. The exalted genres of classicism are freed from the influence of the grotesque tradition of laughter. (Bakhtin, 1984: 101)

The closed and rationalized Cartesian body is therefore severed from its sensual connections with the world and its collective associations with other beings. Alone and in perpetual doubt of sensate experience and the certainty of any knowledge, the self is plagued with that ontological insecurity so redolent of modernity (Giddens, 1990, 1991). No longer is there the hearty collective laugh of the carnival to dispel fear; no longer the ambivalence surrounding bodily existence and the dividing lines of the inner and outer. The person of rationalism and classicism is firmly encased in his or her closed bodily shell, alone with his or her doubt, uncertainty and fear. This is not to say that all of human life has at its base these existential fears and dreads, but that they have become a chronic condition for modern humans in the West.

Accompanying and strengthening these changes in the experience of the lived body there was also a change in the perception of time as the world of the carnival began to fade. Where carnival celebrated cyclical time, with feasts located at points of crisis or of death and renewal, the new experience of time that emerged towards the end of the Renaissance was of linear time. While this created an awareness of history and historical change, it severed the cyclical linkage of death and birth, of decline and renewal, which was so predominant in carnival time. In the linear frame of time, death is antithetical to life, marking its ending rather than renewal, and for the individual this means that their death is no longer the point at which they are taken back into the body of the ancestral people; rather, death is the annihilation of their being. For medieval people, the universe was ordered according to a hierarchical structure, where heaven was the highest realm and the underworld the lowest. During the Renaissance this hierarchy was dismantled and its elements were transferred to a single, linear plane. The emphasis was no longer on higher and lower, but upon forwards and backwards in space and time. Now death becomes an ending, and one that the individual must confront alone.

The Civilized, Armoured Body

Bakhtin's view of the transformation of bodily experience during the Renaissance is complemented by Elias (1978, 1982). Elias's concern is with the changing form of manners displayed in court societies through the Renaissance period, but this also allows a glimpse into the world of the Middle Ages and the forms of behaviour that 'civilized' society attempted to outlaw. One of the main things to emerge from Elias's study is the way in which the medieval body becomes subject to greater restraints within the developing societies of Renaissance Europe. The restraints that are placed upon people are largely emotional restraints, which is to say that they are aimed at the more basic responses to other people and their actions. The more open and volatile displays of emotion that were common in the interactions between people of the medieval period came gradually under stricter control and there was an increasing demand placed upon people, originating in the courts of the aristocracy, to think before they expressed their feelings. This form of 'civilized', or polite, behaviour was seen as a mark of respect for the feelings of others, and one always had to be sensitive to the effects of an action or expression upon another person. It is important to stress here, though, that this is not simply a suppression of emotion; rather, it is more of a deferral and differentiation of feelings. That is to say, in the Middle Ages, emotions were expressed more strongly yet were less nuanced and complex; one could feel friendship or enmity, desire or aversion, good or bad, but there was little differentiation of such emotional states or feelings, few gradations between such polar oppositions, and little scope for ambivalence in them.

This differentiation increased with the modulation of emotional control, which worked at the level of the body in two ways. First, a finer modulation of emotion meant that people had to be continually conscious of their bodily gestures or facial expressions, so as not to do anything to offend another person; this also meant being attuned to the minutiae of gestures and expressions in others, in order to gauge more accurately their feelings and

responses. Here, Elias (1978) notes, we find the emergence of the psychological attitude within people, which is the ability to try to fathom the 'inner'
thoughts or feelings of other persons that may be hidden behind a mask of
politeness or demure. Emotions therefore become psychologized and move
to an 'inner' plane. Instead of remaining part of the responsive aspects of
peoples' interactions, they become something to be felt but not always to be
shown.

Secondly, control of the body also meant control over those bodily
functions that others might find offensive. Elias's first volume of *The
Civilizing Process* is a rich catalogue of the types of bodily processes and
actions that are no longer acceptable in polite society, such as spitting or
farting. Like Bakhtin, Elias also notes how sex acts, along with urination and
defecation, are now confined to specific chambers of houses, having their
own, designated private space. The same is true also of birth and of death
(Elias, 1985). The emerging norms of conduct demanded that, when in
public, individuals should not give off any signs of their bodily needs in case
this might disturb others. This led to the creation of private and public
spaces, which corresponded to a psychological topography of the conscious
and the unconscious, the admitted and the hidden.

Like Bakhtin, Elias also notes the closing of the human body around the
height of the Renaissance period, being expressed, for example, in changing
table manners where people stop eating from communal dishes or drinking
from communal cups. Suddenly, people became more sensitive to the
exchange of bodily fluids which raises the fear of contamination. As the body
becomes more closed to others and fears of contamination are raised,
stronger taboos are placed around bodies and the substances that pass
between them (Douglas, 1966). The demands to observe people in a more
psychological fashion also focus individuals on each other's eyes and faces
in the search for looks, expressions and gestures. The body itself is more
concealed behind elaborate and decorative clothing and becomes a 'danger
zone'. That is, as nakedness is less commonplace in society, the body is
subject to a greater erotic investment as an object of fantasy and wish-
fulfilment, becoming what would be regarded in later centuries as 'sexual-
ized'. Furthermore, bodily sensations are concentrated on visual perception,
which is linked more directly to intellectual understanding, and the other
senses of the body are less central. Smell, touch and taste become less
important senses in a society where knowledge is gathered more from the
distant senses, such as sight and hearing, than through those of close contact
(Falk, 1994). Because psychological understanding is linked closely to the
observation of others, vision came under the control of cognitive apprehension (Mellor and Shilling, 1997).

There is here a unidirectional aspect to the control of the body, for while
the body becomes more closed to others and to the world, and its feelings
more finely regulated and differentiated, at the same time bodily experience
is intensified. We find the creation of inner longings and desires, which were
to become the basis for the Romantic movement in the arts and the object for

psychoanalysis in the sciences. Yet these are bodily experiences that are private; they pulsate under layers of clothing, behind the barriers of reserve, and are expressed only in private chambers of the household. The barriers of reserve and the restraint on feelings become a body armour, frozen into our movements, gestures, posture and musculature. This intensifies the body's surface only at the cost of petrifying it in terms of spontaneous expression. The body becomes more of a communicative body rather than an assimilative one (Falk, 1994; O'Neill, 1985), a signifying surface that both expresses and yet conceals. The court society is a place of masks that hide as much as they show.

However, although the body is becoming more intensified in terms of its experience, this only occurs through it becoming an 'object' of the mind, viewed at a relative distance. This does not simply mean that the bodies of others become the objects for psychological observation, but that our own bodies are also experienced as such. The norms by which conduct is regulated in the relations between people are also those by which we regulate our own feelings and actions. We observe others and ourselves more closely. However, this intellectual observation began to present itself as existing in the form of a separate component of humans, like the heart or brain, so that the act of thinking crystallized into the idea of 'intelligence', 'reason' or 'spirit' which was somehow distinct from the rest of the body (Elias, 1991a: 106). The relation between mind and body, thought and emotion, became conceived in spatial terms. Moreover, the mind was seen as trapped inside the body because of the increased barriers of restraint between people and the doubt about the actual existence of things beyond their comprehension in reason. Humans felt that they were looking out on the world from inside a casing, or at worst, a prison. Elias refers to this through the metaphor of the 'thinking statues', each one of us standing in isolation and silent, inanimate contemplation of an 'external' world with which we feel we have lost direct contact (1991a: 113). The metaphor conveys the new way in which humans experience thinking itself, as something solitary, still and silent. The bodily forms of knowing and thinking which would involve all the human senses – of communication and dialogue, action and movement, touch, sight, sound and smell – are curtailed to thinking at a distance and in an inanimate way. As I have said, it is visual perception and its links to a form of cognitive apprehension – which is to say, purely 'mental' as opposed to sensual – that take precedence. The outwardly projected persona then becomes like a shell or a wall that stands between us and all that is beyond our bodily limits (Barker, 1995).

By the beginning of the eighteenth century in Europe, this experience is fairly well consolidated and is no longer confined to the aristocratic court. The 'civilized' forms of manners and interaction developed in the court are still recognizable today, having been filtered through society with their adoption, in modified form, by the bourgeoisie, spreading to other social classes through bourgeois educators and administrators, and through the teachings of the church. The possibility of the grotesque experience of bodily being has long since disappeared, and the nearest we can get to it today is through the depths of inner experience, which is the legacy of Romanticism. Yet this could not dispel the Cartesian understanding of the body as a closed machine, so that the life of humans has largely moved 'inward' on to a psychic plane, creating the deep subjectivity that we experience as a private possession, removed and distanced from others. Social life is regulated and emotional expression curtailed, yet at the same time the private world of emotion and fantasy is deepened. As Mead (1964) said, emotion is delayed impulse, and the inner-delaying agency is the conscience or superego. This inner psychic censor is nothing more than the internalized social norms that govern and regulate social relations, so that, in contemporary life, conflict is also internalized and expressed as the battle between conscience and temptation (Barker, 1995: 43). However, while the norms that regulate the relations and interactions between people are central to these processes, they stem from wider social changes taking place during the period of the Renaissance.

State Formation and Ideological and Normative Control: a Divided World

A number of changes, then, occurred during the period of the Renaissance in Europe, which drastically altered the experience of human embodiment. The normative controls that people began to operate upon one another, as well as upon themselves, demanding a more restrained and 'civilized' form of conduct, had the impact of closing off the body and encasing it against others in defensive armour. While this laid emphasis on the closed and smooth surfaces of the human body, as opposed to its openings and protuberances, thought and feeling were driven deeper into a private space, both in the social geography of private rooms and places, and in the psychological topography of a private, 'inner' psyche. However, all this is dependent on wider social changes, which many commentators agree is related to the centralization of the state during the Renaissance and its monopolization of the means of violence (Bakhtin, 1984; Barker, 1995; Elias, 1978, 1982). That the state became centralized and secured a monopoly of the means of violence meant that many of the spaces of everyday life within society became pacified. The means of violence no longer belonged to the people, who had to find new ways of influencing the conduct of others. But more than this, nation-states increasingly became disinclined to use physical violence against their own, unarmed populations, and instead a form of ideological control developed. As Barker (1995) claims, this indirect ideological control works as a form of self-discipline through the unwritten laws and norms that govern subjectivity. Rather than individuals being directly coerced into forms of action, they are induced into disciplining themselves through various ideologies.

However, I want to stress here that, between the forms of ideological hegemony and the practice of self-discipline, there are the norms individuals apply to one another within social relations. As Foucault (1979) has remarked, in contemporary Western societies the norm becomes the means through which behaviour is regulated, supplanting the juridical law on which absolutism rested. The absolute monarch had to rely on the sword, on violence, to enforce the law, yet as the disinclination to use violence within society grew stronger as the monopoly on it was secured by the state, a new regulatory mechanism began to emerge. Because the aim of the new form of bio-power was to take charge of life, what was needed was a continuous regulatory and corrective mechanism. It is not so much that the law takes a back seat or that institutions of justice disappear, but rather:

> that the law operates more and more as a norm, and that the judicial institution is increasingly incorporated into a continuum of apparatuses (medical, administrative, and so on) whose functions are for the most part regulatory. A normalizing society is the historical outcome of a technology of power centred on life. (Foucault, 1979: 144)

So, for Foucault, the norm is equated with processes of normalizing, taking place through institutions such as the asylum, the hospital, prison and other forms of administrative organization. The aims of such institutions are to produce docile bodies that are disciplined and ready to be used as labour power. Here we see the two-pronged movements of bio-power: on the one hand, working at the level of populations, adjusting them to economic processes; and, on the other, disciplining yet intensifying individual bodies, creating in them new aptitudes and capacities as free citizens and labourers, without at the same time making them more difficult to govern. The body is, then, at one and the same moment, infused with powers and disciplined. It is given the capacities for self-discipline needed by the citizen who is expected to act rationally and autonomously, entering into free and honourable contracts with others, and is prepared for the disciplines of the labour contract – for the regular and regulated dictates of waged work, and for the sale of the body as labour power, involving the learning of new skills and capacities.

However, Foucault came to recognize the limits of this approach, focused mainly on the techniques and strategies of power, ignoring the 'techniques of the self' through which individuals constitute themselves as disciplined subjects (1986a: 11). His later work was centred upon ethics and how individuals enter into an ethical relationship with their own selves, taking part of the self or its behaviour as the substance for ethical formation (Foucault, 1986a, 1988). As Davidson (1986) remarks, this is a very particular view of ethics, which is centred on the self's relationship to itself, or the techniques of the self used in ethical self-formation. What Foucault is studying is the way in which individuals turn the body and the self into an object, making it the target for the application of regimes, diets or moral precepts. However, a problem with the last two volumes of *The History of*

Sexuality, centred as they are on the cultures of antiquity, is that ethical self-regulation is studied only in terms of the precepts recorded in philosophical texts, ignoring the notion of ethics as dialogical practice among individuals in interaction (Gardiner, 1996). Only in his essay on Kant does Foucault (1986c) make mention of the relation of individuals to one another with respect to ethics, including how people can modify ethical codes through their joint practices.

What is suggested, yet unexplored, is the whole realm of moral inter-actions between individuals and the way in which moral norms are the medium and outcome of everyday relations. I say here that moral norms are both the medium and outcome of moral interactions, borrowing the language of structuration, because, as moral precepts are largely unwritten, they are open to reformulation and re-negotiation in their practical use. Ethical self-formation is an important part of these moral practices, but it is only one aspect of them, and cannot be regarded as the primary element. In this sense, when Foucault (1982) claims that the 'modern state', as it began to develop around the eighteenth century, is one that did not form above people, but integrated them into its very structure, being concerned with individualizing people as much as totalizing the state formation, he was absolutely right. The modern form of regulating behaviour through norms is one that indi-viduals practice upon one another as well as upon themselves. As Elias (1978) points out, the discipline of psychology can trace its roots back to the courts of the absolute monarch and the way in which people had to observe themselves and others more closely, and it did not begin solely in the disciplinary institutions of the eighteenth and nineteenth centuries. Between the institutional practices of normalization and the practices of ethical self-formation, there exists the everyday level of interaction where individuals apply norms to each other in their joint practices.

There is also the idea implicit in Foucault's work that in ethical self-formation people become the subjects of discourses. However, this is only partly true, for Foucault could never explain what made people so anxious, so eager, to speak the truth of themselves through various discourses. The type of discourses that claim to reveal the truth about the self emerged particularly in the eighteenth and nineteenth centuries as writing and speech became the prime modes of expression of the embodied self. The bodily aspects and processes associated with the grotesque body have now become functions, largely stripped of their symbolic content, and language is the primary means through which the self finds expression. The subject becomes an author in discourse and the body sinks beneath the discursivity of the subject (Barker, 1995: 57). As the self is felt to be constituted in writing, the bourgeois subject substitutes for its corporeal body the rarefied body of the text. Thus we get the emergence at this time of the popularity of diaries and biographies among the bourgeoisie, in which the self becomes the subject of cognitive narration (Mellor and Shilling, 1997).

The bourgeois subject, then, narrates both self and world from a private place, and the certainty of that narration beyond the private place of the study or the psyche is called into doubt. From this position there opens up all the divisions which still mark the contemporary Western world: the division between private and public, subject and object, spiritual and material, mind and body, individual and society, and self and others. All these dichotomies are connected through the armouring and division of bodies, both between the bodies of different individuals and within individuals themselves in terms of the division of body and mind. As the individual becomes solitary and private, and his or her own self is understood as a textual narration composed in a private place, the world of materiality and sociality 'outside' that space is felt to be radically distant, as is the materiality of the body. Even the ties between words and things becomes broken so that language itself is experienced as autonomized (Falk, 1994).

Furthermore, this narrated self becomes the ground for all truths, as only the solidity of its textual production can ensure that anything spoken or written about the 'outer' world has a stable foundation in truth. Hence, Descartes's discourse in which he finds the grounds of all truth in the certainty of his own cogito. As Heidegger (1977: 128) says, when humans become the primary and the only real subjects, this means that 'Man becomes that being upon which all that is, is grounded as regards the manner of its Being and its truth. Man becomes the relational centre of that which is as such.' For Heidegger, in contrast to medieval and ancient humans, the modern person makes all knowledge of the world depend upon him or herself – the individual who is at the centre of the relation to the world. At the same time, the world appears before humans as a picture, which is not to say that it is an exact pictorial image as much as an understanding of what is set in place before oneself as a system, as in 'I get the picture.' Heidegger claims that there was no medieval world picture because that which exists is understood as created by God and humans belong to a specific rank in the created order. The being of all that exists is not placed before humans as the objective, in the realm of human knowledge and disposal. In contrast, modern representing means:

> to bring what is present at hand before oneself as something standing over against, to relate it to oneself, to the one representing it, and to force it back into this relationship to oneself as the normative realm. Whenever this happens, man 'gets into the picture' in precedence over whatever is. (Heidegger, 1977: 131)

Thus the world becomes something represented by humans in pictorial fashion, an objectifying act which also inspires people to go forward and master it. So not only does time get stretched on to a linear and flat plane, as Bakhtin (1984) suggested, but space also opens up to modern humans as objective and separate dimensions, to be seen, known and mastered. What is being accentuated here is the importance of vision in modern forms of understanding and the close link that is established between sight and cognitive apprehension, or seeing and knowing.

Rorty (1980) has emphasized how modern thought conceptualizes the mind through the metaphor of sight, as being like an eye – 'the mind's eye'

– which can pick up and mirror an external reality. But it is Foucault (1977) who linked this process to emerging forms of power, especially to the force of surveillance in modern societies. Even in his work on sexuality, where Foucault (1979) emphasizes the importance of discourse in defining various sexualities, 'he insisted on the importance of spatial, visual controls in policing it' (Jay, 1986: 193). Vision, then, is tied up with the power relations and normative controls working on the body, restricting sensate experience mainly to vision, and linking this to rational forms of cognitive apprehension – the only sure route to the truth.

There also emerges in this general trend towards the cognitive representation of a picture of the world what Barker (1995: 86) calls the 'positivism of the object', or Heidegger refers to as the position of realism; that is, of thought being put in a position of having to prove the reality of the outer world, of having to save that which is. For Heidegger, this Cartesian doubt can only be overcome by questioning the truth of being, the notion of the human cogito as the foundation point and guarantor of all truth. However, such a questioning of being turns the project of overcoming Cartesianism into a philosophical, and perhaps ultimately a metaphysical, journey, whereas here I want to suggest a relational approach to the problem. That is, instead of understanding humans as the relational centre of all that exists, we replace this with the understanding of humans as non-central points in the networks of various relations, which encompass relations between people and also with the non-human.

As to the origin of the Cartesian subject, Heidegger agrees with Elias (1991a) that the 'I' of human thought becomes essential when humans become relatively free of religious obligation. Self-liberating humanity comes to posit what is obligatory and, in the absence of any divine ordinance, the guide to truth becomes human reason and its law. But a new certainty must now be created in order for humans to know the truth, and that certainty must rest in the individual subject, divorced from all that is around him or her. It may be claimed that the emergence of an isolated, cognitive subject is not so much the result of secularization as the product of Protestantism (Mellor and Shilling, 1997); nevertheless, what interests me here is the effects of these changes and the loss of religious practice as a guarantor of truth and certainty in the world. Whether through Protestantism or gradual secularization (and it could be argued that the former has led to the latter), humans increasingly feel themselves to be isolated in life with only the power of their own thought to guide them.

As the constitutive subject becomes more central and is seen to be distinct from the body as spirit or essence, the body itself comes to be understood as matter and as a mechanism, or as Descartes put it, an automaton. This situation is one that is gendered; women are equated more with bodily being, with emotions and with the earth, as in 'mother earth' or 'mother nature'. Certainly, the power relations that carve out the division between body and self also involve gender relations, and I will explore this in Chapter 5. Suffice it to say for the moment that there is a tendency in modernity, which affects all genders, towards seeing the body as a mechanism which can be understood, repaired and made to work effectively (Barker, 1995: 72). According to Barker, while the self becomes expressed in discourse, the body is excluded as an expressive being; instead, it becomes the object rather than the subject of discourse. Through those discourses, as Foucault suggested – discourses of medicine, of wealth and populations, economics and sexuality – the body becomes regulated and disciplined, the subject of various relations of power.

Through this process of disembodiment, the self is experienced in Cartesian fashion, as a phenomenon related to its corporeal casing and yet somehow distinct from it. The relation is one that exists across a marked division between two different modes of being. At the same time, there emerged the two aspects of the modern self which haunt psychology to this day: the self as a textual being that narrates its own existence and identity and, behind this, the self as a cognitive and rational being which speaks the truth about itself and the world. As we shall see, contemporary social and psychological theories tend to emphasize one aspect or one side of this self, and generally have problems in conceptualizing the body as anything other than a machine, if they conceptualize it at all.

However, I have claimed here that at the root of this Cartesian division are wider social changes, which intersect the individual and his or her relation to others and to the world. First of all there is the centralization of the nation-state, its monopolizing of the means of violence, and the switch from physical coercion to ideological and normative control. These controls, practised by individuals on one another and upon their own selves, produce a greater emotional distance between people and the feeling that the self is encased inside the bodily armour. The body is experienced as a closed barrier that separates us from others, a sensation expressed in the classical aesthetic of the body as opposed to the grotesque. A wedge is then driven between the immediate sensual experience of individuals in their interactions with each other and with the objects of the physical world, and this divide extends into the body with the division between the body and the mind. Other changes during the Renaissance also contributed to the emergence of the divided and dualistic world; in particular, the effects of secularization upon the population and the transition from the control of feudal and ecclesiastical authorities to social power centred more on norms and self-discipline. While this created the view of individuals as free and autonomous agents, it was at the expense of people acting as the agents of social control upon each other and upon themselves. And yet this view is only partly true, for while relations of power do infuse the relations of communication between people on an everyday level, they do not completely envelop them. Within everyday relations of communication there exist spaces where people can react against and resist official, hegemonic ideologies and produce unofficial ideologies or heretical discourses which challenge the existing order.

The Official and the Unofficial

While power is no doubt an element of both relations of communication and relations that transform the real, there are in all areas limits to the reach of power. It could be argued that more and more of everyday life is continually being drawn into official ideology and normative control, and the hierarchies of the modern state and its bureaucracies are not even subject to the temporary subversion suffered by authorities in the carnivals of the Renaissance. While this is true, other spaces have emerged in contemporary life that can be regarded as the sites of unofficial ideologies or heretical discourses, such as political parties, trade unions and other social movements. Also, official and unofficial ideologies are never separate things for they intermingle and are dependent on one another (Bakhtin, 1986; Bourdieu, 1991; Vološinov, 1986).

I am using the term 'ideology' here, in the way that Vološinov (1986: 91) has described it, to refer to 'systems of social ethics, science, art and religion'. In this scheme, ideology does not simply refer to the ideas of the established ruling groups because others also have their own unofficial ideologies. So ideology, in the meaning of the term employed here, does not indicate a false consciousness or a misleading representation of the world, but rather it defines the beliefs, values or ethics of a group, which can be regarded as elements of a systematic, yet internally contradictory, world outlook (Billig et al., 1988). I will use both the terms 'ideology' and 'discourse' because, although most social theory has now substituted the term discourse for ideology, I do not see the two as mutually exclusive. If we take ideology to be a world outlook, then various discourses can comprise it. For Foucault, discourses are tactical elements or blocks operating in the field of force relations and there can be different, or even contradictory, discourses operating in that field. Discourses are usually centred on the construction of some object of knowledge, such as the population or the human body. Taken together, though, I would say that these discourses form different ideologies, especially where they take on the accent and outlook of a particular social group or class. Foucault believed that it was in discourse that power and knowledge were joined together, yet I do not think this is always the case; power and knowledge can sometimes be joined at a more systematic level where various, contradictory discourses form into the ideology of a group. In this way there can be hegemonic or official ideologies opposed by unofficial ideologies, each composed of various discursive strands. The composition of these strands into ideologies depends on the power relations between the groups involved.

The fact that no system of thought ever stands alone or goes unchallenged can be seen in the emergence of Spinoza's philosophy in the seventeenth century, which contradicted some of the basic tenets of Cartesianism. While never quite turning itself into part of the official ideology dominated by dualism, Spinoza's ideas have survived as a counterpoint to much of

Descartes's philosophy within the canon of classical and rationalist philosophy itself. Spinoza challenged the dualism inherent in Cartesianism, claiming that the mind is the active part of the whole person, who is both body and mind. The body attaches a person to a particular place in the order of time and space, where we are active beings engaged with the environment and, through this active relationship, the object world also makes an impression on us. We are mind-bodies, and the knowledge we create about the world is built upon our active engagement with other persons and objects in the environment (Hampshire, 1987). Humans are understood as active thinkers, whose bodies limit them to a certain finite perspective on the world, yet at the same time the body forms the sensate and emotive basis for evaluative thought.

Along with the more unofficial ideologies within a culture, the body itself also forms a limit to the reaches of power, discourse and normative control. As Foucault claims, modern forms of bio-power have attempted to take life itself into the realms of relations of power and political calculation. However, as I illustrated in Chapter 2, life itself is composed of a series of relations within and between ecosystems, which cannot be reduced solely to the level of power relations. The human body and other biological forms have evolved ecologically and so the bodies of modern humans do not conform strictly to the dictates of modern power. The instilling of the types of manners described by Elias is a form of bodily disciplining that is not bound to work, as bodily functions carry on regardless, causing embarrassment for the embodied person. Harré (1991a) has talked of the powers, capabilities and liabilities of the human body, distinguished by whether they are controllable and to what degree. There are some corporeal powers that are controllable, such as physical strength, which can be built up in the body over time. Other bodily processes, like sneezing, are controllable to some degree, but only in a limited way; an overwhelming need to sneeze or cough may be irresistible. Finally, there is what Harré calls uncontrollable liabilities, such as getting an attack of indigestion or the growth of a tumour. While some within the fields of alternative or holistic medicine might argue that the latter are not really uncontrollable, what Harré is pointing to is that they are not controllable at the level of everyday conscious intentions. An attack of indigestion is something that feels as though it takes us in its grip and is out of our immediate control. No matter how well trained the body becomes, then, there are always some bodily processes that can escape attempts at self-discipline. For Foucault (1979), the death of the body forms the ultimate limit to forms of bio-power, which aim to control and administer life, for as yet there is nothing that human beings can do to prevent death. Thus the body itself forms the very limit of bio-power. This is why death becomes one of the most secret and private events for modern people.

However, a valid criticism aimed at Foucault and other Foucaultian analyses of the body is that they tend to understand the human body only as an object of knowledge and not as a knowing being or a thinking body; that is, as a being centrally involved in the experience of life and the production of knowledge. This plays on the dual function of the body as both an object of knowledge and as an expressive and communicative body. These two aspects are obviously interlinked, a factor often overlooked in various forms of social constructionism.

Bodies, Persons and Minds

The human body, then, is both an object of knowledge and a knowing, sentient being; we sense, touch, feel, hear and see ourselves as individuals located in space and time, and so experience ourselves as a continuous being. However, through relations to others and in the establishment of a relationship to our own self, we can see ourselves from a distance and also act and perform differently in different contexts. Harré (1991b) has divided this experience into the body located in time and space which experiences itself as a unified being (Self-1), and the various selves that we display in different social contexts (Selves-2). The relationship between these two senses of self can be evidenced in the saying 'I no longer know who I am.' Here, 'I' plays a dual function, referring to the location from which one can speak as a unified physical and social being (Self-1), and yet refer to the other sense of self (Self-2) which is oneself as an object of knowledge, the thing which in the quotation has become uncertain. For Harré, both senses of self are produced through the discourses of the local moral order, pertaining to the rights and obligations one has as a person within one's community. Within local moral orders we are held to account for our actions by the others with whom we are locked in various interactions, and the accounts we give of our actions must be framed in terms of local moral precepts. Humans are motivated to do this because they have a basic desire for respect and honour within their communities, and this is achieved by being known as a morally worthy member of society. Thus, through our accounting practices we turn ourselves into moral agents as both Selves-1 and Selves-2; as the embodied person who constitutes him or her self through the theories within his or her culture of what it is to be a morally worthy and responsible person, and as the various selves who act in different contexts to maintain that reputation and self-image.

Like Foucault, Harré follows a Kantian view of morality and ethics – the object of study is the ethical formation of the free and autonomous subject. This is achieved through the knowledgeable relation one establishes with oneself, through the application of local ethical codes. The difference between them is that Harré focuses more on the interpersonal communication between people in joint actions, where people act intentionally to accomplish all kinds of tasks. Norms and conventions are presupposed as playing a central role in the management of interaction, and these norms then become applied to the self (Harré, 1993). However, while Harré tends to assume this as a universal outcome of human interaction – achieved on the level playing field of communicative relations and everyday conversations – Foucault understand the relations of communication to be interlinked with power. In an essay on Kant and the Enlightenment, Foucault (1986c) talked of the relations of control over things, over others and with oneself. These types of relations of control mark out the axes of knowledge, power and ethics, all of which are interconnected. So whereas Harré tends to uncouple everyday relations and conversations from relations of power (which happen some-where else in a 'macro-social' sphere (1993: 126)), and also from the relation to things (in his division between practical and expressive orders), Foucault sees the intimate connection between power and communication, therefore also understanding the close links between power and the ethical self-relation. Also, the free and autonomous subject of the Enlightenment is an historical creation, and one that is still in the process of formation. Thus, the modern subject is still, to a degree, in a state of immaturity, tending to look to external authorities and to obey the dictates of hegemonic powers. For Foucault, to extend the Enlightenment and the drive towards greater individual autonomy and maturity would mean working at the current limits of our freedoms. This would involve considering how the growth of capabilities for autonomous action can be disconnected from the intensifica-tion of power relations, and how people can act freely within the framework of rationally organized practices, reacting to what others do and modifying the rules of the game as they go along (Foucault, 1986c: 48).

I want to pick up these themes, filtering them through the relational perspective. From this viewpoint I suggest that the embodied location of the individual, in both its spatio-temporal context and within social relations, can be regarded as the person (McNamee and Gergen, 1999), upon whom is conferred rights and duties, along with individualizing marks, names and numbers. It is around these symbolic markers (including the ethical codes and norms), as well as through our own sense of bodily location, that we identify ourselves as a specific person. Against Descartes, then, it can be argued that the body is central to the identity of the person and that personhood does not simply reside with the 'mind'. The person has a fairly stable identity that changes only slowly with place and time; like the body itself, it has a more enduring, though not unchangeable quality, a bit like the image of a person's face as it gradually ages.

In contrast to the more stable aspects of a person's character there are also the various selves that develop which are more context dependent and can change from situation to situation in the space of a day. The perspectives we have on our own embodied person can change as rapidly as our viewpoint changes, creating the impression of a variety of selves, or different ways of viewing and presenting ourselves in different social contexts. Like the person to which they are related, the various selves only emerge through the ethical relation we establish with ourselves, and so they configure around a relationally and spatio-temporally located body. While persons and selves cannot be reduced to the body, because they have their origin partly in the symbolic realm, nor can they exist without their embodied location. The difference between persons and selves is that the latter allow for a degree of reflexive distance from embodied personhood and for the ability to take a more universal, although still partially situated, stance towards other people and things.

In the ethical self-relation, something else emerges – another aspect of selfhood – which is the internal witness and judge, the part of the self that stands above all the others and evaluates them. This forms out of the paradox that Benjamin (1990) has pointed to when she claims that, to be a free and autonomous agent, the Western self must first be recognized as such by another. In so doing, the independent agent must cede agency to another. Put another way, we can only make ourselves free and autonomous agents through the political and moral precepts of Enlightenment culture, which holds out independent agency as the highest value to be attained. These are the values of the general culture and not of our own making. To be recognized as an independent agent, then, we must always form ourselves in the values and the 'eyes' of the Other, and take that Other into ourselves in the process of ethical self-formation. There is always, then, an aspect of the self which is not-I or Other. I have referred to this previously as the 'upper-I' (Burkitt, 1991), but Bakhtin refers to this, perhaps more accurately, as the 'supra-I'.

> Something absolutely new appears here: the supraperson, the *supra-I*, that is, the witness and the judge *of the whole* human being, of the whole *I*, and consequently someone who is no longer the person, no longer the *I*, but the *other*. The reflection of the self in the empirical other through whom one must pass in order to reach *I-for-myself*. (Bakhtin, 1986: 137)

However, it is the attitude of self-discipline, developed in the ethical self-relation and the emergence of the Other within the self, which has, from the Renaissance period onwards, alienated Western selves more and more from their bodies. The body is thought of as a machine, rather than the basis of a sentient, thinking being. Instead, the self is intensified as that realm of inner experience, the deep subjective 'interior', which is experienced as the very essence of the human soul. Although inextricably related to embodied personhood, the self comes to feel ever more detached from it as an existence in its own right. The self is expressed largely through text or in symbolic communication and this has led many in contemporary social theory to talk of the self as a purely textual construction. Either that or the self is equated, in truly Cartesian fashion, with only cognitive mental functions, in which case the nature of embodied personhood is once again ignored. The body in contemporary Western society becomes a closed body, its communicative role hiding as much as it reveals of what is experienced as belonging to the person and the selves inside its armoured shell.

Nostalgia and its Dangers

One of the dangers in the type of historical analysis I have engaged in here
is that it can be read as nostalgia for a lost age of the body and sensuality. I
am not suggesting that we should return to the type of society where one
could experience the body in grotesque fashion. In many ways, the carnival
spirit this bodily form belonged to was a reaction to the strictly dogmatic
and sometimes violent external controls operated by feudal and ecclesiastical
authorities, and by the early state formations. What Beck et al. (1994) call
reflexive modernization brings with it doubt, anxiety and uncertainty, as well
as individual isolation, yet this has also brought us many freedoms which
must not be overlooked. We do not want to return to the control of experience, its interpretation and validation by external authorities, of the type that
existed in medieval times or in the early Renaissance. Instead, we must seek
out other forms for the construction of knowledge, which are democratic and
relational. As Heidegger (1977) says, when we get the division between the
individual and the collective, one positive aspect of this is that the collective
is recognized as having worth. The collective has then been given rights
which, although they may be part of a modern form of bio-power, are still
worthwhile and, in terms of the individual, they do hold out the possibility
of maturity, of the ability to distance oneself from authorities.

The individualism that is set over and against the collective, and the
anxieties of doubt that the individual suffers, must not be confused with
existential dread which can only be kept at bay by shots of ontological security
(Giddens, 1990, 1991). The lone individual, with no means of verifying the
reality of the world except the security she or he finds in his or her own self
and fortified body, is an historical creation the origins of which I have partly
described here. There would also be dangers in trying to break down some
of the distance between people and their levels of self-control, as this, too,
has its positive aspect in terms of the sensitivity to the feelings of others and
the general pacification of relations, although this can be an ambivalent
process (Burkitt, 1996). The problem of wishing to return to earlier forms of
close-knit communal association is that they can be highly exclusionary,
so that they involve not only the desire to belong together 'but the pursuit
of identity through "burning others together"' (Mellor and Shilling, 1997:
27).

We seem to have reached a paradoxical stage in this analysis where many
of the dualisms I set out to identify and to criticize are now being recognized
as having some worth and to contain values that need saving. However, as
Benjamin (1990) has suggested, the experience of paradox, of ambiguity and
contradiction, is a creative one and not something that we should run from or
attempt to eradicate. Others have taken this analysis further to suggest that
dualisms need not necessarily be broken down, but we should attempt to live
life on the borderlands; that is, instead of aiming to eradicate difference, we
live at the points of intersection that are meant to draw sharp boundaries

between categories, occupying the borderlands between apparently different entities (Scott, 1998). An example of this is the notion of hybridity as suggested by Haraway (1991), which, translated to humans, would mean that we no longer maintain the rigid dichotomies between the human and the non-human, society and nature, mind and body, demanded by the classical canon, and instead focus on the areas where these categories fuse. Put in my own terms, we need to focus on relations rather than the duality of things to understand what binds people and things together and, at the same moment, seeks to draw differences between them. In overcoming Cartesianism, the aim would be not to critique being, as Heidegger suggested, but to under-stand how we are constituted and divided relationally. The emphasis is then placed on the relations between people and things which begin to produce new relations, other points of contact with the world, and emergent forms of classifying things. It is in these active relationships that we seek to order the world and to create forms of categorization, yet, as Bauman (1991) has pointed out, as we do so the more opportunities for ambiguity open up. For Bauman (1991), ambivalence means the possibility of assigning an object or event to more than one category, which is a normal function of the linguistic practice of naming and classifying. Yet the more we classify, and the more tightly we try to draw the dividing line between things, the more possibility there is for ambivalence, for some aspect of the person or object escaping the assigned category and seeping into another. This is a side-effect of relationally and linguistically created differences; yet, in my view, a way of falling into the trap of dualism is to focus on the relations in which different things are assigned different categories, or in which supposedly different entities are created, such as the mind and the body. Thus, to understand these entities, we do not engage in an autopsy of the things themselves, for their supposed 'essence' does not reside within them; their quality stems from the relationships in the socio-natural ecosystem which creates and sustains them. From the human point of view, linguistic categorization is part of the relation we have to other people and things, but it is one that can never completely encapsulate what exists in our world – either human or non-human – so that people and things constantly escape it, retaining an element of ambivalence. Relations and the inherent ambivalence of things then become the main tools of analysis.

Conclusion

In this chapter I have suggested that, with the consolidation of rationalism and classicism as official ideologies of Western societies, the experience of the ambiguous and open body is lost, and in its place there emerges the closed body of modernity, where the emphasis is placed on the body's surfaces rather than its openings to the world. This is the communicative body, a signifying surface that expresses but at the same time conceals part of itself behind its armouring. Such a body emerges in the division between self and Other which begins to grow more marked with the increasing reliance of the state on normative controls. These are applied to the bodies of individuals in state institutions such as prisons and schools, but they also come into play in the everyday interactions between people who watch each other's behaviour and apply moral norms to others and to themselves. Individuals then become the watchers and the watched, surveying others as well as their own selves.

An emotional distance is then created between self and others, along with a division within the self between mind and body; that is, between the self who watches from a distance and the embodied person who is surveyed, which is now viewed as a material object whose existence can be regarded as partially separate from the seemingly disembodied self. Norms are applied to the self in the process of ethical self-formation and this creates the appearance of a spatial distance between thought and active, sensate, emotive being, which is associated with the body. The self then comes to associate its existence with the cognitive rationality that seems to be central to its very being, and with the text through which it narrates its own biography and reassures itself of the certainty of its identity.

As Heidegger (1977) said, the self now comes to be experienced as the relational centre of all that is. However, in order to try to overcome this, I have suggested the relational perspective, where humans are decentred from their pivotal place in the universe and instead we focus on the relations within an ecosystem between people themselves, and between people and things. Here humans are, like other things in the world, non-central points in the networks of relations. The experience of the division between body and mind is therefore formed as non-corporeal dimensions created within corporeal relations of power and communication. As such, they are not universal and inevitable phenomena, but totally dependent on their social and historical context.

But if this is the case, and the Cartesian subject is not a universal manifestation of humanity, then people do not always and everywhere act as dual beings. Indeed, there is a long tradition in Western thought that not only places this dualism in its social and historical context, but also aims to reconceptualize humans as whole, unified beings. It is to some of these ideas that I now turn.

4 The Thinking Body

Of primary concern in the last chapter was the development of the body as an object within the recent history of Western societies, where one's own body becomes the target of knowledge and discipline (imposed by the self or by the state). The increasing trend towards ideological and normative control, and towards self-discipline, creates the experience of the body as a machine, to be mastered and used. However, human bodies in the Western world do not exist solely as the objects of knowledge, but also as the primary foundation of the knowing subject – the person and selves. Although the sense experience of the body has been attenuated, with modern Westerners restricted largely to sight and hearing as the main modes of sensory contact with the world, the body still remains the basic ground for thinking. Here, then, I want to explore the notion of the thinking body (Ilyenkov, 1977) located in the many levels of time and space, which I set out in Chapters 1 and 2. My focus here will not be on the body as object, which was the subject of the last chapter, but on the body as a thinking and knowing being located in the various ecological systems and their inter-relations. In doing this I will seek to expand the relational view set out in Chapter 3.

This relational view was presented as a way of overcoming the Cartesian division of body and mind, along with the division between humans and the world, in which the 'external' or 'object' world is set over and against the 'subject' as a picture. This is what Heidegger (1977) referred to as the realist view of the world; that is, there is a real world just beyond human reach, one that subjects can only come to know through a more accurate subjective picture of what objectively exists. This notion is expressed in contemporary realist philosophies, where there is the idea that structures exist in the world which are partly independent of human knowledge, and that knowledge changes in order to account for these structures or to reveal them. Aspects of the world are always partially hidden and are laid bare by the penetration of the rational cogito (Bhaskar, 1989, 1991).

Opposed to this rationalist realism is the approach known as social constructionism, which argues that knowledge of the world is produced in the discourses which actually construct the objects we take to be the 'things' of our world, and these discourses are part of relations of power or everyday relations of communication. Recently, Danziger (1997) has claimed that social constructionism can be divided into 'dark' and 'light' varieties, the dark versions linking knowledge to power in the manner of Foucault, while the light versions are more associated with the social psychological styles of constructionism which view knowledge as part of everyday relations and communicative interactions (Gergen, 1994a; Harré, 1993; Shotter, 1993a, b). However, both varieties do have one thing in common, in that they are, as Gergen (1994a) puts it, 'ontologically mute', because they do not claim the certainty of the existence of objects beyond their construction in language. That is to say, humans can never know with certainty the existence of a world beyond their linguistically formulated knowledge of it, and so constructionism cannot bolster us with ontological security. Unlike realism, constructionism does not posit a transcendental ontological realm that exists independently of human knowledge, one which we can more accurately represent through increasingly rational forms of knowledge. Instead, the appearance of such a reality is created by the forms of knowledge that humans have constructed and which they reconstruct through history in their communicative interactions.

My aim here, though, is to move beyond some of the oppositions between these two approaches, questioning the division made between ontology and epistemology in realism and also the extreme ontological scepticism found in varieties of constructionism. Although few constructionists would subscribe to such extreme ontological scepticism that they would deny the existence of any material forms, nevertheless constructionism is not always successful in addressing the relationship between the human and the non-human, nor, as I suggested in Chapter 2, the multi-dimensional nature of experience in which knowledge is the product of the relations of humans within their ecological niche. While Gergen (1994a) has created a relational form of understanding in constructionism, and Foucault has written of relations of power – and, to a lesser extent, the relations and movements of life – constructionism in general has found the question of material relations vexing. In building on the relational approach, I will offer variations on this theme by considering selves not just in relation to others, but also in their relations to the non-human world. As Latour (1993) pointed out, this relationship produces another dimension of life that subverts the traditional opposition between nature and society, an aspect of life in which artifacts, quasi-objects and hybrids emerge; that is, objects which are at one and the same time, natural, discursive and social. This helps us to overcome the resistance that can sometimes be found in constructionism to address questions of the natural world and the way in which it influences knowledge (Murphy, 1994).

As I said in Chapter 3, the focus here is not on oppositions and dichotomies, but on the relationships and transformations that occur in what Elias (1991a) called the three basic co-ordinates of human life: the position of the individual in the social structure, the structure of social relations and the relation of humans to events in the non-human world. As social action gradually changes these co-ordinates, these relationships, the non-human world becomes partially humanized as cultures infuse it with meaning and give objects and artifacts a specific purpose. But, equally, the human world is always intermingled and interdependent with the non-human world, which emerges in various ways in our relationships and practices. Similarly, as I claimed in Chapter 2, the 'mind' is not an entity separate from the relationships that define humanity and human selves – a realm of pure intelligence or rationality, gazing on its surroundings from some degree of separation. Instead of this view, I will consider ideas that suggest that there is no such 'thing' as the mind, considered as something unique to humans alone and separate from the body. Indeed, as Bateson (1973) and A.N. Leontyev (1981) made clear, mind is itself immanent in the ecosystem, as a sensitivity to everything with which it is related, and as an ability to orient itself within those relations. As such, what we regard as the basic processes of 'mind' may not be unique to humans, but can be found in all living matter. Thus, the position I will be taking here rests on a rejection of the dichotomies between mind and matter, subject and object, and I will explore ideas that seek to overcome these dualisms.

I will begin by organizing my discussion around relations of communication and relations that transform the real, as these are, I believe, at the centre of dichotomies that plague both the 'lighter' forms of social constructionism – the style of constructionism I am focusing on in this chapter – and realism. A discussion of these dichotomies helps me to define my position more clearly and to explore other ideas that have moved against dualism. I begin, first of all, with a discussion of the constructionist view of relations of communication.

Relations of Communication

Social constructionists who understand the world as constituted by human beings in everyday relationships or conversations want to move beyond the notion of the world as a picture which Heidegger described as so central to Cartesian thinking. In order to do this, the human subject is not made the object of a metaphysical critique, and instead the focus of understanding the world is relocated on to relationships and conversation. Furthermore, the existence of 'things' such as the 'mind' are understood to be nothing more than predicates employed in everyday conversations. They are aspects of the language of subjectivity, used by people to describe elements of their joint social practices, and they do not indicate actual mental substances or cognitive structures that stand as their real referent. Constructionist social psychologists disagree on exactly how to treat these mental predicates: for some, they are internalized by individuals and form the very concepts through which people think, speak and act (Harré and Gillett, 1994). For others, they remain the predicates used in everyday speech to give meaning to certain actions, and can be understood as part of a situated, discursive engagement which provides a 'tool kit' for comprehending their use (Shotter, 1993a, b).

According to Gergen (1997), such predicates can be dispensed with by psychologists altogether, who should focus instead upon the relations in which such terms are used and take on their meaning.

However, most social constructionists agree that language is not a means of picturing, mirroring or representing a reality that exists separately and independently of it, but is a form of communication that only has meaning in the relevant cultural context. The conversation between people does not represent some ontological realm that is unchanging, and which acts as the foundation for linguistic meaning and knowledge; rather, conversations create and sustain everything that the social group takes to be the ontological foundation of life, the taken-for-granted 'reality'. Words do not stand for things but are an element of the constantly contested meanings in the arena of social life, involving claim, counter-claim and disputation. Within the social sciences, then, there can be no appeal to independent 'facts' or 'realities', or to underlying cognitive structures, as a guarantee of the validity of knowledge. All knowledge is generated in a community of speaking subjects and is an aspect of communication within relations and inter-dependencies. As Gergen (1994a: ix) puts it, 'because disquisitions on the nature of things are framed in language, there is no grounding of science or any other knowledge generating enterprise in other than communities of interlocutors. There is no appeal to mind or matter – to reason or facts – that will lend transcendental validity to propositions.'

Constructionism, then, is opposed to realist philosophies, which suggest that language can create an analogue or model of structures that generate events in the world, ones not observable on the surface of appearances. In this realist view, there is an ontological realm of transcendentally ordered structures waiting to be discovered if only we could devise a scheme of representation for them. However, this raises the problem of how we could be certain of the existence of something – be it an object or underlying structure – that exists beyond the range of our knowledge and outside the linguistic boundaries of understanding. Instead, constructionists insist on the realization that objects of knowledge cannot be independent of the accounts given of them, and that our understanding cannot be separated from the socio-linguistic practices in which it is achieved.

Furthermore, social constructionism rejects the notion that a single, rational individual, engaged in solitary reflection upon the world, produces knowledge. Understanding is not achieved through the penetration of reality by outstandingly rational, individual minds, who are detached and disengaged observers, but through the communicative construction of knowledge by individuals who are acting together. It is feasible, then, to have an account of the joint production of knowledge which does not refer to individual mental events or cognitive frameworks, but is instead focused on the network of communicating persons. Just as constructionism has subverted the realist notion that hidden causal and generative structures produce events, so it also undermines the cognitivist position in which unseen mental processes or structures are construed as the causal mechanisms that produce the actions of the individual.

Knowledge, then, is created in relations and joint activities and not by a Cartesian rational cogito poised, inanimate, to grasp a transcendental world just beyond its view. We do not create knowledge and understanding through logic but through a sociologic. As Gergen says, 'there is good reason for privileging the reality of the social' (1994a: 47), by which he means that language, knowledge and text is best understood as part of a broader social process. However, constructionism does tend, on the whole, to have a problem in dealing with the reality of things – that complex materiality that I have been referring to throughout this book as the relationships within and between ecosystems. It has become caught up in the 'turn to language' that has enveloped much of the social sciences and which tends to reduce all social analysis to that of the text. As Gergen says of this reduction of social life to signification: 'The play of signifiers is essentially a play within language, and this play is embedded within patterns of human action in what we call material contexts' (1994a: 262). Furthermore, 'it is human interchange that gives language its capacity to mean, and it must then stand as the critical locus of concern. I wish then to replace *textuality* with *communality*' (1994a: 263–4).

Yet, this insistence on language as embedded in social relations, which are themselves located in material contexts, has yet to be fully developed in constructionism. Gergen (1997) has suggested that while social constructionism remains explicitly concerned with discourse, he is attempting 'to theorize more fully enriched patterns of relational performance (including the bodily activities of the participants, along with the various objects, ornaments and physical settings necessary to render these performances intelligible)' (1997: 740). However, what remains in question here is how a form of constructionism explicitly concerned with discourse can begin to theorize, or grant any kind of existence to, what is essentially non-discursive, i.e. patterns of relations, bodies, objects and physical settings. In terms of embodiment, Shotter (1993b) has stressed the material and sensuous aspect of relatedness and joint action in his notion of 'knowing of the third kind', which accounts for the actions of individuals in terms of practical, sensuous, joint actions, involving tacitly understood commonalties of feeling and meaning. Humans are thus understood as responsive to one another in their joint actions, by drawing on tacit and corporeal levels of understanding through which the social world is constantly made anew. While Shotter (1993b) stresses the material and sensuous element of relatedness and joint action, he has done so only in respect of the human world. What is missing from constructionism is an attempt to explicate the meaningful relationship of humans to the non-human world, and thus to show how our constructed, communal reality can also be in many complex ways a changing (as opposed to transcendental) material reality. This brings us to the other co-ordinate of human life – relations that involve the non-human.

Relations that Transform the Real (I)

One of the ways in which the realist position, as expounded by Bhaskar, has certain advantages over constructionism, is in taking the relationship of human groups to their complex material contexts more seriously. Like some varieties of constructionism, Bhaskar's critical or transcendental realism takes the relational formation of the social world to be its primary character-istic, yet 'the natural and social worlds [are] conceived as in dynamic inter-relationship' (Bhaskar, 1991: 148–9). However, 'the faster dynamics . . . and the associated spatial features of social life impart to it a more geo-historically specific character than the arcs of biological, geological and cosmological being within which it is successively inscribed' (Bhaskar, 1989: 185). This inscription marks the interrelation between the social and natural worlds because it is not just social relations, but also the geo-physical context, which provide a structured location for praxis. In Bhaskar's *transforma-tional model of social action* society is the ensemble of positioned practices and interrelationships reproduced or transformed by activity. So while no one ever makes their relationships from scratch, because we all come into a world which is historically already made for us, people have the power either to reproduce or to transform their society with the materials at hand. Similarly, following Marx, humans are able to transform nature through their labour, and so Bhaskar has some notion of relations that transform the real. This also includes changing the basis of human nature, for individuals are embodied minds who are partially the products of nature, but also of historically developing ensembles of social relations through which we appropriate stocks of skills and competencies (Bhaskar, 1991: 163; Geras, 1983; Sève, 1978).

However, despite this notion of relations that transform the real, Bhaskar maintains a distinction in his work between ontology (the nature of being and the existence of things) and epistemology (the nature and source of knowledge). The reason for this is that he believes it important that we understand that there is a realm of the objective existence of things that is independent of human knowledge and action. Bhaskar accuses philosophers such as Rorty and constructionists like Shotter of falling into what he calls the *epistemic fallacy*, which is the definition of all being in terms of our knowledge about it, thus reducing all of existence to human knowledge. Instead of this, Bhaskar wants to retain in his work a distinction between the transitive, social-epistemic dimension and the intransitive, ontological dimen-sion. This means that, while socially constructed knowledge is transitive, often going through rapid and dynamic changes in terms of the way things are conceptualized, the ontological domain remains relatively unchanged by this. The causal laws of the structured ontological sphere are transcendental, while knowledge is a social process the aim of which is to produce a model of the laws that generate phenomena in the social and natural worlds. This is why the approach has been labelled 'transcendental realism'.

However, in my view, Bhaskar is wrong to take this position because in the distinction between the transitive and intransitive he has separated out what appear to be two distinct realms and, despite his own best intentions, divided the ontological from the social. That is, reality appears to be governed by its own laws in some independent realm that is distinct from humans, and transformational activity seems confined only to the social-epistemic. Yet Bhaskar has himself shown that this is not so; unfortunately, the philosophical dualism he adheres to does not allow him to build upon the notion of relations that transform the real, and he is left in static theoretical dichotomies. If, instead, we follow a sociological line more akin to constructionism, then we can see that relationships between humans, and those between humans and non-humans, mean that there is no break between the ontological and epistemological. Social relations are lodged in material contexts, and knowledge is another dimension of those contexts. Knowledge can be constructed in many different ways but it is always knowledge-in-the-world, to paraphrase Heidegger, and therefore the non-human is always absorbed in knowledge. The best examples of this are artifacts, quasi-objects and mediating tools, which I have already talked of but will return to later in this chapter.

One final point about Bhaskar's critical realism is that, while he clearly sees the self as socially and historically constituted, he nevertheless has a residual cognitivism in his approach. It is claimed that the production of knowledge depends on the utilization of antecedently existing cognitive materials (Bhaskar, 1989: 68), which comes perilously close to the idea of a developing rational cognitive system, capable of penetrating the layers of appearance and creating models approximating to the transcendental causal mechanisms of the ontological realm. We seem to be edging back to a form of rationalism here which posits the (albeit collective) mind laying bare reality as it is in itself. This is seen most clearly in Bhaskar's critical use of his philosophy, where he claims that to transform society into a more equal and just socialist system depends on the knowledge of underlying social structures, so that 'the world cannot be rationally changed unless it is adequately interpreted' (1989: 5). But as Gergen (1994a: 75) points out, realism cannot say how underlying structures could ever be identified so that the validity of the rational, structural account could be established as an adequate model of the generative mechanisms supposedly in operation. And, as Shotter (1992) says, this also means that Bhaskar tends to put theory before practice: he sees action flowing from a rational, cognitive analysis rather than from communities of shared practice or moral values. Instead of this position, I want to place action before theoretical reflection and as prior to cognitive comprehension of the world. To do this, I will consider the work of Merleau-Ponty (1962) on the bodily preconditions for action and thought, but towards the end of the chapter I will tie this into ideas about the bodily transformation of the world through human practice.

The Active Body

In his phenomenological studies, Maurice Merleau-Ponty attempted to capture some of the relational and active aspects of human thought and consciousness. For Merleau-Ponty, thinking was not the product of some disembodied mind located somewhere outside the material world, beyond time and space; nor was it simply the result of a body reacting to its surroundings. Instead, thought is part of the active relationship between humans and their world, so that prior to the Cartesian 'I think', there is an 'I can' – a practical cogito which structures not only our relationship to the world, but also the ways in which we think about it. Prior to thought and representation, then, there is a primordial coexistence between the body and its world, which grounds the possibility of developing conscious awareness and knowledge. Space and time are not something that the body is *in*, in the sense that the relation between them is distanced and intellectualized, but rather there is a *unity* between the body and space–time.

> In so far as I have a body through which I act in the world, space and time are not, for me, a collection of adjacent points nor are they a limitless number of relations synthesized by my consciousness, and into which it draws my body. I am not in space and time, nor do I conceive space and time; I belong to them, my body combines with them and includes them. The scope of this inclusion is the measure of that of my existence; but in any case it can never be all-embracing. The space and time which I inhabit are always in their different ways indeterminate horizons which contain other points of view. (Merleau-Ponty, 1962: 140)

So, here, Merleau-Ponty is not only declaring the unity between the body, space–time and consciousness, but also drawing our attention to how consciousness is always situated in a particular location, and that, because of other perspectives, there are always different points of view on the world. We can never attain 'objective' knowledge of a world that exists separately from our own subjectivity, for there is no such knowledge to be had: a disembodied view of the world is a view from nowhere and is therefore impossible for humans to attain. All knowledge is embodied and situated, created within that fundamental unity between subjects and objects which is the product of having an active body. We never understand the world from some passive and disinterested spot, but always from within an active and related perspective. Action is therefore the key to understanding human being, for objects are not located in a transcendental spatial framework, but instead are varyingly situated in relation to the agent's specific field of action (Hammond et al., 1991). This active perspective involves not only the fundamental and variable relation between the body and its objects, but also between different human bodies located in space and time, and therefore between different subjects, so that the human world is primarily a social world. This entire relational unity, this being-in-the-world, is the context for human thought and knowledge.

Thus Merleau-Ponty also talks of 'sentience' with reference to the human body and the way in which it is embedded in the various ecological niches. Sentience can be described as the body's sympathetic and responsive relation to its environment, which can be regarded as 'mindful' even though it is non-rational and pre-linguistic. This is similar to A.N. Leontyev's (1981) notion of sensitivity, in that the basis of what we have come to call 'mind' is the body's responsiveness to its ecological situation, and the way in which it is able actively to negotiate this oriented space. Thus the body could be said to be a thinking body and to have intentionality prior to the emergence of language and self-consciousness. The body reaching out to grasp an object is one of the basic forms of intentional action, and no cognitive representation is needed for such performances. Thinking and intentional activity are therefore pre-linguistic and pre-cognitive, and prior to the self-conscious subject there exists the bodily subject which is its foundation. No cognitive form of apprehension of the world could exist without the bodily subject and its performances. Merleau-Ponty therefore opposes one of the central aspects of the cognitive, Cartesian subject, which is that Descartes presented the thinking subject as a spectator, viewing his or her world from an intellectual distance. For Merleau-Ponty, we are not spectators in the world, for we are always enmeshed in a lived relation with it, grounded in the activity of the body. Furthermore, this active relation engages all the senses – not only vision – so we do not picture the world but live it through our bodies.

However, Merleau-Ponty's understanding of the body is not based on any notion of pregiven bodily senses. He believes that sense data in themselves cannot be the basis of thought for there is no initial distinction between the senses, which form a primal unity in all bodies – a synaesthesia. Thus, the senses have to be differentiated and organized for them to have any meaning for us, a process that takes place in bodily action – in active perception. That is to say, a body that is active in the world brings together the senses in a coherent way, and the formation of habits plays a part in this process of perception. Action and emotion, then, are the things that distinguish among the sense data. Yet this distinction and differentiation of the senses is never complete and absolute, for the senses continue to infuse one another to varying degrees, so, for example, there is always some tactile sense in vision, and vice versa. Like thought itself, the senses are only differentiated through our active relations to the world, so that as these relations change there emerge different forms and permutations of sensate experience.

The relations inherent in the lived world, in which thought and intentionality are immanent, are what Merleau-Ponty calls 'internal relations'; this means that they are not causal relations between independently existing subjects and objects, but rather they are meaningful relations in which people and things only have an existence and an identity in relation to one another. Human action is purposive and intentional because it is part of this meaningful pattern of internal relations and can never be understood independently of them. Also, it could be said that because these intentional and meaningful patterns involve inorganic as well as organic matter, then not only humans can be said to display 'mindfulness', and that intentional structures are endemic in the various ecosystems (Plumwood, 1993).

The basis of human thought, then, is not some abstract mind or cognition; rather, it is the human body and its accumulated actions, which form into habits. The body and its habitual actions are not mechanical processes, such as simple physical reflexes, but are forms of knowledge – ways of carrying on effectively in the world. However, while this bodily knowledge is not mechanically produced, neither is it constituted as self-reflexive and fully articulated understanding. Habits are repeated actions that take place in an oriented space, and are, in a sense, non-cognitive forms of thought which are prior to the emergence of cognition. An example would be learning to play a musical instrument where the thinking is in the feel developed for the instrument, rather than in any abstract thought about it. Here we find a notion that sets Merleau-Ponty's phenomenology apart from theories of the mind: *thought is not structured by anything that could be considered as a 'mind' which is somehow distinct from the body, whether this is a set of cognitive structures or categories, or innate ideas. Instead, it is acquired bodily actions or habits that make thought possible.* A similar notion also exists in the work of Pierre Bourdieu (1977, 1990), who talks of the *habitus*, a set of learned dispositions which a body may reproduce within an appropriate social context or 'field'. These dispositions are not automatic mechanisms, but are, as Theodore Schatzki describes the same concept in Wittgenstein, 'more like a condition which can or might be expressed in certain circumstances' (1993: 303). This helps us to build on an idea germinating within Descartes's own philosophy, that the mind is not like the captain of a ship who steers a vessel which is not part of him or herself, for the body is part of our own personal identity. However, if we take this notion seriously, then it challenges the whole distinction between body and mind, for as Schatzki claims, with reference to Wittgenstein, the body is not a vessel or mechanism to be steered by the mind, but rather thought expresses itself in and through the body, which can no longer be conceptualized as a machine. Rather, it is the body that thinks; so, as Varela et al. (1991) point out, thought must be seen as 'embodied action' – an aspect of the sensory body.

Merleau-Ponty, then, rejects any notion that the 'I' is located in another dimension to the body acting in space and time. The original sense of 'I' is the 'I can', a practical sense of the body's active possibilities, and therefore the sense of identity possessed by humans is not based on disembodied thought, nor in the early visual representation of the self (as in Lacan's notion of the 'mirror phase'). Instead, the sense of self we develop is primarily based on the feel we have of our body and the way it connects us to the world. As Gatens (1996) says, this means that the images we develop of our bodies and of our selves – those representations of the body as a unity and as a type – are based on the sense of being embodied and the way in which this is mediated by cultural representations. Thus the imagined or imaginary body is never identical to the actual body, yet it is based on its faculties and its developing capacities.

Merleau-Ponty also claims that the body is the basis of meaning and understanding and also of the ability to project ourselves into possible or imaginary situations. The symbolic function therefore rests on bodily being. However, while Merleau-Ponty has convincingly established the bodily basis for meaning and intentionality, in my view he has never adequately explained the way in which this could be linked to the development of symbols and the realm of the imaginary; that is, the capacity to imagine what could be rather than what actually is. Johnson (1987) has had more success in explaining how our bodily knowledge of the world can infuse and inform symbolic and linguistic concepts, as, for example, the experience of bodily balance in a gravitational field underlies our concept of balance in legal justice. Yet Johnson is less successful in explaining the development of cultural meanings and how these feed back to influence body image and experience. I will argue here that we can only understand the mutual influence of the body and culture upon one another if we adopt a multi-dimensional approach.

There are also other problems with the phenomenological approach to the body. First, while Merleau-Ponty illustrates how the thinking body emerges in the ecological relations of life, he does not consider how various forms of power relations have affected the body throughout history. More specifically, he does not take into account the transformation of the experience of the body from the grotesque to the closed body. An understanding of the effects of power relations on the bodily habitus can be found in the work of Bourdieu, and his work will be considered later in this chapter. Secondly, while the phenomenological perspective makes activity its central concept, it does not consider the way in which human activity transforms its spatial and temporal situations and thus reorients the contexts of activity. It is true that phenomenologists see the world as a product of human meaning, but they have less to say about the transformation of the social relations and material contexts in which such meanings are situated. Furthermore, it can be argued that the transformation of the world, both materially and in meaning, is an integral process, achieved through the invention and production of artifacts – tools, technology, symbols, signs and language – which mediate the relation between humans and the non-human world. An understanding of this relation and its transformative power, along with the way in which it changes the experience of embodiment, can be found in the work of Ilyenkov. Finally, Merleau-Ponty's phenomenology does not link the body and the symbolic in any thorough way, and I will argue that this needs to be done through the notion of multi-dimensionality. In the next sections I will work through each of these points, beginning with the effects of artifacts on our being-in-the-world and the bodily development of knowledge and meaning.

Transformation of the Real (II): the Thinking Body and its Artifacts

Although Merleau-Ponty (1962) began to account for artifacts in his phenomenology, the two artifacts he focused on were the body itself and language. He did not consider the other realm of material artifacts noted by Ilyenkov (1977), which were the material objects or tools that humans construct to serve particular, practical purposes. For Ilyenkov, it is the realm of artifacts as a whole which transforms the human bodily experience of the world, including all invented objects, utensils, dwellings, weapons, tools and technology, as well as language and other signs. Indeed, symbolic systems are not to be given primacy in Ilyenkov's scheme of things, as they are in most varieties of social constructionism, and instead language is understood to be another form of artifact – a variation on all those other human inventions that have transformed the human world. Artifacts are important if we are to consider the phenomenology of the body, for they actually change our way of being-in-the-world, our bodily practice and orientation in the various levels of space and time. Just as language can change our understanding of the world, and therefore also our perception of it, so other artifacts can change our bodily experience. A tool such as a hammer or screwdriver can change the experience of our arms and hands, and also change the things that we can do to the material world; similarly, driving a car supplements our bodies in a way which gives us a totally different feeling of space and time (as in the distance between two points and the time taken to travel between them), and also a different feeling of mobility, the experience of travelling through the world at speed. These are only two examples of the way in which artifacts can change our bodily experience of the world and, at the same time, change our knowledge and understanding by altering our perspective on reality.

This is why, for Ilyenkov, the world as conceived by Descartes and Kant is to be rejected. There is not a level of pure, disembodied thought, or a transcendental mind, which must somehow make contact with a world that is external to it. Ilyenkov is against Kantian transcendentalism, which sees the structures of human comprehension as already contained in the *a priori* principles of mind; instead, he claims that the world is given structure through the forms of social practice in which people come to experience and understand it. As Bakhurst (1991: 197–8) says of Ilyenkov's position:

> human practice transforms the natural world into an object of thought, and by participating in those practices, the human individual is brought into contact with reality as an object of thought. Each individual enters the world with the forms of movement that are constitutive of thought embodied in the environment surrounding him or her. It is not that each mind must find the world anew for itself: we are born into a world that history has made cognizable.

Here we see the expression of what Bakhurst refers to as Ilyenkov's radical realism 'that treats the thinking subject as located in material reality, in direct contact with its objects' (1991: 215). So Ilyenkov's brand of radical realism would oppose the style of realism put forward by Bhaskar, in which the ontological and the epistemological are kept analytically separate, for, in Ilyenkov's scheme, ontologically, our changing relations in the world also change the possibilities for epistemological understanding. Furthermore, like Merleau-Ponty, Ilyenkov sees thought as movement and action within this reality, aided and mediated by artifacts. What his radical realism highlights so well is how social action is always placed in a material context and that social relations and practices are the structures embodied in our understanding of reality. One could say that reality is always reflected in human meaning and knowledge, and that these things are also an intrinsic part of human reality. This radical realism led Ilyenkov to challenge another aspect of Cartesian dualism, that between body and mind. We have already shown how, in Descartes's scheme, the mind is seen as producing thought and action, while the body is mute and unthinking. But if we reject such notions of the non-corporeal, as Ilyenkov insists we should, then we arrive at a very different view where:

> There are not two different and originally contrary objects of investigation – body and thought – but only one single object, which is the thinking body of living, real man . . . Living, real thinking man, the sole thinking body with which we are acquainted, does not consist of two Cartesian halves – 'thought lacking a body' and a 'body lacking thought'. In relation to real man both the one and the other are equally fallacious abstractions. (Ilyenkov, 1977: 31)

Ilyenkov (1977: 34–5) goes on to fine tune this idea, stating that:

> Between body and thought there is no relation of cause and effect, but the relation of an organ (i.e. of a spatially determinate body) to the mode of its own action. The thinking body cannot cause changes in thought, cannot act on thought, because its existence as 'thinking' is thought. If a thinking body does nothing, it is no longer a thinking body but simply a body. But when it does act, it does not do so on thought, because its very activity is thought.
>
>   Thinking is not the product of an action but the action itself, considered at the moment of its performance, just as walking, for example, is the mode of action of the legs, the 'product' of which, it transpires, is the space walked. And that is that.

Harré has noted a similar thing using Streets-Johnstone's idea of dance improvisation as an act of thinking. 'In such thinking, movement is not a medium by which thoughts emerge but rather, the thoughts themselves, significations made flesh, so to speak' (Streets-Johnstone in Harré, 1991a: 29). Thinking, then, is not separate from the actions or movements of the body, for thought *is* bodily action. Furthermore, as Ilyenkov points out, thinking is not something that goes on in the head of an inanimate and isolated person, as in Rodin's representation in his statue *The Thinker*. Here we see a lone man sat motionless, head resting on chin, lost in solitary contemplation. It is not that Ilyenkov is denying the existence of such thinking, only that this is not the primary mode of thought. The immobile, lone thinker is only possible because of the active process of learning how to think and the social conditions that give us something to think about. As Ilyenkov (1977: 37) points out, thought does not arise from within the person as water appears from a wellspring in the ground, but rather:

> to explain the event we call 'thinking', to disclose its effective cause, it is necessary to include it in the chain of events within which it arises of necessity and not fortuitously. The 'beginnings' and the 'ends' of this chain are clearly not located within the thinking body at all, but far outside it.

This 'outside' in which the thinking body is located is the social world of interrelations, practices and meanings, so that what a thinking body is actually capable of doing is orienting itself in its community of meaningful praxis. Thought is therefore lived in and through its embodiment in public activity, in the person's meaningful social relations with others and with objects. The term 'mind' is deconstructed by the refusal to see it as a 'thing' or an 'entity' opposed to the active body, so that Ilyenkov relocates thought processes in embodied practices mediated by artifacts. Thought processes follow the course of the person's practices within the life activity of the social group. This activity, structured by social relations and conducted largely through artifacts, is the means by which humans are not only able to think about their world but also to change it.

Beyond the Concepts of Mind and Body, Culture and Nature

Through the work of Ilyenkov, then, we can begin to see how human bodies and their practices, located in space and time, become the basis for thought and for the transformation of the social and natural world. Ilyenkov also attempts to conceptualize how practice involves the production of artifacts that constitute both tools and signs; human-made objects are symbolic and, through this route, meaning becomes extended to non-human objects. As I have already noted, Elias (1991b) has referred to this as the symbol dimension, which cannot be separated from the other dimensions of space and time.

According to Merleau-Ponty and Ilyenkov, thought originally belongs to the spatio-temporal dimension and is extended through the symbolic realm. Thus, thinking involves a body engaged in spatial and temporal activity, one that is related to other people, animals and objects, and which carries out a series of socially defined activities; a body always thinking in the sense that it is aware – to some degree – of its location, movements and the things it is seeing or hearing. For humans, we are not only partly aware of these things, but we become conscious of many of them and this consciousness is the ability to reflect on one's sensations and thoughts; to ask, 'Why am I feeling this'?, or 'What exactly am I seeing here'? The ability to reflect consciously on thought or sensation, which are initially spatially located, comes through the symbolic dimension. This dimension is blended with space and time, for symbols are used as a means of communicating with others: only later do we use this medium as a means of communicating with ourselves, by thinking consciously using the tools of symbols and language, or, put more simply, by talking silently to ourselves.

This idea is one that is now very familiar because of the impact of such thinkers as Mead and Vygotsky. However, what is often ignored is that they also believed that language is, initially, a spatio-temporal activity and is therefore a material phenomenon. For example, both Mead and Merleau-Ponty thought that language had its roots in gestures through which the individuals within a group adjusted their conduct to one another. For Mead, gestures are linked to the social instincts of human beings and are dependent on the body adjusting its actions to those of the others within the group (Mead, 1934; Burkitt, 1991: 32–6). For Merleau-Ponty, such gestural meaning is the foundation of language and speech, for this is derived from the place that words occupy in the context of action, spoken by people taking part in communal life. The meaning of words and the knowledge of how to use them is also gestural in the sense that it is not lodged in the human intellect, but in the practical use of language in everyday life. Words persist within us rather than being stored in a place called the 'mind', and in this way they belong to the body as much as they belong to any intellectual capacity. Again, this taps into the idea of language as a material phenomenon.

> What remains to me of the word once learnt is its style as constituted by its formation and sound . . . I do not need to visualize the word in order to know and pronounce it. It is enough that I possess its articulatory and acoustic style as one of the modulations, one of the possible uses of my body. (Merleau-Ponty, 1962: 180)

So, for Merleau-Ponty, language is a form of material action within the world, and it is produced from a certain bodily sense that has been developed in individuals in social practices. However, while the symbolic dimension may be rooted in the gestures of spatio-temporal activity and in the production of artifacts, the more elaborate codes of writing and speech can also be used to transcend space and time, by communicating symbolically with people who are not in our immediate presence (or communicating with future generations through stored knowledge). Similarly, we can use symbols to distantiate our own thinking from an immediate space–time location and abstract it into the realms of imagination, fantasy or fiction. But this process of abstraction does not rely on a spirit, essence or location that we can label as 'mind', for thought spans all the dimensions of human life – space, time and symbols.

This raises some complex questions about the nature of the material world. Whereas Descartes's philosophy tended to dichotomize the corporeal and material, on the one hand, from the spiritual and the mindful, on the other, the multi-dimensional approach opposes notions of spirits and essences which are fleetingly attached to, but of a different order from, the material world. Nor does it support crude notions of materiality where everything can be reduced to this one dimension, so that human thought and action is simply a reflex or reaction to immediate sensuous experience. The work of thinkers like Merleau-Ponty and Ilyenkov is reminiscent of Marx (1845/1977), who saw through this trap in his *Theses on Feuerbach*, where he tried to steer a course between materialism and idealism – materialism being the idea that human consciousness is contemplation of an objective and independent reality, while idealism is the equally false notion that consciousness alone is the active force shaping the human world. For Marx, the resolution of this dichotomy was to assert the primacy of an active humanity that is in constant relations of transformation with material circumstances, an idea pursued by Ilyenkov. In this way we can see that human thought and action are never dictated by the material world, for people act to transform the world into something different. However, social action takes place in given material contexts – an ecology of natural and human-made resources, tools and culture, including the power of the human body and its prostheses (such as various forms of technology) – which set the scene for activity and the possibilities of change. Furthermore, this material world will always be diffracted in some way, and therefore be present within the symbolic and artifactual dimension.

Although Marx did not develop any theory of language in association with human action and thought, he was aware that consciousness was created through language (Marx and Engels, 1970: 51). If we add language and consciousness into the picture, then we come to a very complex notion of materiality which complements Marx and rejects the Cartesian view of mind and matter as opposing substances. As Elizabeth Grosz has said, new conceptions of materiality and corporeality need to be developed, 'notions which see human materiality in continuity with organic and inorganic matter but also at odds with other forms of matter, which see animate materiality and the materiality of language in interaction, which make possible a materialism beyond physicalism' (Grosz, 1994: 22). Grosz has attempted to create this new conception of materiality and corporeality through the work of Deleuze and Guattari, whereas I have chosen to formulate it in terms of the work of Ilyenkov. However, the general aim is similar, in that the new conception involves an idea of the human body as productive, along with a notion of what Haraway (1991) and Latour (1993) have called 'hybridity', where there are no clear-cut boundaries between people and things, but rather the identities of subjects and objects are created through their relationships.

Again, artifacts become important at this juncture, for Haraway makes a similar claim to that of Ilyenkov: artifacts are not just material objects, but are always symbolic because they are 'an active, meaning generating axis of the apparatus of bodily production' (1991: 200). Artifacts, which would normally be seen as inert matter, are here given the power of agency, thus challenging the accepted conception of matter. When the world is raised to an artifactual level, objects can 'speak' to us in meaningful ways and invite and enable practices, no longer remaining as mute and lifeless. Thus, the distinction between subject and object, actor and acted upon, begins to break down, as do the imagined barriers between 'nature', 'society' and 'technology' (Stone, 1991). This is why, for me, artifacts are so important because, like the humans who produce them, they are the inhabitants of the multi-dimensional world. They are also the pivots between the material and symbolic dimension of life because, like the human body, they are always both material substance and the bearer of symbolic meaning. Artifacts are the foundation of human culture and yet they are material objects that have the function in human activity of enabling the transformation of the material world. As Latour has said of artifacts and quasi-objects, they are 'simultaneously real, discursive and social. They belong to nature, to the collective and to discourse' (1993: 64). Furthermore, artifacts connect and mediate the relation between humans and the various dimensions of existence, changing our relations to space and time, and our understanding and experience of it. Just think how modern means of transportation, such as aeroplanes, and means of communication, such as telephones or networked computers, have shrunk the time it takes to travel bodily around the world or to send messages to others.

The concepts of multi-dimensionality, hybridity and artifacts are also useful in attempting to avoid the dichotomies between culture and language, on the one hand, and material reality or nature, on the other. Much of contemporary social theory seems to be troubled by this distinction, especially the debates that have emerged between social constructionists and realists over the relationship between language, or discourse, and 'reality'. Whereas realists tend to hold on to the notion that there is a material reality separate from human culture with its own internal causal mechanisms and structures, constructionists want to overcome this dichotomy by concentrating on the discourses people use to try to understand the world and the type of stories they spin to achieve such understanding (Edwards et al., 1995).[1] However, realist concepts tend to separate material reality and its hidden causal powers from human cultures, and fail to account for the transformation of materiality in practice. The simultaneously material and cultural status of humans and artifacts is also ignored. The varieties of constructionism also have similar problems because, in concentrating primarily on discourse, there is a tendency towards one-dimensional thinking and an inability to encompass notions of the material. Language tends to be the only artifact which is considered in terms of the role it plays in human practice, thereby relegating the importance of the thinking body and the various technologies that mediate its practices. In this largely linguistic and discursive approach, where materiality can be seen as a product of various texts, Cartesianism reappears in the form of doubt about the existence of anything other than the centrepiece of the analysis, which in Descartes's case was the 'mind', while in the case of the constructionists it is language. The product of both these ways of thinking, however, is what Marx called idealism. This is because ideas are seen as the only forces acting to construct the world, whether they be mentally or linguistically produced, and the active role played by the thinking body in producing forms of culture and reality, through relations mediated by artifacts, is ignored.

In Cartesian philosophy and social constructionism, the mediated nature of experience – through the mind in Descartes and through discourse in constructionism – separates people from the world because they have no direct access to reality. However, if we understand the mediated nature of our belonging to the world as multi-dimensional, we can conceive of this as a series of flows with many directions – artifacts connect us to the world in deeper ways, while also allowing us to feel more separated from it. The artifact/symbol, and the conscious thought that it constructs, also belong to the other dimensions of space and time; and while it does not directly reflect them – but, rather, 'diffracts' them, as Haraway (1991) says – the symbolic deepens our understanding of, and our relationship to, the practical and embodied. The symbolic also makes possible the realm of imagination, or the imaginary, through which we attempt to *understand* the world in various ways. Through this medium we are connected to the world more deeply because we can attempt to understand it and our own actions within it in an imaginative way, and we can give meaning to the world that it does not have of, or within, itself. But we are also partially separated from the world because the artifact/symbol creates an ability to 'stand back' and distantiate ourselves from reality. It gives us the capacity to disembody and imagine.

Thus, the artifactual and symbolic does not simply separate us from the other dimensions, ripping apart bodies and minds, natures and cultures, but connects them in richer, more consciously thoughtful and imaginative ways. It is correct to say that through the artifact we construct a shared under-standing of the world which shapes our experience of it, and which enables and limits our practices, but it is not strictly true that we entirely construct our reality. The constructed and the non-constructed form a continuum with various degrees of hybridity along it, ranging from non-constructed objects such as rocks or stones, which are given symbolically created meanings, to artifacts and other signs fashioned by humans for specific purposes, which have no prior existence. The natural, or the non-constructed, also plays a part in affecting or directing our knowledge, for human projects are always embedded in the dynamics of nature. For example, in recent times, the scientific knowledge of disease has led to the development of antibiotics to combat certain viruses which infect humans and other animals, yet these have led to the emergence of antibiotic-resistant strains of particular viruses. Now medical knowledge and practice has to readjust to these viruses to take account of them and develop new ways of dealing with them. The material and symbolic dimensions are therefore locked in a constant interaction.

Another example of the interconnection of the five dimensions is the way in which the human body generates metaphors that form the basis of meaning. The active physical experience of being in the world, and of how material things react to or resist our actions, is the basis on which we can generate metaphors that extend to the human world. Johnson (1987) has noted how the experience of compulsive forces in the world, of objects affecting each other's course and direction, lends itself to the human metaphor of how we can be active causal forces or be the subject of such forces. We can be either active agents making things happen in the world, or passive patients who are the recipient or the reactors to the actions of others. Both these experiences are extrapolated from bodily experiences and are used within social meanings to make sense of our lives and to orient ourselves in the world. Thus, the basis of meaning is not to be located in the rules that order cognition, nor in the grammatical structure of linguistic sentences, but in the bodily pattern and order of active perceptions.

However, one thing we need to account for is the constraints that operate upon the body, particularly within social relations. Remember, it is my point here that we are not only living in relations of communication and relations that transform the real, but along with these we are also living through relations of power. In the contemporary period in Western societies these relations of power have begun to close the body, so that we must begin to account for the effects of power upon our embodied experience and metaphorical constructions.

The Thinking Body and the Habitus

I have already noted how both Merleau-Ponty and Bourdieu understand habitual action to be the basis of our bodily orientation in the world and also, therefore, of our understanding of it. However, instead of continually referring to habit, Bourdieu uses the term 'habitus' to refer more precisely to the importance of socially instilled bodily dispositions. For him, the habitus is the system of structured, structuring dispositions that are historically constituted in social relations and practices, and which tend to reproduce themselves when the body is called into action in various social contexts. Habitus is therefore:

> systems of durable, transposable dispositions, structured structures predisposed to function as structuring structures, that is, as principles which generate and organize practices and representations that can be objectively adapted to their outcomes without presupposing a conscious aiming at ends or an express mastery of the operations necessary in order to attain them. Objectively 'regulated' and 'regular' without being in any way the product of obedience to rules, they can be collectively orchestrated without being the product of the organizing action of a conductor. (Bourdieu, 1990: 53)

Habitus is constituted, then, by dispositions that are durable, transposable and structured. Thompson (1991) also adds that dispositions are inculcated and generative. By inculcation, Bourdieu means that many of the dispositions which lead to practices are instilled in us from the very earliest years of childhood, through the everyday training processes of teaching a child how to walk, talk and behave with appropriate manners. Children then pick up modes of comportment and gestures, accents and linguistic expressions, and forms of behaviour and skills at interaction that may stay with them for the rest of their lives. It is in this sense that we can say that dispositions are durable because, even if we become consciously aware of them and wish to change them, this is an extremely difficult thing to do. Most of us may well go through our entire lives unconscious of many dispositions that predispose us to certain actions. Such dispositions are said to be structured because they reflect the social relations of the society in which we are brought up. The dispositions learned by working-class children will be markedly different from those learned by the middle class and, when reproduced as practices in various situations, will instantly give away the background of the person. These unconsciously displayed signs of status and distinction will angle people to certain positions in the division of labour and class structure (Bourdieu, 1984). Thus, habitus is socially structured and, when it is reproduced in practices, will tend also to reproduce the social system of which it is a product.

However, habitus and the dispositions that compose it should not be seen as reproducing the social order in a mechanical fashion. Bourdieu uses the term 'disposition' differently from the way in which the term is traditionally thought of in psychology. A 'disposition' is not a mechanism located in the psyche that automatically produces behaviour. Dispositions are created in the relationship between habitus and the context or 'field' in which the person acts; in other words, between the background of a class of people who are inclined to certain practices and the contexts in which they produce their practices. This is what Bourdieu (1977) means by generative structure: that a person acting through his or her dispositions in novel circumstances can produce practices that are original and unexpected – just like a jazz musician will produce a novel improvisation when his or her learned musical technique is applied to a standard tune. Novelty can also be created because dispositions are transposable, so that a disposition learned in one context or field can be applied and adapted to action in another. Thus, the outcome of practices structured by the habitus cannot be described as a mechanical reproduction of the system or as the continuous production of novelty; instead, practice occurs in the application of a set of dispositions to a changing network of social relations and contexts. This makes it possible to produce 'an infinite number of practices that are relatively unpredictable (like the corresponding situations) but also limited in their diversity' (Bourdieu, 1990: 55). Bourdieu sums up his ideas on the habitus as follows:

> The habitus, a product of history, produces individual and collective practices – more history – in accordance with the schemes generated by history. It ensures the active presence of past experiences, which, deposited in each organism in the form of schemes of perception, thought and action, tend to guarantee the 'correctness' of practices and their constancy over time, more reliably than all formal rules and explicit norms . . . This infinite yet strictly limited generative capacity is difficult to understand only so long as one remains locked in the usual antinomies – which the concept of the habitus aims to transcend – of determinism and

freedom, conditioning and creativity, consciousness and the unconscious, or the individual and society. (Bourdieu, 1990: 54–5)

We escape the above antinomies, according to Bourdieu, by using the notion of habitus, for this does not produce practices as much as orient them; it does not determine action but provides the practical sense with which people act in various situations. As in Giddens (1984), the notion of practical sense or practical consciousness is meant to signify neither full consciousness nor total unconsciousness, but rather an inclination about *how* to do things as opposed to knowledge of *why* one is doing them. For Bourdieu, this practical sense flows through the body so that, unlike Giddens, he places more emphasis on the primacy of social structure and power relations, rather than on the agent's practical knowledge of rules (Livesay, 1989). This position moves away from the subjectivist stance towards which Giddens's theory tended to veer, stressing instead the unacknowledged conditions of action that structural and relational contexts create. The emphasis is shifted from the cognitive realm of thought and reflexive use of knowledge to the bodily production of practice that shapes thoughts and feelings. 'Bodily hexis is political mythology realized, em-bodied, turned into a permanent disposition, a durable way of standing, speaking, walking, and thereby of feeling and thinking' (Bourdieu, 1990: 69–70).

Bourdieu, then, also envisages understanding as a practical process – a way of being-in-the-world through embodied activity rather than cognitive reflection. For him, practical belief is not a state of mind but a state of the body, and enacted belief, 'instilled by the childhood learning that treats the body as a living memory pad', is the product of quasi-bodily dispositions and operational schemes which generate through transference 'countless practical metaphors'.

> Practical sense, social necessity turned into nature, converted into motor schemes and bodily automatisms, is what causes practices, in and through what makes them obscure to the eyes of their producers, to be sensible, that is, informed by a common sense. It is because agents never know completely what they are doing that what they do has more sense than they know. (Bourdieu, 1990: 69)

However, one of the things often obscured by this practical sense is that embodied social necessity, which orients us within our practical interactions and helps us to make the world meaningful through metaphor, is composed of social relations of power and domination. Ingrained in the bodily dispositions of each one of us are the social relations of our society – in this instance the class relations endemic to it which produce individuals with differing styles, abilities and tastes. The social relations that create the habitus and its many variations are therefore relations of power, and these are deeply inscribed in our personal dispositions, even though we may remain unconscious of this fact.

Social power thus works through human bodies by inscribing in them certain dispositions and capacities which enable people to act in certain ways, yet also set the limit upon their abilities and aspirations. In so doing, it marks individuals out as members of a particular class or group, in the way in which they talk and act or carry themselves physically, their deportment and carriage, their manners, the way they give off a sense of confidence or a lack of it, their tastes, judgements and lifestyles; all these things are inscriptions of the habitus. Bourdieu refers to this as a 'technique of the body', a phrase he has in common with Foucault (1986a, 1988) and also Marcel Mauss (1979). However, whereas Foucault focuses on techniques of the body, created by individuals following moral codes and precepts, Bourdieu is concerned with the powers of the body to act in given ways, powers instilled by social relations from the earliest years of infancy, which are the foundation for later forms of thinking and moral practices.

Inscriptions on the body through the social habitus apply not only to social distinctions involved in class relations, but also to other power relations such as those that construct gendered bodies. Thus, in most cultures, women and men are expected to use and manage their bodies in very different ways. The forms of domination used by men against women are reflected in bodily postures, movements and gestures; for example, the lowering of the head and eyes, in women, is taken to indicate submission to domination, whereas men are expected to raise their head and not avert the eyes, indicating their more powerful status (Bourdieu, 1990). (In the metaphorical sense, the 'upward' movement is associated with the male, the 'downwards' movement with the female.) Body concepts also vary, with men tending to perceive their bodies as larger than women generally do. Bourdieu seeks to emphasize how this type of learning, which affects men and women's perception of their bodies and selves, does not occur at the cognitive level but at the bodily level. This type of bodily knowledge is *not* something one *possesses*, like cognitive knowledge, it is something one *is*. In the next chapter I will deal with gendered relations of power and the way in which they infuse human bodies.

Conclusion

In this chapter I have tried to chart a different course on the question of human embodiment and knowledge from the ones followed by constructionists and realists. I have argued that we must take account of the part played by human embodiment within the ecosystem when considering experience, language and knowledge. We cannot convincingly maintain an extreme ontological scepticism, concentrating only on communicative relations and discourses, nor can we support a division between the ontological and epistemological realm which preserves at its core a Cartesian rationalism and cognitivism. The division between ontology and epistemology can only be fused through the concept of the active body, which possesses sociophysical powers of transformation; that is to say, through collective action humans not only transform the world, we also reformulate our bodies in the process. The artifacts we create give us new powers, not only to change nature, but also to supplement and augment our bodies, making us into prosthetic beings or hybrids. In such conditions of mediated action, thinking bodies are always connected to a transformed materiality and sociality. There is no absolute separation between nature and culture, body and mind, materiality and knowledge, for these can be understood as dimensions, interconnected through relations and practices mediated by artifacts, involving the thinking bodies of persons and selves. However, relations of communication and relations that transform the real are also interconnected with relations of power, and these not only help to produce capacities in the human body, they also attempt to limit the proliferation and application of those faculties.

The human body is ultimately inexhaustible and unknowable because it is open to endless transformation and reconstruction. However, strands of philosophical and social scientific knowledge can be brought together to take us beyond the dualistic Cartesian world and help us to grasp the multidimensional aspects involved in the transformation and reconstruction of bodies and their social relations.

Note

1 Edwards et al. (1995: 29) stress that humans have an experience of reality through perception and bodily action, a position they label as 'experiential realism'. However, apart from this, their focus is entirely on the discursive realm and, contrary to what I have been saying in this chapter, the impression is given that there is little of interest for social constructionists in embodied experience.

5 Feminism and the Challenge to Dualism

So far in this book I have been writing about the body as if all human bodies were identical and the experiences drawn from them were the same. This more abstract project was an attempt to write about general themes of Cartesian dualism within Western culture and the challenges to it. However, over the past thirty years, one of the main challenges to Cartesian dualism has come from feminism, a movement – both academic and political – which has insisted on the difference of human bodies and that the Cartesian assumption of a single body reducible to the metaphor of machine is part of the power relations which have closed women and minority groups out of the systems of power and control. It is the model of the male body which is dominant and equated with the body politic, so that the metaphor of the government ruling an otherwise unstable population is related to the mind governing an unruly body, and also with the rational male ruling the irrational female (Gatens, 1996). As women and minority groups are shut out of government, they are often equated with the dangerous, irrational, bodily forces, such as emotion or barbarism, which may overthrow rational mental controls. The image of the body is therefore at the heart of social and political struggles and, in recent times, gender politics has been a central arena of conflict.

One of the ways in which recent feminist writings have contested in these struggles is by questioning the whole range of dualisms which surrounds the dominant Cartesian culture, the main target being the binary dualism between male and female. This seemingly irreducible opposition is itself claimed to reside in the simple and unquestionable fact of bodily being: one is either male or female and it is as simple as that. However, feminist authors are at the forefront of questioning this apparent ontological fact, asking questions about those troubling boundary cases where the sex of the body cannot be determined on the simple and crude basis of clearly defined genitalia. Is it chromosomes, hormones or anatomy that is the deciding factor in the case of sex and gender? Butler (1990) has been one of the most critical thinkers in this field, challenging the notion of male and female as irreducible, unitary entities based on the biological constitution of the body. Instead, for Butler, the body is constructed in the realm of power through the acts called out by the signifying system in which it is embedded. This is a signifying, communicative body, but it is animated only by the power of disciplinary mechanisms lodged in various discourses. Bodily being and bodily performances can therefore be read as a text in which are inscribed the marks of power. However, I will argue here that this emphasis on the body as a discursive product fails to account for the power invested in the productive body; or, in other words, it fails to account for the body as a producer as well as the body as product. As some feminist writers have pointed out, the metaphor of the productive body is even more appropriate for women than for men.

However, as Davis (1997) claims, these debates reveal a tension at the core of contemporary feminist studies, where there are strong arguments for a feminine experience of the body which cannot be reduced to maleness, while at the same time wanting to avoid relapsing into another type of essentialism. If what is on offer is the idea of the body as a surface on which a text is written, then the materiality of the productive body slides below the surface of a purely textual analysis where emphasis is placed on the signifying system rather than the lived body. In this chapter I want to outline some of these dilemmas in order to draw from feminist accounts a way forward in dealing with this apparent dualism between the body as a disciplined subject and the body as a producer capable of acting upon and changing its social and political arrangements. I will begin by looking at the more textual analysis of writers like Butler, gauging whether such an approach can be married to more phenomenological understandings.

The Textual Production of Gendered Bodies

Butler (1990) argues that power operates through the production of a binary frame for talking and thinking about gender and sexuality. The terms that this binary frame constructs, such as 'man' and 'woman', 'heterosexual' and 'homosexual', are not innate dispositions and therefore natural facts, but the categories that culture has created for the everyday performance of gender identity. At the very beginning of her book *Gender Trouble*, Butler (1990) asks the key questions that will guide her study: 'Does being female constitute a "natural fact" or a cultural performance, or is "naturalness" constituted through discursively constrained performative acts that produce the body through and within the categories of sex?' (1990: viii); and, 'How does language itself produce the fictive construction of "sex" that supports these various regimes of power?' (1990: ix). In other words, what we take as ontologically given in our everyday lives – the reality of sex and gender – is to be explored as a linguistic construction which can be deconstructed. This has given rise to the current debate within the social sciences about the reality of sex as opposed to the cultural variability of expectations surrounding gender performance (Hood-Williams, 1996, 1997; Willmott, 1996).

The main point that Butler is making in her work is that sex is not a 'reality' lodged in the body as a biological given, one that is somehow separate from the cultural strictures of gender performances, and which cannot be changed or challenged in any way. For Butler, drawing on her reading of Foucault, the fantasies which construct the illusions of gender identity and sex are disciplinary productions of cultural sanctions and taboos, and it is the juridical law that plays a large part in the formation of human sexuality. There are, then, no primary essences of masculinity or femininity lodged in the body which give rise to gender identity; rather, masculinity and femininity are created through bodily performances that are produced and regulated by the law and through other discourses on sex and gender. Butler (1993) claims that it is in the performance of gender that our bodies are materialized in the way that they are, so that, through the corporeal significations that we are all compelled to act out, the body is made real in a literal sense. The law embodied in the symbolic

> can only remain a law to the extent that it compels the differentiated citations and approximations called 'feminine' and 'masculine'. The presumption that the symbolic law of sex enjoys a separable ontology prior and autonomous to its assumption is contravened by the notion that the citation of the law is the very mechanism of its production and articulation. What is 'forced' by the symbolic, then, is a citation of its law that reiterates and consolidates the ruse of its own force. (Butler, 1993: 15)

What I take Butler to mean by this is that the symbolic law is invested and continually re-enacted through bodily performances, so that it, along with the gender identities it supports, has no existence outside concrete performances. The symbols are created and reproduced by their citation and reiteration in embodied performances. The very notion of the agency of gendered subjects has then to be recast outside the traditional framework of humanist discourses, for the body acts not because of any essence of individuality contained within it – a soul, a mind or an identity – but because of the power invested in it by the symbolic order. Instead of seeing the body as a vehicle steered by the agent inside it, and so getting into a debate about whether the body is inherently active or passive, for Butler the body and its powers of agency are constructed in the same stroke through discourses. Thus, rather than being a voluntary process, agency is conceptualized as a reiterative or articulatory practice, immanent to power. The agent who is able to resist existing structures of power cannot be located outside the reach of power, for the agent is its very product. Power operates through the discursive system of heterosexual hegemony to materialize gendered bodies as either masculine or feminine and, in the process, produce a domain of excluded and sanctioned sexualities.

However, what Butler has to explain from this position is how bodies are constructed and turned into agents by the regulatory discursive mechanisms, and also how some of these agents can come to oppose and resist the system that has created them. As to the question of the human agent, Butler has dealt with this in two very different ways. First, she turned to the works of Freud, particularly *Mourning and Melancholia*, which was reinterpreted to explain how men and women are motivated to adopt the required gender performances according to hegemonic heterosexual discourses. This is done through the creation of sexual desire within the symbolic order and through the identificatory processes of the Oedipus complex. However, unlike Freud, who spoke mainly of the incest taboo and the regulation of heterosexual desire, Butler introduces the notion of a prior taboo that seeks to regulate, yet actually creates, homosexual desire (just as the incest taboo does not actually regulate, but also creates, the whole structure of heterosexual desire). Just as the heterosexual hegemony creates the binary distinction between masculine and feminine, it creates in the same process the opposition between heterosexual and homosexual desire, claiming both of these dualisms to be ontological foundations of identity rather than discursive constructs. Through the homosexual taboo, a boy or girl must renounce any desire for the same-sex parent, just as they are forced to separate from the parent of the opposite sex through the incest taboo, turning their desire instead on to members of the opposite sex outside the family. Through the process of separation, Freud believed that the original identifications with the parents become internalized in the psyche, so that they are never really lost or renounced, and both men and women retain the psychic imprint of masculinity and femininity. However, Butler asks the question about the fate of homosexual desire, which cannot be turned towards individuals outside the family in the way that heterosexual desire can because of the blanket taboo against homosexuality. Instead of seeing this as internalized in the psyche as a repressed desire, Butler believes that it is incorporated in the habitual acts of the body, thus preserving what one has been forced to give up in exactly the same way Freud described the melancholic preservation of lost love. Thus, a boy is made to love the father by the paternal law, while at the same time he is forced to give up not only the object of his love, as he is with the mother, but, in the case of the father, the very love itself – homosexual love. This loss is dealt with by preserving it as a melancholic incorporation on the body; in this instance, the perpetual re-enactment of the masculinity the boy once desired, but the desire for which he had to renounce. Masculinity is therefore not an innate tendency – the expression of some inner sense or essence of manhood – but is a continual performance that must always be reproduced, lest the love that had to be disavowed reappears again. It is such gender performances, not only of masculinity but of femininity as well, that produce the impression of inherent sexual and gender specific tendencies, yet these are only incorporated fantasies – illusions created through repeated bodily acts.

The second element of this explanation of agency and performativity is to be found in Butler's more recent work, where her view of human sexual identity and agency is elaborated through Althusser's (1971) notion of interpellation, which is adapted to explain how the subject is hailed in language (as opposed to ideology) by being called a name (Butler, 1997). The creation of the sexed subject involves the interpellation, or hailing, of the subject by the discourses that create and regulate the heterosexual order. The call that comes out from language does not find an already constituted subject with bodily desires who recognizes itself in the call of its name; rather, this interpellation in language constitutes the sexed and gendered subject and its desires. The body is inserted into discursive practices and is both materialized as a gendered body and subjected as an agent with reiterative powers.

However, there are many problems with Butler's understanding of the body. Let me only briefly mention the old critique of Althusser's work, which has not been settled (or even addressed) by Butler, that it takes a subject who is already at least partly constituted as such to recognize the call of its name in ideology or language. This means that ideology or, in Butler's case, discourse cannot be solely responsible for the constitution of humans as subjects. One could say that it is the introduction of the subject into discursive practice that begins the whole process of performativity and subjectification, and yet it still seems mysterious as to why certain subjects recognize themselves in certain names or interpellations. Even less clear is how the Foucaultian reading of Freud (which has problems in itself) fits in with the Althusserian view of interpellation. Both these theories are used to explain the construction of the embodied subject and yet both are very different: is it identification, incorporation or interpellation that is the key to understanding the regulatory construction of subjects, and, if all three processes are involved, how do they mesh together? The use of an Althusserian/Foucaultian reading of Freud, removed from the historical context of Foucault's discussions, which are then transposed to the level of abstract philosophy, is also fraught with the danger of multiplying more insoluble theoretical dualisms, particularly over the issue of the construction of embodied desire. If the gendered, desiring body is a creation of the symbolic laws and discursive taboos, why did these form in the first place? What would law or taboo have to operate against or regulate if desire and the body are only ever constituted within its confines? Left as abstract questions separate from an account of the *historical* figurations in which laws and desires have emerged (Burkitt, 1998), such questions raised by Butler's work spin around in an endless circle of dualism.

Perhaps, though, this indicates still deeper problems in Butler's philosophy, especially for the type of perspective on embodiment that I am trying to develop here. Given what was said in Chapter 3 about the view of the person which emerged in the nineteenth century from the tradition of classicism, where the self came to be viewed as purely a textual narration and the body was submerged beneath the text, language therefore becoming 'autonomized' and separated from the material realm, there are traces of this lineage in Butler's views. *Gender Trouble* is a curious book: in it, despite all the discourse about the body, one never gets the sense of a lived, material body. Its anti-humanist framework seeks only to show how the lived body as currently gendered is but an illusion – a fiction – and that social analysis should instead focus on the discourses that produce this illusion. The experience of being a body is irrelevant compared to the mechanism through which the body is constructed. The criticism of a lack of materiality in Butler's analysis was addressed through the notion that it is discourses which actually materialize bodies and invest them with their powers of agency (Butler, 1993). Yet this does not fully answer the criticism because discourse is still idealized as the precondition through which all material forms in the world are constructed. As with the nineteenth-century diarists, Butler's writings submerge the bodily and the material beneath the text and autonomize language as the precondition of all being, and, in Butler's case, of the material body itself. When the body appears in her work, it is only so far as the body – or its parts, gestures and movements – signify through their performances, caught as they are, reiterating in a chain of signifiers.

Once language is autonomized and cut loose from any moorings, every-thing can be collapsed into the symbolic realm. Bodies are only material so long as they signify, power only works through discourse, the agent only has agency and identity through its naming in language. I have already criticized this type of discursive reductionism as it operates in other forms of social constructionism and have contrasted this to the type of approach I am trying to establish here, which is multi-dimensional. The symbolic realm is always integrated with the material, and while it is impossible to separate them, they should not be collapsed together. Also, I have tried to show that relations that transform the real, relations of communication and relations of power are interconnected but not identical to one another. For example, in communication, spaces can emerge or be created where people can construct ideologies that oppose the established hegemony, and these can exist alongside other spaces where people are compelled to reiterate it. Saying this, I realize, of course, that I shall be accused by anti-humanists of the most naïve form of humanism, and that I have fallen into the trap of voluntarism. Not a bit of it. Because I am proposing that relations of production, communication and power are linked but not identical, it is possible for such spaces to appear, and it is also possible for the subject to be socially constructed in relations yet not always caught in the web of power. Because anti-humanists tend to collapse discourse and power, there emerges the problem of how the subject who is discursively constructed can ever oppose or transform relations of power.

Butler (1997) tries to address this difficulty using Derrida's theories about the iteration of language. Following Derrida, iteration is thought to create spaces between the marks of a text, or between the different performances of an utterance, which open up a break from the originating context of the discourse. This is how change becomes possible in the (re)iterative perform-ances of the discursive system because each different performance occurs in a space that has broken away from previous performances. Although the subject is one who can only iterate from a text he or she did not author, he or she cannot foresee the consequence of his or her performance or utterance as it breaks from the context in which he or she speaks and percolates into others. Language and performance is therefore constantly changing. How-ever, while this sounds a little like my own suggestion of the different spaces in which ideology can be created, there are major differences. While I would claim that the different spaces in which people perform or utter are social spaces, for Butler these spaces are those to be found within the text. It is language that creates the possibilities of change, not individuals bound into constantly shifting and reforming social relations and contexts. As Giddens (1987) has pointed out, Derrida confuses space with the temporality of text in his analysis of the play of differences intrinsic to signification. This means that 'the "extending" of writing is involved in the spacing of sounds or marks, but this is the very same phenomenon as their temporal differentiation' (Giddens, 1987: 91). The implication of this is that Derrida – and Butler too – has little conception of the way in which language is embedded in the relations of communication across time and space, involving what Bakhtin (1986) would call the dialogical; that is, the dialogue within and between communities of speaking subjects. Using ideas drawn from Derrida, Butler's notion of resistance is centred on the citational and iterative power of language, and how it both positions and breaks away from the *individual* speaker. Thus resistance is founded in the structure of language rather than in its use among collectivities. The same is also true for Butler's account of the normative ways in which sex is produced, for these regulatory norms exist only in discourse and not in the relations and interactions between social beings.

Something of Butler's collapsing of relations of power and relations of communication is evident in her critique of Bourdieu (Butler, 1997: 145–7, 152–61). While she has some sympathy with Bourdieu's notion of performances emanating from the habitus, which is history incorporated into the body, Butler has difficulty with his distinction between the linguistic and social dimensions. For Bourdieu (1991), authority is not always accorded to people purely from their interpellated position in language, and instead it can be grounded in a person's position in the social hierarchy. This view of power troubles Butler because it suggests that authority can have bases in something other than the purely linguistic, and that power is not completely synonymous with the utterance. For her, the theoretical distinction between the social and linguistic is difficult, if not impossible, to sustain. However, I do not read Bourdieu as saying that the power of language always comes from a non-discursive source, but that it is possible for power to have other dimensions. For example, authority could come from the position one occupies in an organization, from qualifications or, at the extremes, power could be rooted in physical violence or coercion. From the multidimensional perspective I am developing here, while I agree with Butler that it is impossible to *separate* language from elements one considers non-linguistic, it is equally impossible to *reduce* everything to the one dimension of language. In the power of a prime minister or president, the head of a large corporation, a scientist or academic or a military commander, language is clearly implicated in the way they create and maintain their status, but it is not everything: organizational control, economic resources, access to information, institutional support and the means of violence are also other aspects of their power. While it is possible to speak with authority simply through the force of one's utterance, this does not mean that language is the only root of power.

Butler is also critical of Bourdieu for what is claimed to be his 'conservative' view of the performative, in that the concept of habitus rests on the notion of an embodied, practical sense which is not always open to discursive scrutiny and, thus, to critical reflexivity and resistance (see also Kögler, 1997). Because of this, it is claimed, people are always bound to endless performances of the same, established social practices. Yet this completely ignores Bourdieu's notion of transposable dispositions and generative structures which were described in Chapter 4, by which he accounts for changing performances in terms of the way in which agents will reformulate their practical skills and knowledge according to the demands of different social contexts. Because agents act in a multitude of social contexts, innovative practices can emerge and heretical discourses can develop. However, according to Bourdieu, before such critical voices can overthrow the established hegemony, there has also to be a corresponding crisis in existing social relations – in the social, political, institutional and economic structures through which the official order is maintained and current forms of domination are legitimized. Otherwise we could not explain how established ideologies can defend themselves from highly persuasive critical voices for so long, nor exactly how one ideology succeeds another. If this were down to discourses alone, is it the most credible discourse that wins out in the end? Because of all these factors, it is difficult, in my view, to maintain a singularly discursive view of power and resistance.

Ironically, though, Butler cannot maintain this position herself, especially when it comes to the way in which the binary construction of sex is inherently unstable. She says:

> the limits of constructivism are exposed at those boundaries of bodily life where abjected or deligitimated bodies fail to count as 'bodies'. If the materiality of sex is demarcated in discourse, then this demarcation will produce a domain of excluded and deligitimated 'sex'. Hence, it will be as important to think about how and to what end bodies are constructed as it will be to think about how and to what end bodies are *not* constructed and, further, to ask after how bodies which fail to materialize provide the necessary 'outside', if not the necessary support, for the bodies which, in materializing the norm, qualify as bodies that matter. (Butler, 1993: 15-16)

So, after all the labyrinthine contortions to try to maintain the notion that bodies are not ontological givens but are only materialized as sexed through discourses, we now learn that some bodies fail to materialize as they should or simply do not fit into the constructs created by the regulatory norms – in other words, they are *not* constructed. And those bodies that fail to materialize as they should presumably have something about them as bodies that resist normative materialization, otherwise every body would be constructed as correctly gendered in the heterosexual hegemony. As Davis (1997) says, the body must serve to some degree as a point of differentiation in the gender system, both as a mark of the binary opposition of male and female and as a challenge to it, for there are bodies that do not fit into that simple dual categorization.

Where does this leave us now in the consideration of gendered bodies? For me, we have to begin to consider the materiality of the body and the way it is lived, and how the lived body is not only a surface for signification, a puppet of discursive norms, but also a body that signifies in relation to other bodies. Put back into the context of a dimensional metaphor, we live the material body in the world as well as in the symbolic dimension, and we must begin to understand how the body allows us to signify – what it contributes to that signification – as well as how the symbolic realm changes our experience of embodiment. Fortunately, such work has already begun in feminism.

The Material Body

There have been other attempts to deal with the material body in feminist writings, and here I want to refer specifically to the work of Grosz (1994), who accounts for the multi-dimensionality of the body, both as a material and symbolic construct and as a corporeal and psychic entity. This is done by exploring the ways in which the body's psychical 'interior' is established through the social inscription of bodily processes. Grosz uses psycho-analytical ideas to show how the psyche is only established through the creation of a unified body image, while at the same time that psychic imagery is patterned along the lines of many organic bodily processes. Freud, for example, showed how the emergence of the ego is dependent upon the construction of a psychical map of the body's libidinal intensities and is, in this sense, a bodily tracing. However, the ego is not simply a copy of the actual, physical body, for it is continually being augmented by the products of history and culture, the artifacts and symbols which extend the body beyond the immediacy of its spatial and temporal location. There is always the problem, then, of the relationship between the *Innenwelt* and *Umwelt*, between the imaginary body and its objective realities. This is only one of a number of tensions which mean that we never attain the solid and stable identity that is the ideal. In the imaginary, we see the operation of the multi-dimensional approach: subjects are connected to their world in deeper ways through the symbolic, but are also partly separated from it because they only have mediated access to reality.

On this basis, though, Grosz (1994) can begin to account for the construction of sexuality and gendered identity through the symbolic re-transcription of bodily forms and instinctive processes. Instincts are bio-logically given responses that are transmuted into historically and culturally specific drives through their incorporation into the symbolic and psychic realms. Similarly, the type of body one has influences the way in which one can experience masculine and feminine positions within the social order, so that it is possible for a man to experience a degree of femininity and a woman a degree of masculinity, but these experiences will be very different when lived by physiologically different bodies. Thus, the body itself plays a major role in the performance of gender, but we must not forget the way in which the body is literally written on at the anatomical, physiological and neurological levels by the patriarchal culture in which we live. We never simply 'have' a body, for it is always the object and subject of signification, and of attitudes and judgements, which are socially formed. While, for example, Merleau-Ponty (1962) recognizes the importance of the lived body, he fails to understand the differences in lived experience that having a male or female body may make, and he also does not recognize the differences in value judgements made about those bodies in patriarchy. His view is therefore implicitly male orientated because it displays the way in which men can take themselves as generic persons who are representative of all humanity. Men can therefore divorce themselves as subjects from their body and their sexuality, associating themselves with the disembodied mind and with reason, while women are seen as synonymous with the body.

Thus, Grosz is reluctant to say that sexual difference is based on the inscription of uncoded matter, yet she realizes that the body is historically and culturally pliable. In this sense, she is working with a notion of the re-formed body, one that is:

> an open materiality, a set of (possibly infinite) tendencies and potentialities which may be developed, yet whose development will necessarily hinder or induce other developments and other trajectories. These are not individually or consciously chosen, nor are they amenable to will or intentionality: they are more like bodily styles, habits, practices, whose logic entails that one preference, one modality excludes or makes difficult other possibilities. (Grosz, 1994: 191)

Having said this, though, Grosz does continually engage the textual metaphor in a manner not dissimilar to Butler, and this sometimes gives to her understanding of the body a sense that corporeality is more constructed (or written) than constructing. This problematizes the vision of the productive body that is very strong in parts of her work. In this, Grosz borrows from Deleuze and Guattari (1984, 1988) who theorize production as consisting of those processes that create linkages between fragments of bodies and fragments of objects. These 'assemblages' are the consequence of social practices that create a series of flows, energies, movements and intensities between subjects and objects. The question is no longer one of 'what is the body'?; rather, it is a question of what the body is capable of and of its capacities. The ways in which fragments of bodies join together in practices with other things create what Deleuze and Guattari have referred to as machines, meaning

> a nontotalized collection or assemblage of heterogeneous elements and materials. In itself, the body is not a machine; but in its active relations to other social practices, entities, and events, it forms mechinic connections. In relation to books, for example, it may form a literary machine; in relation to tools, it may form a work machine. (Grosz, 1994: 120)

While there is much in Deleuze and Guattari's approach – and therefore also in Grosz's – that is compatible with my aims in this book, and while I agree with the spirit of what is being said above, the mechinic metaphor that is being employed raises certain problems. It is clear from Grosz's interpretation that when Deleuze and Guattari refer to machines, they are making reference to the *active relations* between bodies and social practices, entities or events; in which case we have to ask whether the metaphor of the machine is an appropriate one. Why use such an alien metaphor when we can actually talk of mapping social relations and activities? And the Nietzschean philosophical background to both Deleuze and Guattari and Grosz's projects also makes them problematic given my critical comments on Nietzsche in Chapter 2. It seems strange to rely on a philosopher whose work is so saturated with notions of the biological roots of power and domination (which Nietzsche clearly associates with men, giving his work a misogynist hue), when one is trying to construct theories of the malleability of the body and the potential for challenging patriarchal power relations. What also seems to have disappeared in the adoption of these various approaches is a notion of the lived body and how gender relations are not only inscribed upon it, but that the body can become a site around which to contest patriarchal power in everyday life.

The Lived, Gendered Body and the Symbolic

The question of gender difference and the role of the body and its signification have been pursued by a number of feminist writers. As Gatens (1996) has claimed, although our bodily experiences lack any fixed significance – that is, the body does not generate the same symbols in every culture, nor are male and female bodies represented in the same way – they are likely, in all social structures, to be privileged sites of signification. This reclaims the idea that it is embodied persons who signify, and that the body will contribute something to that signification through its lived experience, one which will always be somewhat different for women and men. This is not to deny the tension between sameness and difference in the gendered experience of embodiment (Benjamin, 1995), nor that masculinity and femininity are not mutually exclusive; it is simply to draw attention to the fact that the gender positions, available in different degrees to both men and women, will be lived slightly differently by different bodies. For example, women's experience of menstruation provides a lived bodily experience that is not open to men and which is counter to many currently dominant forms of social organization and signification (Martin, 1989). As Gatens puts it, 'there is a contingent, though not arbitrary, relation between the male body and masculinity and the female body and femininity' (1996: 13). This means that the male and female bodies are centrally involved in generating the cultural symbols and experience of masculinity and femininity, but that such symbols and experience are never fixed or determined by biological being, varying from culture to culture. As Butler pointed out, this also creates problems in contemporary Western culture for those whose bodies do not fit this polar model, as there are few images of transgendered individuals available to us.

Gatens also goes on to claim that women are closed out of the symbolic system and made subservient in societies where the dominant images are those of the masculine body. In Western modernity, the image of the nation-state is that of the male body, so that the 'body politic' shares many features with the imaginary masculine body. By the notion of 'imaginary body', Gatens means precisely that contingent, though not arbitrary, relation by which the body is linked to the various forms of its signification. In the terms I am using here, an imaginary body is not an illusion but an image of the body that is lived in the five dimensions of space, time and symbols. For Gatens, the imaginary body is created within the body images established in a culture as they relate to each individual body through its lived experience; yet the imaginary body also relates to the body politic as an image of the state and society, which is understood along the lines of a model of the human body. The images which infuse, form and inform Western civil societies are largely those of the male body, and women are granted access to the public sphere only so far as they can emulate the powers and capacities associated with male privilege. This is why attempts to grant women equal access to the public sphere through equal opportunities legislation have often had disappointing results. It is not that women are biologically unsuited to work, management or politics, but that 'the political body was conceived historically as the organization of many bodies into one body which would itself enhance and intensify the powers and capacities of specifically male bodies'. Because of this, 'female embodiment as it is currently lived is itself a "barrier" to women's "equal" participation in socio-political life' (Gatens, 1996: 71).

Furthermore, the metaphors generated both from and about women's bodies do not easily fit into the images of the closed body which have been largely dominant since the classical age. Male bodies are more readily viewed as closed bodies, tightly encased within armoured boundaries, whereas, through processes such as menstruation and birth, women's bodies are imagined as permeable and subject to changes of shape and cyclical processes (Pateman, 1988). Women's bodies are also open to penetration and 'invasion'. There is much, then, about the embodied experience of women which creates fears in society, as female bodies threaten to escape modern forms of power and regulation. Perhaps this is why they have been such a focus of the medical disciplinary gaze since the nineteenth century. Foucault (1979) has illustrated how both women and children are more likely to be the targets of medical regulatory practices than are men, and perhaps this is because their bodies are seen to be more prone to 'irregu-larities' than the disciplined and closed bodies of mature males. There is also the worry about children, whose bodies may fail to develop into the correctly gendered form, and doctors today still regularly perform 'corrective' surgery on children who are not specifically gendered as distinctly male or female at birth. However, through the imaginary body, only men are allowed to reach maturity as independent and whole beings, as human subjects (Gatens, 1996).

Martin (1989) powerfully details the fragmentation of the female imaginary body in her study of women's experiences of the medicalization of their body processes. Martin begins by observing the change in metaphors describing the human body during the seventeenth century, when the medieval model of both male and female bodies as based on analogous structures began to be challenged by notions of their inherent difference, and by metaphors of the body as a machine. This culminated in the nineteenth century with the rise of metaphors of the human body as a production process, like a small business or a factory. The body began to be understood along the lines of the industrial system, a metaphor with particular implications for women's bodies that are directly productive when giving birth. A model of the body also developed in tandem with this, which conceptualized it as an information-processing system with a hierarchical structure, just like a factory, a business or any other modern form of organization.

Because a healthy, adult female body was understood as a productive system, anything thought of as a failure in production was categorized as pathological. Thus, menstruation and menopause are understood in medical models as a failure of production and also as a breakdown in a hierarchical system of authority. Implicit in these images is the notion of an unruly female body that must be observed, controlled and mastered through medical intervention. More than this, in the process of medicalization, women's bodies are fragmented into separate parts and objectified, made to seem separate from the whole woman as a person, and given their own rhythms and motions independent of her control. Using the concepts of person and self that I am developing here, we can say that Martin shows how the embodied woman, the person, is split between an objectified body, which becomes the target of medical, technical intervention, and the various selves which can only look upon this body, having a detached relation to it. The woman has been cut away from her body, leaving only the various parts of her (re)productive system. Thus, in Martin's interviews, she regularly found themes of the self as separate from the body, or of bodily processes as something that the self has to adjust to, go through or attempt to control. Rarely did any women express the view that these were actions that were part of the self as a whole person.

The process of fragmenting and mechanizing parts of the reproductive system is traced back to French hospitals in the seventeenth century – the time when Descartes was writing of the body as a machine – where the uterus was conceptualized as a pump, a machine for giving birth. Martin notes throughout her book how, to this day, both medical textbooks and the women she interviewed talk about contractions as something involuntary, as something which happen *to* women in childbirth, rather than an act they are involved in. Women are alienated from the process of giving birth because the doctor steps in to manage labour just as a manager on the factory floor supervises and controls the labour of workers. Martin thus notes the irony that, in most accounts of 'labour', it is the work that men and women do in producing goods and services that is the main focus of analysis in the social sciences, and the 'labour' that is exclusive to women in producing children (and being their main carers) is largely overlooked. Perhaps this means that 'the complex systems of domination, complicity, resistance, equality, and nurturance in gendered practices of bearing and raising children cannot be accommodated by the concept of labour' (Haraway, 1992: 7). However, Martin shows that there are some elements of the concept of labour that can be used to understand women's experience of childbirth, and of their bodies in general, even though the power relations that govern labour cannot be reduced to relations of production.

Another theme to come from Martin's interviews with women on the subjects of menstruation, childbirth and menopause is that the medicalization of these bodily processes often leaves women feeling alienated from them. These are things that *happen* to a woman's body rather than being aspects of a woman's life, and the way in which women talk about this reveals the separation: rarely did women talk about '*my* labour' or '*my* contractions'. If a baby is delivered by caesarean section while the mother is under anaesthetic, then she can even feel alienated from her child, whose birth she did not witness. Again, women's experiences of childbirth are taken out of their hands and managed largely by doctors, using new medical technology. Martin argues that we need to look at the relations of production which dictate who uses this technology and for whose benefit. A time-limited birth and a healthy baby are often the main aims in the use of medical technology, which is fine at one level, but at another it completely ignores women's experiences during pregnancy and birth and tends to separate the unit of mother and baby.

It is not just the technological management of these processes, however, which affects women's experience of their embodiment. The imaginary body created in medical understanding promotes the view of the body as mechanical, objective and fragmented, and these images are lived through embodied experience. Yet Martin also found in her interviews that these views of the body, although predominant, were not all encompassing and that many women did give phenomenological accounts of their bodies. These were based on their own experiences of the lived body as it blended in with more informal advice and received wisdom passed on by other women, often relatives. This kind of experience was more common among working-class women who did not have as much access to childbirth literature and medical services as the middle-class women in the study. For Martin, then, class and race are also important factors both in the way in which medicine affects women, as well as in the way they create an understanding of the body and build up resistance to the dominant medical view.

But another type of phenomenological understanding emerged from the women's experience of being embodied as women: for example, many reported feelings of creativity and powerfulness in their pre-menstrual period which counteracts the more stereotypical image of women as incapacitated, irritable or emotional. For those who did report a loss of concentration, lack of co-ordination and loss of efficiency around menstruation, Martin asks the question whether it is women's bodies that are really the 'problem' or whether it is the organization of society that really makes things difficult for women, with its rigid systems of discipline and its mechanical view of work-time. This may be the source of a lot of women's anger during menstruation, along with any domestic or relational oppression they may suffer. What Martin is indicating here is that women's bodies are not just the objects of power relations and discipline; they are also the centres of resistance around which women can draw alternative experiences and images. Women's bodies are more likely to be the basis for metaphors of cyclical time and openness, and this is out of kilter with modern social organization. Martin asks 'are women, drawing on the different concepts of time and human capacities they experience, not only able to function in the world of work but able to mount a challenge that will transform it?' (1989: 138). Her answer is a resounding yes.

However, the main opposition focused on in Martin's work is the alternative literature on childbirth and the creation of new birth imagery and, with it, new conceptions of the female body. Against the medical texts, which stress the fragmentation and depersonalization of women's bodies, the new metaphors in this literature stress the woman's wholeness and her active participation in giving birth. Beyond this, the emphasis on wholeness, the underlining of notions of woman as an *embodied person*, oppose the dualisms in Western culture more generally, particularly the dualism between the mind or self and the body. For Martin, then, women do attain a critical standpoint, signposting the way to a different type of culture beyond opposition and dualism, and which is in contrast to the rigid boundaries that men develop around the self. As Nancy Hartsock claims,

> The female construction of self in relation to others, leads . . . toward opposition to dualisms of any sort, valuation of concrete, everyday life, sense of a variety of connectednesses and continuities both with other persons and with the natural world. If material life structures consciousness, women's relationally defined existence, bodily experience of boundary challenges, and activity of transforming both physical objects and human beings must be expected to result in a world view to which dichotomies are foreign. (Hartsock, 1983; quoted in Martin, 1989: 198–9)

While we must be careful of the dangers of romanticizing or essentializing women's experience by regarding this as 'closer to nature' and therefore outside culture, we can begin to see how – in the terms of this project – women may have a different *relation* to others and the natural world, meaning that their bodily experiences can never be as detached from the world as men's can be. However, this is one of the main advantages of an approach like Martin's: she presents an integrated understanding of the biological and the social. She is not saying that the body determines our experience or structures its own cultural images, but that bodily experience is always cultural and vice versa – ideologies are always lived in the body. The norms of medical or other discourses do not simply construct or regulate the body, creating the limits of sex and gender, because other embodied ideologies or discourses, which are more informal and everyday, feed back into the system creating points of opposition and resistance. Medical and other official ideologies, while dominant in many women's understanding of their bodies, are not all-determining; there are other sites for the construction of discourses in the everyday relations to other persons and to the non-human, in which contrary ideologies may appear.

We also find in the writings of Hartsock and Martin an extension of the concept of the productive body that I am constructing here, for women's bodies are directly productive in a way that men's never can be, giving birth to new life, new bodies, new persons. Feelings of openness may always be more accessible to women than to men, and while women also have the same experiences of transforming the real, they also have an experience of bodily production in pregnancy and birth that may never be possible for males. In contrast to Butler's ideas, I would suggest that this shows why feminism needs a concept of the lived body and of the productive body, one that is a constructor as well as the constructed. This opens the dialogue not only to the informal voices of many women, but also to those who speak from various positions where the experience of gender may be more ambiguous and non-dualistic.

The use of the concept of the lived body has also been advanced in feminism by Young (1990), who wants to acknowledge the effects of both the controlling and marking of bodies in relations of power and, at the same time, retain a notion of lived experience from which resistance to the structures of oppression can be drawn. However, at this point it is worth noting the problematic nature of the term 'experience' within the social sciences, for if used in its everyday sense, experience can suggest unmediated, first-hand knowledge which escapes power and ideology in one fell swoop, revealing the unalloyed truth about the world. Yet, as I have already pointed out here, even movements that oppose established structures of power and ideology are themselves locked into relations of power, and they also construct ideologies around their own understanding of social contexts. Despite these problems, Young puts forward an excellent case for retaining the notion of experience, for while

> No experience or reality is unmediated by language and symbols; nevertheless, there are aspects of perception, action and response that are not linguistically constituted. By the term 'experience' I also wish to evoke a pragmatic context of meaning. Meaning subsists not only in signs and symbols, but also in the movement and consequences of action; experience carries the connotation of context and action.

> Perhaps more important, with the term 'experience' I wish to distinguish a certain mode of talk, a language-game. The experiential language-game is specifically first-personal, or subjective. Talk about experience expresses subjectivity, describes the feelings, motives, and reactions of subjects as they are affected by the contexts in which they are situated. (Young, 1990: 13)

Much of importance is being said here, so let me try to unpack some of these points as they relate to my project here. When Young says above that no experience is ever unmediated by language and symbols, yet there are aspects of embodiment that are not linguistically constituted, this is a very similar point to the one I have been trying to illustrate through the multi-dimensional approach. The body itself partly constitutes the symbolic system through its movements and actions within the networks of social relations. This symbolic system then becomes another dimension of experience, one which can never be separated from motility, activity and relations between material bodies; it is a dimension which can expand human knowledge in ways that incorporate the material, yet is never limited or determined by it. In the different social contexts where people find themselves in relations of communication with one another, there is always scope to generate new ideologies relating to those contexts that will not be wholly encapsulated by the current ideological hegemony, and these everyday or behavioural ideologies are drawn from what people regard as personal experience; that is, the way they have come to understand the contexts in which they act, through a mixture of official and unofficial ideologies as they relate to their own embodied personhood. This is, as Young claims, a language-game that expresses a sense of embodied personhood, one's location in relations and social contexts. It also expresses feelings, motives and reactions that are not purely linguistic phenomena but, as we shall see in the next chapter, are complexes composed of the different dimensions of human life. The notion of experience has some currency for the social sciences, then, for while it does not denote a pre-social, individual, truthful understanding, it does capture the way people understand themselves and the world through symbolic forms as they relate to the contexts in which they are bodily located.

In this scheme, people and their various selves are constituted in relations, interactions and language, but there are always contextual spaces where individuals can negotiate new forms of understanding with one another that oppose accepted ideologies. As Young says, 'the concept of the subject retains this aspect of agency as creative, as the life activity that takes up the given and acts upon it' (1990: 13). So, Young is describing something akin to what I have been outlining here in terms of both the communicative and the productive body, one who acts upon the world in order to change it. For Young, the concepts of experience and the subject have a dual function in that they allow for the realization and understanding of forms of oppression, and also for the possibility of resistance and change within those relations of power. In building a more phenomenological approach to embodiment, one that does not want to ignore the effects of relations of power on the body,

Young begins to develop a theory similar to Bourdieu's, which is aimed somewhere between (post)structuralism and phenomenology. Account is taken of the effects of power on the body, particularly in terms of habitual actions that create dispositions and contribute to a sense of identity, and yet the performative is not reduced solely to the structures of the signifying system. In movement and action there is also the possibility of transcendence, of the realization of the restrictions of the bodily habitus and an awareness of the potential to break through it, if only partially. The body does not break free of all forms of habitus but realizes alternatives that are already partly present in lived, daily experience. Thus, in Martin's work, we can see how women are aware of the restrictions placed on their bodies, in medical interventions and through discourses on menstruation, pregnancy, childbirth and menopause. Yet, they also sense – if only dimly – an alternative form of lived bodily experience in other metaphors and practices.

A similar form of understanding appears in Young's own phenomenological studies, in which she describes the lived feelings of restriction, yet also of possibility, in the current Western embodiment of femininity. In her essay 'Throwing Like a Girl' (1990: ch. 8), she describes the confinement that women experience as a literal feeling of being restricted in the body. According to Young, although women's bodies are more open than men's, girls and women occupy space in a very different way. Where men tend to use most of the space available to them in any activity, and do so in a bolder way, especially when playing sports, women's body movements tend to be more restrained and hesitant. This more tentative approach restricts women's physical capacity, as they tend to underestimate their strength and capability in many situations. This accords with Bourdieu's remark that, through the experience of the habitus, men tend to overestimate their size and strength, whereas women underestimate theirs. The body then becomes a thing rather than a capacity, making Merleau-Ponty's idea of embodiment as a sense of 'I can' an ambivalent experience for many women, who may tend to withhold full bodily commitment in their actions.

However, it must be realized that Young is not claiming that this is a universal experience for all women. First, different women will experience their bodies in different ways, as will different men, so that the feelings Young is describing will not be sensed by all women to the same degree, and some of these feelings of restriction in the body may well be common to many men. Young is simply claiming that there is a general tendency for this to be more a part of women's experience than of men's. Secondly, it is not suggested that women in every culture will experience greater restriction in their bodily motility and capacity, but that this is a general tendency of femininity in contemporary Western cultures. It is in this respect that we see the indivisible nature of culture and the body as it feeds into sex and gender identity. Thus, when Young refers to the modalities of feminine bodily existence, she is referring to 'a set of structures and conditions that delimit the typical *situation* of being a woman in a particular society, as well as the typical way in which this situation is lived by the women themselves' (1990:

143-4). In patriarchy, women experience a situation that is inherently contradictory, for as human beings they are free subjects, but as women they must deny a degree of free subjectivity along with their powerful capacities, in order to be subjected to men. This reflects in bodily comportment.

Like Martin, Young has also noted the alienation many women experience during the medical interventions in pregnancy (1990: ch. 9), yet on a more positive note has begun to describe some of the outlawed and disruptive aspects of feminine bodily experience. For example, in her account of 'breasted experience', Young (1990: ch. 11) describes how the pleasure and sensitivity of breasts opposes the phallocentrism of patriarchy. According to Young, women's breasts and nipples are centres of pleasure in themselves, especially when suckling a child. While breasts are objectified as symbols of male pleasure and desire, women can get pleasure from them without men, and can find sexual satisfaction through their breasts without the phallus. Thus breasts are threatening to the male-dominated social and sexual order and are more often strapped in and hidden in Western cultures. The bra, which is often regarded as a 'shaping' device, is actually a part of this restraining culture, for the fluidity and changing shape of breasts is an offence to the norms of patriarchy, emphasizing as it does the smooth, muscular, armoured surface of the closed body. Furthermore, located on the chest, which is often regarded as the centre of personhood, women tend to associate their personal sense of being with their breasts and feel a great sense of loss in losing one or both breasts in a mastectomy. Thus, Young is illustrating how, in both a positive and negative way, the body is active within culture as both a signified and a signifying capacity, one which is constructed and normalized in social practices and the habitus, yet at the same time is given – and makes for itself – the potential to change relations of power. The body is not simply a product of relations of power, but also of relations of communication and transformation, and as such is equipped with a variety of dispositions, capacities and potentialities that allow for agency and the constant possibility of social change.

Conclusion

While the body, then, should not be seen as an ontological foundation for sexuality and gender identity, it nevertheless has a contingent relation to them, contributing to the experiences through which we live out our sexuality and gender. As Grosz (1994) pointed out, the body is an open materiality, a set of potentialities which may be developed into dispositions and capacities through the habitus – that incorporated history which generates bodily styles, habits and practices. Power relations work through the body in this way, creating dispositions that lead to the performance of a specific gender and, in the process, both marks and controls bodies while also investing them with certain powers and capacities. These develop not only in relations of power, but also in relations that transform the real and in relations of communication, so that power is never able fully to contain the lived, productive body. Its performances are never wholly tied to the symbolic, or to any other single dimension of human life. In the varied experiences of the lived body, in the different contexts in which it applies its already developed dispositions, there is the possibility of realizing the potential for change within the social order, not by breaking free of the habitus, but by realizing alternatives to established power relations and ideological hegemonies that are already partly present in lived, daily experience.

Feminist writers have begun to show how this is already happening for many women in their embodied, lived experience of various contexts in patriarchal power relations. The medicalization of women's bodily processes, especially around reproductive functions, creates both an imaginary body and a set of practices through which women experience themselves as fragmented and alienated. However, there are other embodied experiences, other aspects of the habitus, which present alternatives to this and suggest the possibility of wholeness in women's bodily experiences and a point of opposition to current medical and patriarchal practices. If these alternatives were to be fully realized, they could present one way out of the dualisms that haunt embodiment in the West, not just for women but for men as well.

6 Social Relations, Embodiment and Emotions

In recent years the subject of the emotions has come more to the attention of social scientists, largely because of the emphasis on embodiment in social theory and because of the feminist challenge to the dualism of mind and body, in which the domination of women involves their equation with the bodily and emotional sphere. Here, I offer my own contribution to the debate around the emotions, which sets out a relational and embodied understanding of the emotions that elaborates upon my own previous work (Burkitt, 1991) and also Kenneth J. Gergen's (1994a, 1995). It is this relational method that I hope will take us forward in developing a multi-dimensional approach to the emotions in which they are seen as complexes; that is, as experiences involving physical, symbolic and relational elements. In this multi-dimensional view, however, it is my opinion that the relations which structure embodied activity are the defining element of the complex experience we call an emotion. This is because, as Bateson (1973) has pointed out, in the Anglo-Saxon world we have given certain feelings names that we then associate with a precise quantity, a thing, which we consider to be the emotion proper. And yet all human feelings are characterized by *pattern* rather than quantity: it is the pattern of the relationship between self and other, and self and environment, which is the subject matter of emotions such as love, hate, fear and anxiety.

Despite this, Gergen (1994a) has pointed out that it is rare for definitions to be offered in studies of the emotions. At the beginning of such studies, researchers do not clarify their ideas of what an emotion actually is and therefore leave uncertain what they are looking for in their research. What is the object of study, how is it defined and how will it be investigated? In the work of social scientists as diverse as Jackson (1993) and Duncombe and Marsden (1993), relational theories of the emotions are implicit, but they never quite reach a more explicit formulation of what emotion is or what a relational understanding of emotion would entail. In the absence of this, the everyday assumptions about emotion that exist within our culture can creep back into the analysis without the authors realizing what is happening. That emotion is somehow part of gender relations is clear from Duncombe and Marsden's (1993) work on the emotional division of labour in heterosexual households, but it is never fully elaborated how feelings are produced in such contexts. Stevi Jackson (1993) comes much closer to an understanding of emotion as produced in relations but is unclear about how this occurs. As she says, an emotion such as love is traditionally seen as an indefinable and mysterious thing, existing somehow beyond rational discourse and breaking out at unpredictable points and in unforeseeable ways to disrupt the rational organization of society. Weber (1947) was one who thought that emotion was an irrational force and thus needed a form of analysis distinct from the usual study of rational modes of social action. However, Jackson comes no closer to defining the object of enquiry despite a bold attempt to do so. She claims that because emotions are not observable phenomena, we only have access to emotions through the mediation of the discourse of our culture, so, as in the case of love for example, 'there is . . . no way of exploring love except through the ways in which it is talked and written about. Language itself, moreover, contributes to the cultural construction of emotions and is a means by which we participate in creating a shared sense of what emotions are' (Jackson, 1993: 207).

And, yet, to say that we only have access to emotions through the mediation of discourse suggests that something called 'emotion' exists beyond discourse, but can only be described through it. Jackson, then, seems to fall into the trap of seeing emotion as some extra-cultural object. In the next sentence, though, it is said that because we can only explore emotions such as love through discourse, then language plays a role in constructing emotions by creating a shared sense of what they are about. Now, this is correct in the sense that emotions are only definable in terms of cultural meanings and the social contexts in which we find ourselves. However, there is a danger of a form of discursive reductionism here if emotions are defined *only* as discursively created experiences. Is emotion simply discourse, in which case the study of emotions would be just a part of discourse analysis, or is there something more distinctive about the study of emotion, especially given that emotions are embodied experiences? Jackson seems to suggest both these options, stating that there is no way of exploring emotion other than through language, but then saying that language only *contributes* to the cultural construction of emotions. What other factors, then, are involved in this construction? Jackson (1993: 212) goes on to say:

> Our subjectivities, including that aspect of them we understand as our emotions, are shaped by social and cultural processes and structures but are not simply passively accepted by us . . . we actively participate in working ourselves into structures and this in part explains the strength of our subjection to them. We create for ourselves a sense of what our emotions are, of what being 'in love' is. We do this by participating in sets of meanings constructed, interpreted, propagated and deployed throughout our culture, through learning scripts, positioning ourselves within discourses, constructing narratives of self. We make sense of feelings and relationships in terms of love because a set of discourses around love pre-exists us as individuals and through these we have learnt what love means.

Here we can see some of the confusion that surrounds Jackson's work on love and emotion. First, it is never clearly stated what the social and cultural processes and structures are that Jackson is referring to, and so the allusion to working ourselves into structures we then become the subjects of is rather puzzling. Secondly, there again emerges the idea that feelings and relations can only be made sense of through sets of discourses, only now there are added scripts and narratives. Also, prior to the above quotation, Jackson quotes Rosaldo, who claims that, 'feelings are not substances to be discovered in our blood, but social practices organized by stories that we both enact and tell. They are structured by our forms of understanding' (in Jackson, 1993: 212). If the forms of understanding are what Jackson is referring to as 'structures' then this certainly lends weight to Craib's (1995) claim that this form of constructionism leans towards subjectivist cognitivism. But what is also a problem here is the way in which the object of study is confused at various points. What exactly is it that we are studying in work on the emotions: is it relations, practices or various forms of discourse? While all these things are undoubtedly interrelated, the question is *how are they interrelated and what implications does this have for the study of emotion?* Furthermore, what is the role of the body in the construction of emotion? I want to suggest that the central object of study in research on emotions are relationships, and that embodied practices and discourses are both structured by them and also take their meaning from them. Here, I will present emotions as complexes, ones that are essentially relational but have bodily elements, as well as cultural elements, as necessary components.

The physical aspect of emotion is something that Craib (1995) attempts to pick up in his comment on Jackson. For Craib, who approaches these matters from a psychoanalytical perspective, there are a range of emotions rooted in our biological make-up, but which also have a cultural and historical dimension. The basic emotions are therefore shared among all human beings, yet are culturally elaborated so that they are socially and historically nuanced and thus variable. However, at root, the emotions have a life of their own which may not fully accord with cultural norms or with cognitive categories. In this way we can have feelings that we cannot adequately express, or experience contradictions between thought and feeling. However, the problem here is that Craib gives to the emotions their traditional role – as individualistic experiences that arise internally, perhaps organically – so that there may be a clash between inner and outer processes. Equally, emotions themselves may be contradictory, causing degrees of subjective turmoil that need working on for some kind of resolution or acceptance to be achieved. Thus, for Craib, 'what seems evident about emotions in terms of their own – as opposed to social – dynamics is that they are necessarily contradictory' (1995: 155). Here we can see clearly the division between the inner and outer worlds, the social and the individual, which is elaborated further as follows: 'people – men and women – are by definition engaged in at least two interlocking forms of emotional work: the "internal" work of coping with contradiction, conflict and ambivalence and the "external" work of reconciling what goes on inside with what one is supposed or allowed to feel' (Craib, 1995: 155). The split between the social and emotional is displayed so evidently here. It seems that in trying to avoid Jackson's social reductionism Craib has strayed back into individualism and a dichotomy between self and society. Here, I want to argue that it is possible to retain the notion of emotional contradiction and avoid reduction-ism, through a relational account of emotion. Before I do that, I want to make one last point. In his commentary Craib uses the division between social and emotional dynamics to stress that there is no simple relation between an emotion and its expression. However, I want to try to get away from the idea that emotions are expressions of something 'inner', so that the expression is an outer register of an inner process. Instead, I will claim that, if emotions are expressive of anything, it is of the relations and interdepend-encies that they are an integral part of, and in this sense emotions are essentially communicative: they are expressions occurring *between people* and registered on the body, rather than expressions of something contained inside a single person. At the same time, though, we must account for emotions in part as lived embodied experiences, available to us as persons (Denzin, 1984). I will outline below how I think the relational approach can encompass these elements.

Emotions in Relations

I will contend here that what is involved in the production of emotion are relations and the practices and speech genres that can be found within them, rather than processes internal to the individual which are only later expressed at some appropriate (or inappropriate) moment. So, for example, in this view, aggression is not an emotion that initially arises inside people, from some deep inner well and in accordance with its own mechanics, but is produced in the relations of which the aggressive person is part. Relations of conflict may stir in people feelings of aggressiveness towards certain others with whom they are interdependent: those who may not have fulfilled their responsibilities in the relationship, who may have betrayed or undermined it; or those seen as outsiders or a threat on the basis of national, ethnic or racial prejudice. And yet the aggressiveness comes from the interrelations not, originally, from inside the person. As Elias says, 'it is not aggressiveness that triggers conflicts but conflicts that trigger aggressiveness' (1988: 178). Thus any aggressive action, gesture or talk is not the result of aggressive feelings; rather, the feelings are the result of relations. Furthermore, these relations are always social and cultural, specific to a particular place and time, and within them only certain actions or utterances will be labelled as aggressive. This applies not just to aggression but to all emotions. Gergen sums up the relational approach to emotions in the following way:

> Emotional discourse gains its meaning not by virtue of its relationship to an inner world (of experience, disposition, or biology), but by the way it figures in patterns of cultural relationship. Communities generate conventional modes of relating; patterns of action within these relationships are often given labels. Some forms of action – by current Western standards – are said to indicate emotions. (Gergen, 1994a: 222)

Here we see distilled many of the central elements I want to hold on to
here: emotional discourse gains meaning within cultural relationships, and
these involve patterns of action that are often said to indicate certain
emotions. Borrowing from Leontyev (1978), I would say that different
actions display distinctive emotional colourings: acting out the emotions – or
what Gergen calls 'emotional scenarios' – *are* the emotions themselves. In
other words, nothing pre-exists the emotive action that could be called the
emotion proper, which is then expressed through the action. Instead, the
emotion is the action itself and is governed by the relations in which it
occurs. As Gergen says, emotions do not have an impact on social life; 'they
constitute social life itself' (1994a: 222). So, emotions do not come from
outside relations and impact upon them, they are constituted by the relations
that compose social life.

As for the discourse that occurs within these relations, rather than seeing
discourse as positioning the subject within its already structured frame, I
propose that emotional discourse can be seen as an example of what Bakhtin
(1986) calls *speech genres*, which exist in the flow of human action. In
contrast to Foucault's use of the term discourse – to denote tactical elements
or blocks deployed in the field of power relations, which construct objects or
identities – for Bakhtin, speech genres encompass:

> All the diverse areas of human activity involv[ing] the use of language. Quite
> understandably, the nature and form of this use are just as diverse as are the areas
> of human activity . . . Language is realized in the form of concrete utterances (oral
> and written) by participants in the various areas of human activity . . . Each
> separate utterance is individual, of course, but each sphere in which language is
> used develops its own *relatively stable types* of these utterances. These we may
> call *speech genres*. (Bakhtin, 1986: 60)

These genres are not limiting because the possibility of their diversification
is boundless: the reason for this is that the scope of human activity is
inexhaustible and thus speech genres will multiply as the horizons of social
relations and activities expand. The concept therefore illustrates how individuals are not in any simple way the constructs of discourses because
people are also language users. In this way, *individuals actively use speech
genres to orient themselves in their relationships and interactions and to
give expression to them*. Also, speech genres are heterogeneous because each
different sphere of human activity will have its own repertoire of speech
genres. This could be the military command barked out on the parade
ground, the technical language of limited scope used in scientific or business
reports, or the declarations of love between two lovers.

What Bakhtin is also demonstrating is that emotion cannot be solely a
linguistic construction, for the words in which emotion is expressed are
often neutral. That is to say, the words in a language are not themselves the
carriers of emotion: it is the embodied person located in a relational context
who feels an emotion and uses the speech genres of his or her culture in
order to express that emotional scenario. However, this is not a simple
matter of choosing the right word to express the context one is embedded in,

for a person may choose a word or expression which is the opposite of what he or she is feeling and use his or her vocal intonation to signal that the utterance is ironic. The utterance, then, is not just a word taken from an established speech genre, but is a complete utterance that is the expression of a person's embodied location in a relationship or context. An exclamation such as 'He's dead!' is an expression of shock or surprise, tinged with either deep regret or glee, depending on one's relationship to the person who has just died. Emotion, then, is not so much to be found in the speech genres as in our whole bodily bearing as we utter words. For Bakhtin (1986: 87), then:

> emotion, evaluation, and expression are foreign to the word of language and are born only in the process of its live usage in a concrete utterance. The meaning of a word in itself (unrelated to actual reality) is, as we have already said, out of the range of emotion. There are words that specifically designate emotions and evaluations: 'joy', 'sorrow', 'wonderful', 'cheerful', 'sad', and so forth. But these meanings are just as neutral as are all the others. They acquire their expressive colouring only in the utterance, and this colouring is independent of their meaning taken individually and abstractly. For example, 'any joy is now only bitterness to me'. Here the word 'joy' is given an expressive intonation that resists its own meaning, as it were.

Expressive intonation is, then, determined by the context we are in and by our relations to the people and things within it. This illustrates that emotion cannot be reduced to language alone, nor can it be said that words are the sole means of identifying emotions. Given this, I now want to go on to explore the idea of emotions as complexes constituted in relations. That is to say, emotions are multi-dimensional and cannot be reduced to biology, relations or discourses alone, but belong to all these dimensions as they are constituted in ongoing relational practices. As such, the focus of the study of emotions cannot be on objects understood as 'things', and instead we must reconceptualize emotions as complexes composed of different dimensions of embodied, interdependent human existence. In the first section, I want to suggest how emotions may be seen as composites of embodied practice and the speech genres that accompany such practice. In the second section it is claimed that emotions need also to be understood in terms of techniques of the body which are both physical and cultural. And, in the third, how emotions can only be made sense of within the power relations of specific cultures located in historical space and time.

The Embodiment of Emotion

While emphasis on the cultural construction of emotion is commendable, stressing as it does the malleability and historical nature of emotions, the attempt to escape from biological reductionism perhaps leads this approach to be too reticent in addressing issues of embodiment and the dimension of bodily sensation. The idea that emotions are cultural and historical is not inimical to an understanding of how emotions involve bodily processes. However, some constructionists are ambivalent about the degree of naturalness in emotions. For example, Claire Armon-Jones (1986) is cool about attempts to understand certain basic emotions as natural, bodily-felt sensations (a position similar to the one Craib is proposing). This is because she feels it important that emotions are understood as acquired within cultures, while perceptions and sensations are natural phenomena and not skills developed by training. Within constructionism, the argument for this distinction is made on the basis that emotion cannot be defined by its sensory quality. Crying and weeping are observed at both funerals *and* weddings, and yet crying for joy is a very different experience from crying for grief. If the sensation does not define the emotion, then the cultural rules and conventions that guide our interpretation of events must play the definitive role.

However, I believe that this is a one-dimensional view: sensations may well be necessary *components* of emotion while not being the defining feature. I also think that sensations and perceptions are not simply natural phenomena that are closed off from cultural conditioning, as Constance Classen (1993) has shown in her socio-historical and cross-cultural analysis of the changing world of the senses. Instead of the view of sensation as natural and unchanging, we need to understand how sensate experience is formed in social activities, making it *both* biological and social. This is part of the problem in Craib's analysis of emotion. While he is willing to contemplate certain basic emotions that are culturally elaborated, it soon becomes clear that at root these can be separated from cultural dynamics, making them individual experiences which can be opposed to the influence of social relations. We must replace this view of the biological aspects of humanity with an understanding where biology and sociality are inseparable, meeting as they do in the human body itself – a view I am developing here. From this perspective, emotions can be seen as socially constructed while also having sensate, corporeal components that are necessary to the lived bodily experience of that emotion. Would we say we had experienced fear if our hearts did not race and our palms sweat; that we were in love if there were no sense of light-headedness or elation; or that we were depressed or miserable without the feeling of physical drag, of everything being just too much trouble to bother about? I think not. The physical component of an emotion is vital to our experience of it. Emotions can have a familiar physiological pattern to them, recognizable to some degree across cultures, while at the same time being in their full expression culturally constructed and thus particular.

This also means that emotions are not based on introspection through a cognitive scanning and interpretation of inner sensations. Rather, sensation and thought can arise at one and the same moment within specific social contexts as a learned bodily response or disposition. Here, I am following the notion of disposition as found in the work of Bourdieu (1990) and

Wittgenstein (see Schatzki, 1993): dispositions are not mechanical responses to a given situation, but are more like conditions which may or may not become manifested in certain contexts. One could say that a culture provides for people an *emotional habitus*, with a language and set of practices, which outline ways of speaking about emotions, and of acting out and upon bodily feelings within everyday life. Individuals are trained in the emotional habitus from infancy and, through this, develop emotional dispositions that can be expressed in certain contexts throughout a person's life. Emotions, then, are both cognitive and pre-cognitive: they involve culturally informed interpretation, but are also bodily dispositions instilled through social practices. For example, in Wittgenstein's (1953) account of feeling joyful, he claims that we recognize this emotion through behaving and thinking in a joyful manner, not by reflecting on an inner state or attitude of joy. The emotion, then, is not a cognitive interpretation of the situation, nor of some inner physiological stirrings, rather it is *a bodily expression within a situation* that gives us joy. Wittgenstein says that 'joy designates nothing at all. Neither something inner nor something outer' (1967: 487), by which I take him to mean that joy is not the expression of an inner or outer cause; instead, the expression *is* the joyful feeling. Joyfulness is *not* having the attitudes or cognitions of feeling joyful, *but is joyfulness itself*, a condition that can be expressed in joyful thought or action. Furthermore, these conditions are not found inside a person but are aspects of the conditions of life within which a person exists.

Here we can see how emotion need not be reduced to either an inner organic or a psychological process, for it encompasses both these things within the contexts of everyday life. Individuals do have a psychological and physiological life, but this is fragmentary and intermittent, and is held together in a meaningful way only in the 'weave of behaviours' that compose the practices of social life. Because emotions involve human corporeality, there may well be a basic patterning discernible in many displays of emotion across different cultures, and yet these patterns are drawn out and elaborated in very different ways. While Craib may be right on this point, his next move – to give emotions an inner existence separate from cultural norms or cognitive categories – does not necessarily follow. Embodied emotional experience may flow from the social contexts in which people are enmeshed, and yet still be against some more generally prescribed norms. Either that or people may feel a conflict of emotion stemming from a particular situation. On hearing the news of a misfortune befalling a rival, one may be torn between the need to show some feelings of sympathy for the person and the secret feelings of pleasure at the news. Emotional conflict, then, does not arise from internal states of ambivalence; instead, it emerges within social contexts which are themselves inherently ambivalent or filled with conflict. People in such situations may choose not to express a bodily felt emotion, but that does not necessarily make the affect an 'inner' experience. In such circumstances, a person may think of the emotion in that way, and yet it has been created within relations to others and has a meaning for the person only in that context; otherwise, the emotion would not be identifiable or intelligible.

However, Wittgenstein's notion of conditions of life and his ideas about embodiment tend to be somewhat vague. These concepts can be elaborated upon using Norbert Elias's notion of 'forms of life', which refers to the power structure, culture and practices of a social figuration, along with his ideas of the social habitus and embodiment. When fused with similar concepts found in the work of Bourdieu and Foucault, we have a powerful sociological imagination of the emotions that complements some of the literature in the field (Denzin, 1984; Kemper, 1990a; Scheff, 1990a). This leads us to consider first of all the bodily dispositions and techniques involved in the production of emotion as they are woven into relations of power.

Bodily Techniques of Emotion

The term 'bodily techniques' can be found in the work of Marcel Mauss (1979) and Michel Foucault (1986a, 1988), but here I am using the term to refer to the postures, movements, gestures, expressions and general powers of the body to act in given ways. These techniques and powers are instilled through social relations from the earliest years of infancy onwards, and are the foundation for later forms of action and thought. This concept is applied to the work of Elias, whose approach is very much in line with the one I am suggesting here, in terms of viewing emotions as complexes that have physical and cultural dimensions. For Elias (1987b) all emotions have bodily, behavioural and feeling components. An example of this is that humans and many other animals share the fight–flight reaction to danger, composed of a racing heartbeat and raised levels of adrenaline that prepare the body for sudden action and produce the sharp reactions to sudden movement. These would be the somatic and behavioural components of emotion. However, in human beings (and in human beings alone as far as we know) there is also a feeling component which is entirely learned, so that a fight–flight reaction can be felt and expressed as anger or rage, as fear, dread or anxiety, or as a combination of these depending on the situation. Elias warns, though, much in the manner of Wittgenstein, that we must not see these behaviours as 'expressions' of any underlying thing called 'emotion', for the expression *is* the emotion and therefore the somatic, behavioural and feeling components are all aspects of the same thing – of emotion itself.

It is only if we define emotion narrowly in terms of the feeling component that behaviour becomes a secondary effect, a mere 'expression' of the feeling or thought. This is in accordance with the commonly held view of individuals as monads whose true self is hidden deep inside, so that, 'what shows itself on one's "outside", for instance on one's face, is merely a derivative or else an "expression", and often not a true or even distorted expression, of what one is inside' (Elias, 1987b: 355–6). Elias seeks a way out of this problem by asking what function emotional expression has for human beings, concluding that it is one of *communication* between people, rather than the expression of a hidden 'inner' world. *Expressions are not, then, the 'outer' signal of 'inner' feelings, but are signs in the networks of social relations and interdependencies.* An example of this given by Elias is of the 'smiling emotion', in which the smile is a signal of friendly intent towards others or the reaction when greeting a friend. The feelings associated with this sign prepare a person for a certain type of action, for the gestures of friendship and the subsequent actions of friendliness. The *relations* between people and the feelings associated with them are part and parcel of interaction, which is composed of gestures, signals and bodily movements. All these things are part of the same communicative process, with relations, behaviour and feelings all interlocked.

Certain aspects of this process may well be unlearned, as smiling tends to be a universal signal with a similar meaning across cultures. Such a gesture can have developed socially but become ingrained biologically through the evolutionary process. Yet at the same time smiling is also a learned response as it can signal a variety of subtly different emotions. In fact, Elias claims that all the unlearned propensities of the human body are mobilized and patterned through learning, so that on no occasion do we see a basic, purely biological emotion that does not bear the imprint of a socially tutored body technique of communicating feeling. In culturation, then, the learned feeling component of emotion may become extremely varied and, with it, the bodily techniques of feeling expression may also become more subtly nuanced. One of the central aspects of Elias's work is that it helps us to understand how learned techniques of body control, such as manners, modes of conduct and the changed forms of feeling and thinking that go with them, are to some degree involuntary. Children are trained in these techniques at an early age and they quickly become spontaneous, along with the feelings associated with them.

A good example of how the bodily techniques of emotion are instilled, briefly discussed in Chapter 3, is Elias's (1978) study of the Renaissance period in Western Europe. Here, educators made an attempt to instruct the nobility on how to raise their children as 'civilized' beings. The most famous treatise produced by such educators was Erasmus's *De civilitate morum puerilium* in which it is claimed that 'the art of forming young people involves various disciplines', a rigorous training of the body in practices that are regarded as 'civilized' in 'polite society'. Furthermore, Erasmus's book, concerned as it is with bodily carriage, gestures, facial expressions and dress, shows how the 'outward' behaviour of a person is read more closely as expressing something of the 'inner' person, his or her character or refinement. However, as Elias points out, these are not indicators of a refined intellect or sensitive spirit, but of the class position of individuals and the habitus in which they have been raised. It is of these social relations that a person's bodily techniques are expressive. Yet Elias is

interested in the emergence of the type of observation that today we call
'psychological', in which a person's behaviour is explained by referring it to
some underlying 'mental' characteristic – the very type of explanation that
Wittgenstein challenges in Western thinking. In everyday terms, the psychological mode of observation emerges in societies where people's behaviour
comes under much closer scrutiny; societies in which individuals are
watched by others for bodily signs that reveal something of their 'inner'
character, thoughts or feelings. This is so because in all social life – in work,
the family and the community – people are now more interdependent with
one another and interactions have to be more finely tuned. People also
demand certain standards of behaviour from those with whom they interact,
standards which are different from those of the Middle Ages, the main
difference being the demand for a style of behaviour we have come to call
'polite' or 'well mannered', which shows a constant concern for the feelings
or sensibilities of others.

The importance of social relations and interdependencies are paramount
here in terms of the mutual demands individuals make upon one another,
thus shaping sensibilities and cultural precepts, such as the rules of etiquette
inscribed in Erasmus's treatise. These precepts and rules are tied to the
relations between the social classes and to the general social structure of the
times, so that the emotions and feelings they compose are intelligible only
within this social context. Relations also structure the practices that instil in
the body techniques and controls, the modes of expression of feelings and
thoughts. Thus, Erasmus's book concerns itself to a large degree with
techniques for the control of bodily processes: with table manners and how
to express one's appetite; on the correct way to blow one's nose and what to
blow it on; on the place for sexual activity and the degree of decorum
surrounding it; on how to fart silently in church; and the way in which
aggressive or angry responses may, or may not, be displayed. The social
controls that become internalized are meant to regulate these aspects of
bodily processes, more often than not unsuccessfully. This lack of success is
an occasion for embarrassment in societies that demand the strict regulation
of bodily functions and see this as a sign of good upbringing and education
– that is, as displaying high social status.

Here, we also see the operation of the modern form of the communicative
body which, as Falk (1994) claimed, seeks to conceal as much as it reveals.
The controls that are placed around the closed body lead to the formation of
techniques which attempt to master both bodily processes and also the
displays of emotion as they are registered on the body's surface. Thus, Elias
(1978) describes how advice on manners came to dictate that not only
should well-mannered people not fart in public, they should also not rock
back and forth in their chairs, or blush with embarrassment, in case they give
away to others in their company the need to break wind. What has come to
be regarded as good manners, from the Renaissance onwards, therefore
recommends that in public individuals must present themselves as both
acceptable bodies and, through this means, as acceptable persons. This is

achieved whenever possible by techniques for the careful control of the body and its registering of emotional responses from within the relations in which it is located.

Such control of the body also contributes to its armouring, to the concealment of certain feelings and bodily needs, which are then experienced as having to be kept 'inside' the person. That is, they cannot find expression on the surface of the body and so are metaphorically perceived as being hidden in the 'subjective' realm, which is felt to be distinct from bodily being. It is through lack of opportunity for expression that emotions come to be experienced as private and subjective, and can become intensified experiences because of the regulations that surround them. As I noted in Chapter 3, it is this state of delayed response that has become emblematic of the emotions for modern people and one of the chief characteristics of emotional experience. Although intense emotion can still be characterized by its expression, for many individuals emotion would be seen as synonymous with the private realm that is partly hidden from public view.

However, despite the information on the control of the body, Elias's main interest is the way in which social interdependencies, practices and expectations lead to socially formed emotional dispositions. Initially, the emotional dispositions of human beings have no innate structure; certain impulses or instincts such as hunger or fear, or reactions such as smiling, are unlearned and have developed in human evolution, thereafter being passed on through genetic inheritance. But even these unlearned impulses are not properly formed until they are elaborated upon and differentiated from one another in the process of social learning. Even then, the affects are not to be thought of as separate, discrete entities, but instead:

> they complement and in part supersede each other, transform themselves within certain limits and compensate for each other; a disturbance here manifests itself there. In short, they form a kind of circuit in the human being, a partial system within the total system of the organism. Their structure is still opaque in many respects, but their socially imprinted form is of decisive importance for the functioning of a society as of the individuals within it. (Elias, 1978: 191)

What Elias becomes concerned with in this fashion is the way in which emotional dispositions are conditioned within the social habitus so that certain feelings are mixed and complement, or contradict, one another. The prime example, used again by Elias, is of aggressive feelings. Such feelings could be expressed openly and be actively enjoyed during the Middle Ages. The battle hymns of the times expressed a joy in war and in hurting and killing the enemy. Remember that, following Wittgenstein, this joy is not an underlying emotion but the way in which individuals could, within their cultures, participate in battle and express themselves in their actions. Killing the enemy was pleasurable; it was accepted as an honourable, even gallant and courageous, thing within society, so one had no need to hide one's pleasure in the exultation that being a good warrior would bring. In the early court societies, it was the primary social function of a knight to go to war and fight, and so to enjoin in battle and fulfil one's function – to practise one's art – was pleasing. Only later, when court societies became more pacified and physical destruction was not so openly celebrated, did the expression of enjoyment in aggressive acts become suppressed. Instead, the enjoyment of war was expressed in terms of the camaraderie between soldiers, or of the just cause for which one was fighting. One can see here the conflict of emotions – any enjoyment of violence became outbalanced by feelings of repugnance at physically aggressive acts.

What Elias's work demonstrates so clearly is the integrity of interdependencies, practices, expressions and feelings; for, as forms of emotional expression change, so does the feeling of what it is like to act in certain situations. It was no longer enjoyable to physically destroy another human being in combat, and scenes of carnage associated with wars and mass slaughter became sights that occasioned disgust. Such sights were no longer for public display and were removed 'behind the scenes' where no one but the perpetrators had to countenance them. With the development of more modern instruments of warfare, such as weapons that could destroy at a distance, even soldiers no longer had to see the horrific results of their own actions. As forms of expression within social practices changed in terms of what was permissible and what was taboo, so the experience of certain actions and bodily functions or behaviours changed; they were experienced in different terms emotionally, associated with different feelings and thoughts. The sight, sound and smell of actions or bodily functions that once were openly accepted became repugnant and to be hidden; what was once a source of pleasurable feelings was now a source of shame. Other writers have also been concerned with how a culture delimits the experiences of individuals, associating certain actions or functions with pleasurable feelings or with repugnant, distressing ones (Douglas, 1966).

Therefore, the emotional life of individuals cannot in any way be separated from culture and learning. There is no 'inner' world of feelings separated from 'outer' cultural norms or values. We can understand how there can be contradictions in feelings created by contradictory or conflicting relations, or emotional expressions which need to be controlled due to the demands of the current situation, without setting up the dichotomy of the individual and the social. Emotional experience is still inextricably bound up with embodiment in relations, and this leads to the third aspect of emotion complexes: that the relations in which emotions arise are always, to some extent, power relations.

Power Relations, Moral Precepts and Emotions

How emotions are tied to relations of power is well illustrated in the following statement from Elias:

> Today the circle of precepts and regulations is drawn so tightly about people, the censorship and pressure of social life forming their habits are so strong, that

young people have only two alternatives: to submit to the pattern of behaviour demanded by society, or to be excluded from life in 'decent society'. A child that does not attain the level of control of emotions demanded by society is regarded in varying gradations as 'ill', 'abnormal', 'criminal', or just 'impossible' from the point of view of a particular caste or class, and is accordingly excluded from the life of that class. Indeed, from the psychological point of view, the terms 'sick', 'abnormal', 'criminal', and 'impossible' have, within certain limits, no other meaning; how they are understood varies with the historically mutable models of affect formation. (Elias, 1978: 141)

The interesting thing about this quotation is the way that it shows how the socially imposed standards of behaviour – precepts and regulations – are instilled in children at a very early age as bodily techniques. The precepts and regulations of a class (or of any other social group) could be said to form the emotional habitus, while the bodily techniques form the dispositions for the production, or suppression, of emotion signals in particular circumstances. The emergence of the wrong emotion signs show, in the eyes of one's peers, a lack of social skill or, worse, some underlying psychological 'disorder' which has disabled the person in learning the required bodily techniques. Either way, the person has failed to learn the expected levels of self-regulation and self-control, and because of this is judged inadequate by those who are more powerful, or whose class or gender upbringing has instilled in them a different set of controls and techniques which, because of their power, are seen as 'superior'.

Also, Elias talks above about the pressures that form people's habits, and it is interesting to note how the techniques and controls that surround the body and emotional life can actually form into habits which are imprinted on the body in the skeletal musculature. We have already noted Reich's (1950) concept of the body armour and how the controls on emotion become ingrained into our posture, movements, carriage, gestures and tone of voice. Reich believed that it was the capitalist economy, with its need to repress and sublimate the sexual instincts into the work ethic and the drive for capital accumulation, which inflicted such violence on the human body. However, as Keat (1986) has pointed out, we do not need to accept Reich's naturalizing of the sexual impulses in order to adapt his ideas about the way in which power relations become rooted in body armour. For example, the notion of the body armour can be used to explain how controls are instilled at the level of the body in modern social institutions or in the well-mannered interactions of everyday life. In both cases, the body must be disciplined into certain routines and habits through relations of power in order for it to be acceptable as a person or citizen. And what these ideas show is the way in which the human body is the site of the interaction between biological and social processes.

However, despite the controls and techniques that operate on the body and the attempts to inculcate the correct habits and dispositions, this process is open to failure. This failure has two main implications for the view that emotions are produced by 'feeling rules' (Hochschild, 1983), a position which cannot always explain why emotions may arise in the first place which are against such cultural rules. First, emotional signals are largely learned and yet performed in specific contexts quite spontaneously, which means that emotional behaviour does not always conform to feeling rules. People may inadvertently break the feeling rules of the particular situation they find themselves in, or they may find it impossible to prevent themselves feeling what they ought not to feel because of spontaneous emotions experienced in their relationship to a situation or another person. Such a view answers one of the main criticisms of constructionist theories of emotions (see Harré, 1986), which is that emotion cannot be produced by people conforming to the feeling rules of each situation – such as happy at parties, sad at funerals, and so on – because then one would never find people miserable at parties and happy at funerals. If we are at a dull party we may feel and look miserable, while at the funeral of a long-time rival we may secretly feel glad. So feelings can often contradict and conflict with the rules of emotion in particular settings because of the *relations* of the people within them (Kemper, 1981). There is also the phenomenon of mixed emotions, of ambivalent or ambiguous feelings held by individuals towards other people or things, and the idea of emotions being structured by feeling rules cannot always account for this.

Secondly, social power relations involving class, gender and race are intimately connected to social precepts and regulations, which play such a central role in the shaping of emotions. Averill (1986) has criticized Elias for seeing the precepts and regulations that orient emotional behaviour as exclusively restrictive, being internalized as self-controls and self-regulations. This is a fair criticism. We can see, for example, in the later works of Foucault (1986a, 1988) an illustration of the way in which precepts and regulations that govern the body are used to *produce* (rather than simply regulate) emotional feelings of friendship, love and sexual desire between men in classical societies. Indeed, if we assume that the learned precepts that orient emotional feeling are only about regulation, then we must also assume the emotions they control are primarily unlearned, and this is not what Elias wanted to convey at all. Better, then, to see precepts and regulations as both productive and restrictive, for, as Foucault so clearly shows, they are the foundations of the techniques of the body, central to the experience of emotion. In laying down the moral requirements of behaviour, they make the person who follows them discipline his or her body in ways of feeling and experiencing through the moral practices they engage in. *Emotional feeling is, at one and the same moment, produced and regulated.*

Because of the productive and regulatory function of moral practices and the emotional feelings that are their products, the entire emotional habitus of a social group is linked to the power and status structure of society (Collins, 1990; Kemper, 1981, 1990b; Scheff, 1990a,b). This involves the domination and subordination of certain class, gender and racial groups. As Elias says when he asks the question why social relations – the 'forms of life' – change, this is also the same question 'as why feelings and emotions, the structure of drives and impulses, and everything connected with them change' (1978: 205). Thus, for Elias, 'forms of life' are inextricably linked to emotions, and these forms are the structure of social relations and interdependencies that mark out the power and status balances in a society. Kemper (1981: 346) remarks that:

> as Elias makes incontrovertibly clear, the process of behaviour change, of prescription, of emotional differentiation resulted from the effort to maintain or enlarge status differences, to demarcate social relations and social structure with unmistakable clarity, so that all would know that just precisely such-and-such was required in order to meet the demands of status due.

Although Kemper is referring here to Elias's writings on Renaissance Europe and his references to the divisions and exclusions between class and status groups, and also those between the sexes, the relation between emotions and power can be seen in many periods of history and with reference to many different groups. Foucault (1986a) also illustrates, often implicitly, how power was tied to gender relations in classical Greece, where those men who cultivated in themselves the culturally defined 'masculine' traits were given enormous privileges. The man who could show he was master of himself, who proved himself capable of ethical action through moderating and regulating his own appetites and desires, was the one selected to become the master of others and to give service to his city. In the style of a man's comportment, the display of his self-mastery, there was found the key to social elevation. It was also the path to the maintenance of his status.

Thus, the ability to master one's desires and to practise moderation was seen as an active and masculine achievement, whereas giving in to one's desires, indulging oneself in an immoderate fashion, was seen as a passive acquiescence to the appetites and was a feminine trait which was denigrated. The whole notion of activity and passivity pervaded the relations between self and others, as well as the relation of a person to his or her own self, and was reflected in the modes of domination and subordination in social relations of power. Here, the masculine was prioritized and given superior status over those traits which were seen as feminine, and the man who displayed these traits in the most clear and unambiguous way proved himself worthy of mastery over women and slaves. As we noted in Chapter 5, the techniques and characteristics that define the male body also become the model of the body politic, and in this way women and other oppressed groups are excluded from positions of power. In this way, emotions and their controls are tied to the power structures of a society, which in turn emerge from the relations between classes, races and genders.

An example of the formation of emotion in the context of power and gender relations, given by Elias (1982, 1983), is that of courtly love, an expression of the bond between two people that resonates well into our own era. It is this relation between two people and the expression of feelings between them that we call 'love'. This emotion only began to arise as court societies became more pacified. In the courts of the ninth and tenth centuries, women were treated roughly by the knights and there was general mistrust between the sexes. The language and feelings of love had not emerged, and could not do so in social relations such as these. As court societies became more pacified, the social importance of women increased. The intellectual life tended to focus around women, whose consorts included clerics, poets and singers. While men remained dominant, women began to create their own circles of power and influence. Interestingly enough, Elias (1982) shows in his study of *minnesang* – a love song or ballad – that it was not the actual relations between men and women of the times which was expressed in these songs, but the relation between a socially superior woman and an inferior man. This would be the poet or singer in the paid service of the lady, whose declarations of fine and noble feelings and intentions had to be couched in the language of deference – words and feelings that would not be the normal currency between women and men of the same social rank, involved in an intimate relationship.

The speech genres of love established by *minnesang*, recognizable to this day in romantic songs and fictions in which a man is at the tender mercy of a woman who is calling all the shots emotionally, had some basis in the everyday lives of courtiers. As more and more men gradually lost their function as warriors, there was less division between the sexes, and the court became a common sphere of social life for both women and men. Here, the power balance had adjusted slightly between the sexes, giving women more influence in social life. Women could also withdraw their affections from men and were not as easily attainable, creating a situation of heightened tensions, longing and desire between potential or actual lovers that is the stuff of romanticism. However, the romanticist picture was and still is only partially true. In real-life relationships between women and men of the same social rank, the men still dominated in the relationship as well as in the wider society. In this sense we could regard the speech genres of love to be idealized as they do not adequately fit the everyday relationships between women and men. People, then, find their relationships only partially expressed in the speech genres of romanticism; they find something of their relationships and thus themselves in the songs and poems, but there is an aspect of them left out, particularly that surrounding continued male domination. Intimate relations thus become idealized in the lore of love, and actual relations are bound at some point to become a disappointment. As Leonard says of the way in which women continue to identify their emotions in these speech genres: 'They sublimate their sexual feelings into a "courtly love" mould, and thereby ignore the passive, dominated role they must occupy in heterosexual courtship' (cited in Jackson, 1993: 210). This may also explain why men find it difficult to use the speech genres of romantic feelings, especially in a long-standing intimate relationship, and why women are the ones who are seen as more skilled in emotion talk and more concerned with the preservation of relationships (Gilligan, 1982). Power relations between the genders still involve the emotions and the controls placed over their expression, as much as they did in the days of ancient Greece. The division of emotion and 'emotion work' in contemporary heterosexual relationships, noted by Duncombe and Marsden (1993), continues to revolve around the inequalities between women and men and the partial eclipse of these inequalities by the speech genres of courtly love.

Conclusion

In this chapter I have put forward a relational conception of the emotions, arguing that emotions are not 'things' internal to the individual and his or her biological constitution, but are to do with the social relations and interdependencies between embodied persons. In so doing I have tried to define the focal point in this study of emotion, which is the relations between embodied persons that form the context where the experience of emotion arises. Emotions exist only in the context of relations and are to be conceptualized as complexes; that is, as irreducible to social structures, discourses or the body. All these elements are constitutive of emotions, which are felt only by active, embodied beings who are locked into networks of interdependence. It is not discourses alone, then, that construct human subjectivity, but the relations in which humans are actively engaged. These constitute the subject and his or her experiences, including the way that people become aware of emotional experience. This involves the way that people learn to use their bodies as sensate beings actively involved in the world, and is where techniques of the body come into play through which sensations and emotions are socially and historically shaped.

The techniques of the body are learned in the emotional habitus that surrounds a child from its earliest days onwards, and will reflect to a large degree the cultural background of its parents, but also the unique configuration of the family group. This will filter the relations of power that structure the habitus: the class and status divisions, and gender and race differences, that form the expectations of the child's behaviour. Through learning the appropriate techniques of the body, often unconsciously, the child develops the means of emotional expression which are used in the communication between individuals of his or her class or group. Techniques of the body, then, forge real emotional dispositions within the person, ones that can appear in situations that evoke particular emotions. It is in this sense that emotions should be regarded as performative, rather than being divided, in Duncombe and Marsden's (1993) distinction, between 'real' and 'acted' feelings. It is always possible for a person to act an emotion they do not really feel, but this does not mean that all emotion is just fake performance, or that acted feelings are not real. What is clear from the work of Elias and Wittgenstein is that practice and emotion are one and the same thing, and there is no division between a genuine 'inner' feeling and its 'outward' expression. *Emotions only exist in action, contained as it is in relations of power, interdependence and communication.* Emotions, like the speech genres in which they are expressed, exist only in the activities between interdependent people. It is only since the Renaissance and the development of the closed, communicative body, that bodily and verbal gestures are read as indicating an inner condition of the person that is hidden from others, and this is because of the increasing complexity of the relations between people and their communications.

Here I have used love as an example of how an emotion develops in the power relations and interdependencies between people. It is only as power relations between women and men begin to equalize that women can demand and become the object of more subtly nuanced emotions from men, ones that are more in keeping with the times and with changing patterns of gender relations. It is perhaps no coincidence that in societies, such as ancient Greece, where women were regarded as only one rank above slaves, so much time and effort was spent by men on the expression of affection towards younger boys; in other words, to those who were near equals (Foucault, 1986a). It is only as women began to attain this position in the West that we find in *minnesang* what today is regarded as the expression of heterosexual romantic love. And yet this speech genre is something of a distortion, expressing as it does the feelings of a subservient man for a woman of superior rank. It is no wonder that so much trouble can be caused by people trying to recognize themselves and their relationships in this genre when it does not fit so many actual intimate relationships. Nevertheless, this is a good example of how the self and emotions are not just a product of positioning within discourses, stories and narratives. Instead, emotion is to do with flesh and blood bodies and selves, actively bound in power relations and interdependencies, whose embodied expressions and feelings are primarily the outcome of those relations. This is the matrix in which emotions appear and can properly be understood.

7 Modernity, Self and Embodiment

So far in this book I have focused on the issues that the body puts back on to the agenda for the social sciences: the emotions, the place of experience and the very nature of personhood and selfhood. An embodied social theory does not turn its back on rationalism and all the elements of the classical canon, associated as they are with reason and the intellect. In working against dualism, a theory of the body seeks to integrate classicism with what has been associated with romanticism, thought with sensuous embodiment and activity, and rationality with the emotions. What has traditionally been seen as disembodied in the classical perspective is now conceptualized as an aspect of embodiment, understood as belonging to the thinking body in the nexus of its relations and activities. In this sense the thinking body cannot be separated from the emotional body, which in turn cannot be separated from the communicative or productive body. These are all facets or capacities that are possible for embodied persons and they emerge in different ways in different cultures. The body is, then, both a cultural product and producer, inhabiting a symbolic world connected to the other dimensions of its experience: to its location in the various spaces and times carved out by its social activity. The symbolic dimension allows us to extrapolate from experience, to build a theoretical or imaginary world that is not identical to immediate bodily experience; and yet, the theoretical must always be in some way related to the sensuous and practical and can never be separated from it.

The question now becomes one of the twists and turns in the relation between the symbolic and the sensuous, and how this is changing in the period of the late twentieth century as our experience of space and time is being dramatically reconstituted. The shift in capitalism towards greater forms of flexible accumulation (Harvey, 1990) and the development of technologies which allow relations to be disembedded from their traditional everyday anchoring (Gergen, 1991; Giddens, 1991) means that our embodied experience of space and time is fundamentally restructured. Some in social theory refer to these changes as ushering in a new era or a new attitude, that of the postmodern, while others stress their roots in modernity and suggest that we are now living in a period of 'high modernity' (Giddens, 1990). While I have more sympathy with the latter than the former, I think we should take heed of Foucault's sobering words when he asks 'What are we calling post-modernity? . . . I must say that I have trouble answering this . . . because I've never clearly understood what was meant . . . by the word "modernity" ' (quoted in Smart, 1993: 5). As I have used the term 'modernity' throughout this book, some clarification of terminology is needed before I begin my discussion of the re-formation of the body in the contemporary historical context.

When defining the period of 'modernity' many sociologists follow Weber's (1930) example, viewing the start of the period when people in the West thought of themselves as modern as beginning with the breakdown of the traditional social order. By traditional, sociologists tend to mean the feudal period where individuals' lives were closely bound up in relations of power centred on the nobility and the church, which were authorities who presented their rule as timeless. The breakdown of this order was seen by the classical sociological theorists – Marx, Weber and Durkheim – as in some way to do with the rise of capitalism, whether this was because of the power relations of property owners and workers, the rise of a capitalist spirit from the Protestant sects or a more complex division of labour that tended to inequality and anomie. However, I have suggested here that many aspects of the contemporary experience we call modern emerged prior to capitalization and in many ways paved the way for the form of capitalism we have in the West. I therefore do not want to set a date for when modernity began, believing instead that we need to consider this term as useful yet problematic, for modernity is made up of a number of contradictory traditions. First, there are the changes I spoke of in Chapter 3, with the rise of the centralized nation-state during the Renaissance period and the slow decline in the power of religious authorities. This brought about a resurgence of interest in the classical forms of knowledge and rationality, and new forms of power relations extolled the virtues of intellect as opposed to the body and its sensuous forms of knowing. The rationalized forms of government and the closed bodies it worked to produce, where greater control is exerted over the body and its processes, were elements that made the rise of capitalism possible in the way we know it in the West. This is the second element of modernity, that power relations in eighteenth-century Europe shifted away from the aristocratic nation-state, as sovereign rulers lost many of their powers (if not their positions or their lives), and towards relations centred on the capitalist economy. But capitalism also required and reinforced, at least until recently, the closed and disciplined body. Even the rise of a romanticist movement in the nineteenth century, with its emphasis on the emotions and the heroic life, did not challenge the private and solitary nature of the closed body.

Given this, the notion of postmodernity is, in my view, even more troublesome than that of modernity, and I have always remained sceptical of its usefulness and validity. Here, I will consider some postmodernist theories of body, self and society, but I will not suggest that in terms of social relations, culture, experience or attitudes we are in a postmodern society or have adopted an attitude of postmodernity. This is because I believe that many elements of what is called postmodernism do not significantly challenge the classical forms of modernity, nor do they address the central problem of our society, which is the integration of both classical and romantic understanding – the rational and the sensuous. I will return to this theme at the end of the chapter. As a way of proceeding, I tentatively suggest that the term modernity can usefully be applied to divergent and various strands of the emergence of relations, behaviours and feelings that people in the West regard as special to themselves. In that sense, they describe the life of the contemporary Occidental world. Yet it must also be remembered that the term modernity, like its sister 'civilization', is one that is value laden, referring to the purported progress and advance of Western societies over those of the East. It is in this problematic situation that I will talk about the fragmented bodies and divided selves of present-day modernity.

Bodies, Selves, Technology and Motion

I have noted in previous chapters how, in modernity, the body becomes closed and more tightly controlled, but at the cost of fragmentation, of losing the experience of a whole body open to its world, replaced with feelings of a mental or personal essence divided from the automaton it must inhabit. In Chapter 5 we saw how the experience many women have of the medicalization of their bodies brings this fragmented body into sharp relief, where, in medical interventions, many women experienced their bodies as being separated from them as a person and divided up into various mechanical functions. In modernity, the body becomes a machine, or like the different bits of various machines, internally fragmented and separated from the public world of others by layers and barriers. The seemingly contradictory desire in modernism to reach or discover some element of permanence or stability may not only be an attempt – no matter how futile – to entrench the modern mechanical, rationalized forms of control deeper into society and into the body, but may also express a genuine desire to set foot on a solid rock in the middle of a rough and unpredictable sea. As Berman (1982) makes clear, the modernist desire for stability and permanence is one which arises in the midst of a society constantly changing and recreating itself, and is a reaction against these conditions motivated by a fear of everything falling apart and disintegrating. Thus the modern subject strives to seek order in the face of chaos, both within its own self and in society.

Although Gergen (1991) does not address the issue of the body, he claims that the postmodern self is different from the modern: while the modern self was said to exhibit essential qualities, such as measurable traits that made up the personality, the postmodern self comes to embrace diversity and change. For Gergen, 'under postmodern conditions, persons exist in a state of continuous construction and reconstruction . . . Each reality of self gives way to reflexive questioning, irony, and ultimately the playful probing of yet another reality' (1991: 6–7). The self and its reality are not constituted by inner essences, as with the modernist self, for instead the postmodern person is refigured within its relationships (Gergen, 1991, 1994a). That is to say, the isolated self is no longer seen as the source of emotionality, identity, creativity or morality, but rather it is persons located in relations which are the focus of study. This is because relations are the original source of identity and feelings. As Gergen (1994b: 75–6) says in respect of argumentation:

> Rather than defining the individual in terms of a unified, rational core – the owner of a coherent logos – we may view the person as *fundamentally multiplicitous*, populated by views and opinions absorbed from the social arena over many years and differing conditions. Whether an individual claims one of these views to be 'my belief', 'my value', or 'essential' and 'true' is not the result of introspective discernment . . . Rather, the claim to possession is the result of social positioning, where the individual is placed at a given time vis-à-vis ongoing relationships.

However, in the postmodern age, even positioning within such relationships is not unproblematic. In an age saturated by new communications and information technology, social relations are mediated to such an extent that they become fleeting and unspecific to either time or place. In this way, the postmodern self reflects a move away from the romantic notion of a deep interior and the modernist idea of essences to what Tseëlon (1992) has called a surface or screen model. Here the self is the product of images that are created in the nexus of relations. Thus, for Gergen, the self must be replaced by the reality of relatedness, in which the notions of 'I' and 'you' are transformed into a conception of 'us'. For Tseëlon, this postmodern idea of self overcomes the Cartesian dualism between public and private, false and true self, for we are left solely with a publicly constituted, socially constructed person, one who lacks a stable and unitary inner core because of the fragmentation inherent in postmodernity. However, whether or not this fully overcomes Cartesian dualism is doubtful, for there remains the problem of the body to be addressed.

I will return to the notion of the body and the self located in relations towards the end of this chapter, but for now it must be said that accounts of the postmodern self are somewhat wanting. Not only do they ignore the issue of embodiment, they tend to gloss over the similarities in the experiences between the modern and the postmodern in order to ground the latter as a distinct form of experience. Earlier this century, writers such as Simmel (1903/1971) were concerned with how modern individuals coped with the sensory and intellectual bombardment of city life, adopting a blasé attitude as a defence against over-stimulation, and Mead (1934) spoke of the continual reconstruction of the self in a social word where meaning was constantly in flux. Of course, postmodern writers would claim that modernists like Simmel and Mead still clung to some vestigial notion of a coherent inner self who could adopt a blasé defence to protect its own integrity, or could reconstruct an aspect of the self from a stable core of identity – the 'I' who could reorganize the different 'me's'. While I would agree that modern technologies have saturated the self in the communication process to a much greater extent, this is an extension of processes that began almost a hundred years (if not longer) ago and does not necessarily mean that some core aspects of identity do not remain, such as the sense of personhood surrounding one's bodily location in, admittedly multiplying, networks of relations.

That the experience of fragmentation and the multiplication of self is only heightened in the contemporary Western world can be seen in theories of modernity which stress that the image is increasingly removed from any referent, creating the impression that representation floats free (Lefebvre, 1971). Indeed, for Baudrillard (1983), this is one of the main markers of postmodernity: that we are now in an age of 'simulacra' where signs are produced only in reference to other signs and there is no real world that underlies them and bestows meaning upon them. As I noted in Chapter 3, according to Heidegger (1977), in the Middle Ages there was certainty about the reality of existence because meaning was underwritten by religious teaching, so that what existed was understood as created by God and was taken as self-evident, its meaning unquestioned. But as Baudrillard (1988: 170) says:

> All of Western faith and good faith was engaged in this wager on representation: that a sign could refer to the depth of meaning, that a sign could *exchange* for meaning and that something could guarantee this exchange – God, of course. But what if God himself can be simulated, that is to say, reduced to the signs which attest his existence? Then the whole system becomes weightless; it is no longer anything but a gigantic simulacrum: not unreal, but a simulacrum, never again exchanging for what is real, but exchanging in itself, in an uninterrupted circuit without reference or circumference.

For Baudrillard, three orders of simulation have succeeded one another since the Renaissance. They are, first of all, the *counterfeit*, which is the dominant scheme of the 'classical' age, from the Renaissance to the industrial revolution. In this epoch, what governs the order of simulacra is a natural law of value in which signs embody their natural referents as a counterfeit of the original. This is the age when the notion of representation first appeared, of a sign as a representative of a natural value that actually existed in the world. Also, the symbolic products of humans could be divided between the original and the counterfeit, the work of the master and its copy: so, for example, in painting one could have the original work created by the master himself, opposed to the attempts to copy or fake the original. All this alters in the second phase of simulation, called by Baudrillard *production*, and which corresponds to the age of the industrial revolution. Here, signs no longer take their meaning from the realm of nature or originality, but from the industrial simulacrum itself. The notion of the counterfeit falls away because all signs in the industrial order are produced and therefore equivalent. No one would say that they possessed the original version of a new model of car, for all cars in that model are identically produced. They only take on different values as commodities in the marketplace according to the commodity law of value and not because they represent some underlying natural value. Technology and systems of mechanical reproduction create the objects and the reality encountered in the epoch of production, and this becomes a reality in itself which does not have to purport to be a representation of anything else.

In the current phase of *simulation*, communications systems and information technology come increasingly to the fore, so that what becomes central is a structural law of value where the code or model in which information and the sign system are encrypted is the main principle. The code or structural model inherent in the simulacrum becomes the reality, as systems for the reproduction of signs substitute for the order of production. Now 'the real becomes not only that which can be reproduced, but that which is always already reproduced: the hyperreal' (Baudrillard, 1988: 146). Signs are no longer a representation of reality, nor is reality produced by the simulacrum: reality *is* the simulacrum; it is that world which has already been reproduced by it. We are in the cybernetic age where the information produced by technologies of reproduction forms a hyper-reality, one that exists entirely within the realm of simulation. Thus, Baudrillard believes that his work challenges the Cartesian dichotomies between the true and the false, an authentic reality and its imaginary representation; in so doing, the notions of an objective world set against the subjective would also be undermined. Even the body is taken up and transformed in the simulacrum where the prostheses produced by soft technologies have turned 'every possible body . . . [into] its immutable repetition – this is the end of the body and of its history: the individual is henceforth only a cancerous metastasis of its basic formula' (Baudrillard quoted in Denzin, 1991: 32–3).

Baudrillard touches here on the current literature on the cyborg, in which the opposition between human and machine is thought to be effaced by the new information technologies and the creation of cyberspace, the world-wide information and computer networks through which people can communicate intimately without being bodily present to one another. Here women can become men and vice versa, and people can speak in a multitude of voices and personas without contradiction by physical appearance or location in the spatial and temporal domains of everyday life. As a user of the Internet says in a British newspaper article, 'It used to be impossible to relate to anyone without the body coming into it somewhere, even if just as your handwriting or your voice. But in these dimensions, you can relate to people in all sorts of ways just by using your mind' (*Guardian Weekend*, 18 March 1995: 33).

However, I want to question whether all of this really does overcome Cartesian dualism and whether an age of simulation has really supplanted that of production. First of all, Baudrillard's idea of the epoch of simulation could be said to be the height of a (post)modern form of Cartesian radical doubt where, unlike Descartes, who came to doubt the existence of anything but his own process of thought, Baudrillard nevertheless doubts the existence of anything except the processes of simulation. The only certainty of existence we have is not the mind but the sign; not the cogito but the order of simulacra. The idea of a multi-dimensional reality, in which humans are embodied physical beings whose ideas and signs are put to use in reality and gain their meaning from that use, is as alien to Baudrillard as it was to Descartes. Instead, we are encapsulated in the technology of reproduction and its hyper-reality just as Descartes encapsulated human beings in subjectivity. In this way, any notion of multi-dimensionality – of one world with many perspectives on it and with different dimensions of experience – is lost. Attempting to argue that the age of simulation also spells the end of the body and its history is an unconvincing attempt to resolve the main Cartesian dualism. Even in the age of the computer and soft technology, humans are embodied beings living in more than just a symbolic world. As Merleau-Ponty (1962) claimed, the sense of self is based on the feel we have of our own bodies and the way in which they place us in the world. Baudrillard's (1983, 1988) ideas also emphasize the reproduction of signs at the expense of the communicative and productive bodies that produce signs in the first place, as well as the technologies of social saturation. It is embodied people who are physically and mentally skilled that produce the machines which reproduce the images of the simulation age. As Stone puts it, 'No matter how virtual the subject may become, there is always a body attached. It may be off somewhere else – and that 'somewhere else' may be a privileged point of view – but consciousness remains firmly rooted in the physical. *Historically, body, technology, and community constitute each other*' (1991: 111; emphasis added).

This is all so different from Baudrillard and, it must be said, his sometimes absurd notions about the end of the body and the end of the social. Rather, for Stone, we are, in Paul Churchland's (quoted in Stone, 1991) words, 'situated biological creatures' who appear on a daily basis as physical social beings. The ideas presented by Baudrillard, and the work of cyberspace researchers, assume that the body is either 'dead' or just 'meat', dissolved in hyper-reality or the computer network. Again, this is very Cartesian, because the 'I', the seat of identity (fragmented or otherwise) has moved elsewhere, out of the corporeal and into the realm of the image or virtual reality. However, once more Stone (1991: 113) reminds us that 'it is important to remember that virtual community originates in, and must return to, the physical. No refigured virtual body, no matter how beautiful, will slow the death of a cyberpunk with AIDS. Even in the age of the technosocial subject, life is lived through bodies.' Furthermore, in forgetting about the body, it is easy to lose sight of how all the new computer technology is still produced by embodied beings and their labour, people who invariably live in Third World countries, predominantly women, and who are subjected to gross exploitation (Denzin, 1991; Stone, 1991). To claim, then, that an age of reproduction has superseded one of production is a gross exaggeration and founded on a perspective that is solidly based in the Western middle class.

I think that Baudrillard's order of simulacrum has some basis to it, but the way in which he has formulated it is wide of the mark. If we see the order as phases in the *production of artifacts*, then a very different picture begins to emerge. I would side with Denzin and Stone above; I believe Baudrillard to be wrong when he claims that labour is no longer a force, but has become instead a sign among other signs. For many people in the world, labour is far more than just a sign; it is something they still have to expend their energies upon and often for little reward: it is still, in the Marxist sense of the word, labour power. Instead of the order of simulacra, I want to suggest that there is an *order of the production of artifacts* in which we can discern three phases that broadly parallel the order of simulacra. In the first phase, which is from the Renaissance to the beginning of the industrial revolution, people feel themselves to be disembodied minds or spirits acting against an external 'natural' world (for reasons we have already considered). However, before the age of machine production, this is the era of the craftsman, the artisan and the artist. Such people see their designs, and their skills at turning them into artifacts, embodied in the objects they produce: there is something of their own personality in the objects they have created. Thus all artifacts, whether objects or signs, have an aspect of the self expressed in them; that is, the skilled, socially developed person who embodies their social relations. Also in these conditions, people's communications related more directly to their everyday, face-to-face interactions, or those of their immediate relationships. Symbolic productions were not as highly mediated as they are today, and did not span such wide vistas of time and space. Thus the life of the social group was embodied more directly in the artifacts and sign systems it produced.

During the capitalist industrial revolution this began to change. With machine production and the rise of more sophisticated communications technology, people no longer felt that their own social being was embodied in the artifacts they produced. This is part of the experience Marx has referred to at several points in his writings as *alienation*. Here, in mechanized and capitalized systems of industrial production, the object produced confronts the person as something alien – as the embodiment of capital rather than of an individual's social skills and abilities. Equally, the artifact does not appear as the product of the social relations in which the person is involved, but as a sign of capital. In this sense, the artifact becomes a very different type of sign embodying different values and meanings; the labour that goes into its creation is seen as brute, physical labour – mindless and soulless, labour that is purely bodily force and does not engage any of the individual's skills and capacities (Sève, 1978). This also goes for other signs produced in the machine age, which, as Baudrillard has shown, can be produced and reproduced endlessly, each sign or artifact displaying a value equal to its identical others. But once more, in the age of mechanical reproduction, we find humans experiencing themselves as Cartesian, divided between body and mind, the body becoming a brute instrument that is used and exploited, while the 'mind' and its creative, imaginative potentials are under-used and under-developed. Here, the body is quite literally mechanized, as Marx remarked, in becoming the appendage of the machine: its movements become routinized and habituated to a degree never before known, with all the requirements this entails for the greater discipline of the body.

The third phase of the production of artifacts I would place much earlier than Baudrillard, and suggest that this occurs in the early part of the twentieth century, where, as Lefebvre (1971) claims, there was a decline of referentials which acted as the basis for artifacts and other signs.

> A hundred years ago words and sentences in a social context were based on reliable referentials that were linked together, being cohesive if not logically coherent, without however constituting a single system formulated as such. These referentials had a logical or commonsensical unity derived from material perception (Euclidean three-dimensional space, clock time), from the concept of nature, historical memory, the city and the environment or from generally accepted ethics and aesthetics. (Lefebvre, 1971: 111)

However, according to Lefebvre, all of this began to break down around the years 1905–10 under the influence of science, technology and social changes, with the result that signs lost some of their main referentials. In this society, 'common sense and reason lost their unity and finally disintegrated; the "common-sense" concept of absolute reality disappeared and a new perceptible "real" world was substituted or added to the reality of "well-informed" perception, while functional, technical objects took the place of traditional objects' (Lefebvre, 1971: 112). While it is difficult to know what is meant here by traditional objects, because humans have produced objects for millennia, Lefebvre is saying something about what it means to live in the age of mechanically produced artifacts, where the technically produced object is central to what people perceive as reality.

But it is not only reality that is changed in the era of mechanically produced artifacts, for perception itself is altered by living in a highly technical age. The senses become more educated and merge as the dimensions of time and space, as well as the symbolic dimension, begin to be radically transformed. The practical possibility of travelling at high speeds reformulated all notions of time and space. There was no longer an inherent opposition between the static and the mobile as people learned to experience the world at varying degrees of mobility. This whole experience is linked to the notions of relativity that dominate contemporary Western cultures, not just in terms of science, but also in the everyday belief that there is not just one standpoint on reality, for the world is seen from many varied perspectives. There are always other times, other spaces, other viewpoints. Also, in terms of the symbolic dimension, experience becomes more highly mediated, with a theoretical attitude to the world mediating between sense perception and conscious awareness. Perception becomes less immediate and instead is increasingly filtered through the gauze of symbolic interpretation. Because of this, objects increasingly become signs as they are incorporated into the realm of meanings, and signs become ever more objectified as they take on the appearance of being concrete. As A.A. Leontyev (1981) remarked, signs can be seen increasingly as quasi-objects, an almost material force in human interactions. However, as mediation increasingly fragments the immediate link between the sign and its referent, the whole notion of referentiality is called into question.

The notion of mediation has been explored in more detail by Anthony Giddens (1991), who claims that human experience is always mediated, especially by language. For Giddens, though, modernity is inseparable from its own media, for it was the printed text that allowed many of the barriers of traditional social bonds, tied as they were to specific places and times, to be broken. The printed text could be produced in large quantities and distributed over a wide area, so that people could read the same text almost instantaneously. Oral cultures are tied to the immediacy of place and time, whereas the printed word is not. In the twentieth century, communication media rapidly expand as the electronic signal allows for the development of the telephone and the radio and, later, television and video. Films and newspapers also become widespread forms of media. Taken together with the new information and computer technologies, these media become important aspects of the reorganization of time and space. Events in far-off places of the world can become as real to us through television or computers as are the interactions that take place on an everyday basis; in some cases, they may seem more real. Thus, social relations become fragmented, broken up by the media of modernity and reconstituted across global vistas of space and time. Interaction is no longer confined to human co-presence in a shared time and physical space, becoming disembedded from such contexts and reconstituted on a global level. Furthermore, the mirror through which individuals identify themselves is no longer that of a purely local community, but is instead a global one where humanity as a whole has become a 'we' against which personal identity as an 'I' is constructed (Elias, 1991a; Giddens, 1991).

I do not read Giddens as saying that in modernity everyday life has completely fragmented, only that far-flung events can be as real to us in the modern age as daily occurrences. But, as Lefebvre (1971) says, everyday life is still one of the main referentials for humans, a grounding which signs can relate back to. Signs do not only refer to other signs within a free-floating simulacrum. Not only does everyday life act as a referential, so does the global network of interrelations. However, according to Giddens (1991), because contemporary media act as disembedding mechanisms, uprooting social connections from local time and space, social life is no longer rigidly structured by traditional precepts or practices. This means that there has to be an increasing self-reflexive monitoring of action on the part of social agents. For Giddens, all human action involves self-reflexivity, which is the conscious and purposive guiding of activity within social contexts. However, in modernity reflexivity is said to be heightened because of the breakdown of pre-established precepts and practices. In such a system, where social life is more fragmented and people are members of many different social groups across time and space, the requirements of social practices are less well defined and more open ended. More scope for decision-making is now left to the individual as to how he or she will act in particular circumstances, as well as over the skills and performances required in situations. Furthermore, the institutions of modernity need skilled and fairly autonomous individuals in order to function properly in a flexible and constantly changing global order, and so knowledge is disseminated to people who use it to structure their own social activities. Also, information is constantly changing in the modern world so that individuals have to be skilled in techniques for learning and using knowledge.

Alongside these changes, Giddens notes a similar trend with regard to modern science, in which reflexivity of knowledge undermines the certainty that Enlightenment thinkers believed the natural sciences would bring through creating absolute knowledge of the social and natural worlds. Instead, modern science is built on radical doubt, where all theories are open to criticism and all knowledge open to revision. Indeed, while most people in the modern world would probably assume that current practices in science create accurate representations of nature and the universe, most would also believe that at some time in the future a more advanced science will better this knowledge and provide answers to the questions we have failed to settle. But here again we come to the question of the multi-dimensional experience of the modern world, where relativity is a key feature. It is possible to hold on to a notion that our relationally created knowledge allows us to transform and orient ourselves and the world in ways never possible before, so it could be said – in a technical sense – that our understanding of nature is more highly advanced than at any time in human history. However, in other ways we become increasingly aware of everything about the world, our universe, and humanity, that we do not know and may never be likely to know. Yet this is very different from Cartesian radical doubt, where Descartes doubted the existence of anything beyond his own thought processes. To recognize that human knowledge will never be a perfect fit with reality and that we will never know all that there possibly is to know, is to recognize the multi-dimensionality of the world. In such a place, where we live in one reality but with so many different perspectives on it, the hope of absolute knowledge has had to be abandoned, and yet this may only enrich rather than diminish human life. It also means that we do not have to abandon all notions of reality.

To return to the other Cartesian problem, the relation between body and mind, Giddens (1991) approaches this problem in a manner similar to other theorists of modernity by claiming that the body is becoming part of the reflexively monitored life projects of contemporary people. That is to say, body and self are entering into a new relationship as the corporeal becomes an aspect of our lives to be shaped according to some consciously formulated plan. This is not just a narcissistic and vain preoccupation with bodily appearance, it goes to the root of modernity and the modern attitude. Here, we find a desire actively to construct and control the body in a fashion similar to the way in which other aspects of life are being brought increasingly under reflexive control. Giddens (1991: 7–8) says that:

> Here [in modernity] there is an integral connection between bodily development and lifestyle – manifest, for example, in the pursuit of specific bodily regimes. Yet much more wide-ranging factors are important, too, as a reflection of the socializing of biological mechanisms and processes. In the spheres of biological reproduction, genetic engineering and medical interventions of many sorts, the body is becoming a phenomenon of choices and options. These do not affect the individual alone: there are close connections between personal aspects of bodily development and global factors. Reproductive technologies and genetic engineering, for example, are parts of more general processes of the transmutation of nature into a field of human action.

However, there are problems with Giddens's approach to the body in modernity. He states above how the body has become part of a person's whole lifestyle, so that a certain body image is aimed for, not just through choice of clothing, but also through body regimes that shape the physical structure of the body itself. Harré (1991a) has also remarked on this phenomenon with particular reference to the cult of body-building. Yet we have already noted, particularly through the work of Elias and Foucault, how body regimes and disciplines are part of the cultural and personal regulation of the body through which agency is produced in many, if not all, societies. Body regimes, involving the production of self-image and modes of behaviour within a cultural framework, are among the main foundations of social life and are not just peculiar to modernity. Also, we can see how, in the above quotation from Giddens, there is a strong sense of an opposition between a 'natural' body and one which is becoming increasingly more 'socialized' in modern forms of practice. There seems to be a basic assumption here that the biological is part of nature and something external to society, while in modernity – through things like reproductive technologies – nature is being transmuted into the field of human action. But what was nature before this transmutation? Could nature ever have been separate from human activity, especially as action must involve human bodies? Like the theorists of cyberspace, Giddens sees modern cultural trends, especially technologies, as doing things to the human body – shaping and transforming it into social and personal projects – but what he ignores is the way in which bodies produce such trends and technologies through their own activities in the first place. Relations and agency, which produce, transform and orient, need a trained, active biological body to begin with. Certainly, the results of that agency may well transform the human body, but it has always been so: it is simply that in modernity this transformation occurs in different ways and with new possibilities.

As Shilling (1993: 201) has remarked about Giddens's conception of the body, he has gone from a predominantly, though not exclusively, deterministic view in structuration theory – where the body was seen as a physical constraint upon action – to an almost voluntaristic perspective on embodiment in his work on modernity. Both Shilling and Giddens agree that the body in modern society is transformed to an extent never known before. However, in his study on death, Shilling (1993: ch. 8) demonstrates that the limits on the transformation of the body, displayed in the fact that modern people are still powerless to control death, also show in clear relief the limits of the power and knowledge of modernity. Giddens sees crises occurring in modernity when individuals are forced to confront 'original nature' through experiences such as facing death. To try to escape the anxiety created by such problems, modern people have 'sequestered' these experiences away from everyday routines and confined them to particular spaces where experts can deal with them. Thus, in contemporary society, death belongs in the province of the hospital and hospice, and should not intrude into daily life; if it did, we would not be able to cope, for we are now de-skilled in dealing with the dead or dying (unlike our ancestors for whom such things were a normal part of life). However, this does illustrate once again Giddens's dichotomous view of society and nature: problems such as dealing with death are seen as part of original nature, which becomes separated from day-to-day life in modernity. Thus, modern societies are internally referential systems of knowledge and power to such an extent that we witness the 'end of nature', which means that the natural world has become a ' "created environment", consisting of humanly structured systems whose motive power and dynamics derive from socially organized knowledge-claims rather than from influences exogenous to human activity' (Giddens, 1991: 144). But this is almost like Baudrillard's claim that we are now at the end of the body. Furthermore, Giddens seems to think that nature is something 'external' to human activity and society; modern systems have become so powerful that nature can largely be shut out or sequestered away. This is confirmed when he says that 'socialized' nature is different from the 'old natural environment, which existed separately from human endeavours and formed a relatively unchanging backdrop to them' (1991: 137).

However, this all creates a number of problems. First, external or original nature is seen as separate from society and social activity so that the two constitute different realms or realities. Giddens does not take account of what I have called here, following Foucault, 'bio-history', a term that refers to the way in which the movements of life and the processes of history interfere with each other. In such a view, biological life has never at any point been separate from history, and the body has always been part of the life projects of individuals with respect to their various cultures. Whether it is the way in which tribal people tattoo their bodies, extend their necks with rings or their lips with plates, or the suggestions that ancient cultures may have had knowledge of contraception (Taylor, 1997), it is clear that the body has always reflexively figured in the cultural lives of individuals. Given what was said in Chapter 2 about the social pressures on the evolution of the body in bio-history, we have to view the modern body as the result of a long process of bio-social selection and so cannot maintain any distinction between the natural and the socialized body.

The second problem to arise from Giddens's understanding of the body in modernity is that it is itself highly modernist, for the body is seen as something which must be brought under social, cognitive and textual control. Otherwise, an individual would be paralysed by existential fears about the unsocialized nature that lurks beyond his or her regulated, cultural cocoon. Certainly it is true, as Elias (1978) also points out, that modern people must control themselves and their bodily feelings in a more constant way or else they would find it difficult to live in a highly rationalized, fast-paced modernity. This applies just as much to the denizens of late twentieth-century cyberspace as it did to the city-dwellers of the early part of this century. However, there is a difference between saying that the need for body controls and disciplines arises from the very style of modern living and that they are necessary in order to create ontological security, to stave off existential fright at the possible intrusion of 'nature' into the highly protected modern world. Furthermore, the narratives that Giddens sees as binding a person's identity are largely cognitive and textual, and it is these narratives that weave people into the protective cocoon of bodily control and socially warranted knowledge claims. It is said that these can only be maintained through the sequestration of the troubling aspects of nature and embodiment, but there are problems with this. One could say that it is the very act of sequestering bodily facts, such as death, and hiding them 'behind the scenes' that creates such anxiety in the first place. We know, for example, how cultures that deal with death in a more open way than in the West have not the same high anxieties about it. This means that the abject fear of death may not be an existential problem in all humanity upon confronting mortality, but may – like all fears and anxieties – be socially induced.

All of this creates difficulties with Giddens's understanding of 'life politics', a form of politics which is common only in late modernity. Life politics is focused on the body, self-identity and the environment, and involves the collective reappropriation of institutionally repressed areas of life – such as birth, sex and death – which now become moral-existential questions to be addressed politically. For Giddens, this is what many of the new social movements are doing: in refusing to focus solely on issues of inequality and injustice, as did the old 'emancipatory politics', they instead combine such issues with things like environmental concerns, as in the 'green' movements. The term 'life politics' is meant to indicate this resurgence of concern with elements of 'original nature'. However, I find it strange that Giddens equates the emergence of life politics with a remoralization of modernity, as if morality is about individuals facing and finding solutions to ahistorical and asocial questions which have been set by nature. As I have already indicated, existential dilemmas, such as the inordinate fear of death, could just as much be a creation of modernity as of the existential nature of life. And I have noted that the body has always reflexively figured in the cultural construction of an individual's self-identity. So why does Giddens see such phenomena as peculiar to Western modernity?

What I am driving at here is that moral questions around the environment and the body have not suddenly returned after their suppression in modernity, for such questions emerge from bio- and socio-history and have always been present in some form or another. As there is no time in history during which humans were not related to nature (something impossible for embodied beings), all politics and morality emerge from the changing relations between people, and with life itself. Indeed, if all of life is composed of relations, so that social relations are always contained within this wider network, then the web of interrelations that makes up and supports life must always be the context for human politics and morality. Political and moral questions will change as the webs of relationships change, both in life and in society. Nature is not given and fixed any more than the human social life that is part of it. The question, then, is not how to re-engage with nature, but what should be our relationship to nature? The question is not whether we should intervene in nature, for our very existence is part of nature and therefore an intervention; rather, the question is what constitutes ethical interventions in nature and what is unethical? Also, because we are always related to nature through social groups, we can never divorce these questions from ones about the organization of human society and what constitutes ethical relations among ourselves as embodied beings. As Marx would no doubt have pointed out, is it surprising that social organizations in contemporary capitalism, which have few qualms about exploiting the majority of the world's population and leaving millions in poverty, also have few concerns about ruthlessly exploiting nature? I will return to such questions about morality in the Conclusion.

The final critical point I want to raise is that most theorists of postmodernity and modernity see changes to the self and its relation to the body as due to the rapidly advancing systems of communications and media technology. Yet they do not always link these cultural changes to those taking place in the power relations of capitalism. Although both Jameson (1991) and Giddens (1990) see capitalist relations as a continuing influence on the cultures of the contemporary Western world, it is Harvey (1990) who has drawn out in the most imaginative way the relationship between current forms of flexible capital accumulation and the advent of what we have come to regard as postmodern culture. This has added to the tendency I remarked on, in what I called the third phase in the production of artifacts, where the object or sign loses its referent to a readily identifiable human community where it could gain meaning in face-to-face interaction. This experience of signs losing their reference point is heightened with flexible accumulation, which has had the effect of breaking up families and communities and scattering human associations more widely across geographical space. Flexible accumulation describes the conditions since the break up of labour control practices, consumption habits and the style of Keynesian economic planning by governments practised until the mid-1970s. At this point, the more carefully controlled and planned political and economic system was superseded by one where there is rapid change, flux and uncertainty (Harvey, 1990: 124). Flexible labour processes and markets also created more geographical mobility, which coincided with the explosion in new communication and information technologies that Gergen (1991) describes as technologies of social saturation. It is these conditions taken together which have led to the heightening of the modernist experience of fragmentation, ephemerality and chaos, and have also led to what Harvey (1990) calls greater 'time–space compression', in which the material practices from which our concepts of time and space flow are drastically changed. According to Harvey, 'since capitalism has been (and continues to be) a revolutionary mode of production in which the material practices and processes of social reproduction are always changing, it follows that the objective qualities as well as the meanings of space and time also change' (Harvey, 1990: 204). In recent years, the practices of flexible accumulation have broken up local communal and familial relations, and have led to the reconstitution of social relations across wider vistas of space and time, the new technologies of social saturation allowing for changed forms of relationships in a new social terrain.

However, all of this has led to a heightened focus on the body and its practices. While the tenor of most modernist and postmodernist writing is highly cognitivist – speaking of the disappearance of the material body in the reflexively constituted life plans of individuals or in the nets of cyberspace – the body is becoming more of a focus within contemporary life, as well as in social theory (Shilling, 1993). I think this is for two primary reasons. First of all, in conditions of flexible accumulation, the body cannot rely on the fixed habits and routines that it could in the earlier forms of modernity. As the habitus becomes more fluid and changeable, bodily dispositions can no longer reproduce practices and performances in any taken-for-granted way, and bodily performances become the centre of conscious attention. While this lends credence to Giddens's notion of reflexive monitoring, this does not mean that a previously natural body is becoming increasingly socialized; instead, it indicates that an already socialized body has to become more aware of its own practices, dispositions and capacities. In an age of flexible accumulation, expanded relational networks, burgeoning communicative systems and geographical mobility, the body's dispositions and capacities need to be transposed into many more varied situations than ever before, making the body and its social performances in various contexts a focus of concern, of discourse and of reflexive monitoring.

However, this is not simply an extension of the networks of power relations and bodily control. As Harvey (1990) points out, time–space compression is also destabilizing those institutional spaces and practices that Foucault studied so closely, which he saw as the capillary points in power relations for the production of docile bodies. These institutions – such as hospitals, schools and factories – still play a central part in people's lives, yet their influence can never be as all consuming as it once was, as they exist directly alongside other spaces and places in which different values, different practices, can be experienced. Thus, as we saw in Chapter 5, the influence of medical institutions and the knowledge generated there is still immensely powerful upon the view people have of their bodies, illustrated here by the experience of women around menstruation, childbirth and menopause. However, alongside such institutions, there exists the everyday knowledge about such bodily processes passed on between relatives and friends, as well as a growing 'alternative' movement composed of various groups of women who are generating another discourse, suggesting different practices and interpretations of the experience of menstruation, childbirth and menopause. As I suggested in Chapter 5, a new space is opening up in which alternative ideologies can be explored and more creative practices can be developed.

But, just as important as social spaces opening up for creativity and activity, we also heard expressed in the words of many women a desire to be treated as a whole person, not just a body divided into many separate mechanical functions. Against fragmentation, a desire to be whole was expressed so clearly, and this is a desire that is often missing from the writings on the condition of (post)modernity. It is not simply a question of the body emerging as an issue for contemporary people because of the need for greater reflexive monitoring and the desire for greater mental control over a material substance. The body is becoming an issue because, in an increasingly fragmentary world, there is a growing desire for wholeness, for integration and for healing. It is not a reactionary tendency, nor an inability to cope with the excitement and possibilities presented by a fractured world, but a critical stance which refuses to take at face value division, rupture and, behind this, various forms of domination and exploitation. In resisting forms of domination and dividing practices, the body becomes a point of focus because it is around the body, as it is located in relational networks, that individuals can integrate the various aspects of themselves into a whole person, and can demand to be treated as such.

This is not to say that these are the only influences behind the resurgence of the body. Mellor and Shilling (1997) have drawn our attention to the importance of the decline of Protestant religion with its strong ascetic control of the body and, with this decline, the rise once more of a modern form of counter-reformation spirit, in which 'baroque modern bodies' seek out opportunities for fleshy pleasures and sensuality. For Mellor and Shilling (1997), this means we are now living in a 'Janus-faced modernity' because the old cognitively based forms of social control are still in place, with their contractual mentality towards social associations, while, at the same time, we witness the rise of other forms of social bonding based on the emotional, bodily and sensual forms that connect people to one another. An example of this can be the existence in modernity of forms of social association based on contract, such as relationships in the workplace, side by side with those relations based on emotional or sensual solidarities, such as tribal communities of soccer supporters or the spiritual union of fundamentalist religions. The difference between these communities is that contractual association is founded on the carefully regulated, cognitively controlled and relatively emotionless everyday world of relations between colleagues or acquaintances, while sensual solidarity is usually cemented and expressed in some form of 'collective effervescence' or epiphany, such as the physical violence

of the soccer hooligan or the congregational revelations of the fundamen-
talists. However, once again, the problem with this Janus-faced notion of
modernity is that, while it may express with some accuracy the duality of the
modern world, it leaves unexpressed the desire for integrity that has always
been a part of modernity, where duality and fragmentation cause distress. It
appears that modernity has created the division between mind and body,
cognition and emotion, rationality and irrationality, and that we are forced to
jump one way or the other at various times and places. The basic dualistic
notion of the body as the seat of irrational, emotional and pre-social forces
(as opposed to the orderly mind) also seems to be accepted. Also, what this
approach fails to account for is the countervailing tendency to move against
all dualism, to seek the connections between what, on the surface, often
appears opposed. It is this striving that expresses itself, both in social life
and in social science, in the turn towards notions of embodiment in
relations.

Conclusion

I have sought to argue here that the current period of Western history,
labelled variously as modernism or postmodernism, is characterized by the
domination of mechanically produced artifacts and new communication
technologies which have reconstituted the embodied experience of space and
time. However, in my view this does not spell the end of the body with its
absorption into a symbolically constituted virtual reality. Nor is the body
totally assimilated into the life plans and lifestyle mapped out by a purely
reflexive, cognitive being. Instead, the body still plays a crucial role in
modernity as the producer of new technologies and also of the meanings that
infuse our technologically saturated society. Artifacts and social meanings
still refer back at some stage to communities of embodied persons. Equally,
life politics is not about confronting 'original nature' within the cocooned
confines of a rationally organized and cognitively reflexive modernity, but is
to do with the re-evaluation of our necessary relationship to nature. After all,
as embodied beings, nature is something we can never escape, no matter
how hard we may have tried to sequester some of the experiences that come
from being a body or from being part of the natural world. Instead of
understanding embodied experience as sequestered, I have tried to outline
here how we are coming to more politicized and ethical views of embodiment and nature because of changing relationships in the human world and
with the non-human. I will elaborate these themes in the following Conclusion.

Conclusion: Relations and the Embodied Person

One of the central themes of this book is that there is no such thing as the 'mind' considered as something separate from the body and its spatio-temporally located practices. The mind is an effect of bodily action and also of becoming a person within the diverse networks of social relations. Embodied persons become identified within their relations to others and also within relations to the non-human world. The sense of personhood we possess is at least partly based on the feel we have of our own bodies, as much as in the symbols which define our unique social identity. As I suggested in the introduction, paraphrasing Whitman, if the body is not the person, then what is the person? The body image and self-image we develop is based on the sense of being embodied and the way in which this experience is mediated by culture. It is also within relations that transform the real, relations of communication and relations of power that we acquire bodily capacities to change the social and natural worlds in which we live. This means that the body must be viewed as an open system, one that has developed in bio-history where social formations affect the relations that support life. In this context, certain aspects of our bodily being have a history that is much longer than any currently surviving social formation, and so the body is not infinitely malleable and open to social construction. However, within these broad limits, the body is open to what Mellor and Shilling (1997) have called 're-formation', so that, in my terms, the body acquires specific capacities and powers within the multiple relations in which it grows, communicates, learns and works. For me, the main medium through which such re-formation occurs is artifacts – prosthetic devices that augment bodily powers and make possible new activities and new ways of life. Artifacts thus re-form the body and the experience of embodiment and, in enabling humans to transform the real and communicate in more elaborate codes via technological media, they also reconstitute the embodied experience of time and space. The artifact is therefore the means through which knowledge is stored and transmitted through the generations, replacing the gene as the mode of cultural transmission and as the instrument of re-forming the body.

Each body takes on an identity, along with capacities and powers, in its artifactually mediated relations and activities, and these create differences between embodied persons that are not innate within biological systems. Rather, difference is created in the relations between human beings themselves, and between the human and non-human worlds. The relational approach I am advocating here does not reduce heterogeneous bodies and identities to a homogeneous unity, but seeks out the relations in which difference is created and sustained. People and things are therefore internally heterogeneous, yet this does not mean they possess fixed or given identities. Identity is constituted in various overlapping networks of relations and, as such, is rich and varied, resisting attempts at rigid categorization that only results in multiplying ambiguity and ambivalence. The relational approach to the body and identity could therefore be characterized as the search for the connection between differences.

For example, Heidegger (1977) noted the change that occurred in human perception in the Middle Ages, where people no longer perceived themselves as part of the world order, instead viewing the dimensions of space as a picture set before them. The world became composed of objective dimensions of space and time set before the perceiving human subject. Space, as objective dimensions opposed to the human realm, was there to be mastered and manipulated as people lost their sense of relation to it, their oneness with the world. In this role, humans enter the picture as masters and creators, occupying the position once filled by God. We are no longer *in* the order of nature, but those who *order* nature. For Heidegger, the solution to the problem of humans taking the place of God was to critique the nature of being itself, of the rational cogito as the foundation stone and guarantor of knowledge. Thus, we must undermine the modern notion that 'man' is the relational centre of the world and question the truth of being. This has inspired many contemporary works in the social sciences to question the nature of man, indeed to pronounce upon his death. Here I suggest an alternative: instead of questioning the nature of being, we focus on the different types of relations – of transformation, communication and power – in which active human bodies are re-formed and identified as persons with certain powers and capacities, and how they are divided from one another. Here, the embodied subject does not have to die; instead, social science is re-centred on the study of relations. Embodied persons are the non-central points in such relations.

Equally, the lived experience of modern social systems mediated by new technologies of communication and social saturation, which allow for disembodied communication and interaction, does not spell the end of the body or of the person. The domination of new technology is reconstituting the embodied experience of time and space in modernity and, in the process, re-forming the body. New technologies are also new bodily prostheses, which offer possibilities for the body not previously available. Again, though, this can occur only within certain limits because the promise of an escape from the body as constituted in bio-history is impossible. Even in the world of virtual reality, there still is, and must be, the embodied, physically related dimensions of interchange and meaning to which the virtual always returns. In this sense, the turn back to the body in modernity is partly a search for such stable ground in a world of fragmentation and a reaffirmation of the historical links in which, as Stone (1991) says, body, technology and community constitute one another. While modern artifacts have expanded the symbol dimension and reconstituted the other dimensions of space and time, these dimensions can never be totally reconfigured by the symbolic because they are not its creation. Artifacts can change our relation to space and time, yet can never collapse these dimensions into the symbolic, reducing all of life to just one dimension. The body and artifacts are themselves multi-dimensional and, as the axes on which the relation between culture and nature turns, are themselves hybrids belonging to nature, society and discourse.

In terms of the body within modernity, the relational search for connection within difference means that I am not advocating a turn either to a purely sensual way of knowing or a purely cognitive reflexivity of the body. We cannot completely abandon the Enlightenment traditions of the West as they are so deeply ingrained in our history. Instead, we need to appreciate the possibility for maturity within the Enlightenment project: how the modes of rational thought and action established in this movement allow for critical distance and anti-authoritarian ideas. I do not want to even hint at the possibility of a return to societies like those of the Middle Ages, where intellectual and sensate experience is rigidly controlled by social authorities. However, there is a problem with classical rationality if this leads to a denial of the fleshy body and the sensual knowing that it makes possible. This form of knowledge is not to be associated with Enlightenment notions of 'irrationality', for bodily knowing has its own rationale, based as it is on the activity of the body in its relations to others and to things. Although rationally constructed knowledge has become more abstract, it is still based on activity – ways of relating to the world – involving sensitivity and other aspects of embodied knowing. While bodily knowledge has become more suppressed with the emergence of the closed body, if some of the controls over the body are relaxed as the structure of power relations begins to change in the late twentieth century – with the opening of more spaces for resistance – then something of the sensuous nature of the body can be experienced again and melded with cognitive forms of rationality. Passion and emotion can then be re-assimilated with rationality as part of the active, thinking body. Indeed, I would maintain that this is how most people function in their everyday lives: by acting on the basis of a sense of what ought to be done, drawn from experience of previous situations and the tacit knowledge this has developed, along with 'gut feelings' about what is right in the circumstances. Most people refer to this as intuition or common sense, whereas it is actually a complex interplay of knowledge and feeling.

Such everyday knowledge is often played down in the Western world where, as Northrop (1946/1979) has pointed out, a theoretical style of knowledge is more dominant, where immediate sense experience is downplayed in favour of hypotheses about hidden causal mechanisms behind events. This contrasts with the Eastern world where more aesthetic and intuitive forms of knowledge are privileged. However, these two positions can never be totally exclusive, for if, as I am arguing here, knowledge is a form of practical engagement with the world, then knowledge can never be separated from spatially and temporally located activity. The knowledge gleaned from practice may be abstracted and elaborated symbolically, yet the practical, spatio-temporal dimension is always diffracted in some way in symbolically formulated knowledge. On the one hand, the sensual is located in the actively constituted experience of time and space; while, on the other hand, theoretical knowledge is derived from symbolic practices that may depart from aesthetic immediacy. Yet because the symbolic is another dimension of space and time, it can never be completely separated from them, and knowledge can always be regarded as practice, relating back to spatio-temporal activities. The best example of this is in metaphor, where the senses of a spatially and temporally located active body are employed in the creation of symbolic meaning. Could we understand an abstract idea without a bodily sense or experience by which to place it and give it meaning, even if that idea ran contrary to embodied experience? I think not, for even in the case of a contrary idea, bodily sensation is used to understand and judge it. So even if we have not had a certain experience, such as the weightlessness of the body in outer space, we can still understand the concept of weightlessness by our very sense of being weighted.

In terms of the classical and Romanticist movements of the nineteenth and twentieth centuries that still influence our knowledge today, the attempt to synthesize aesthetic and theoretical knowledge means that we must avoid swerving in the direction of a classical modernity or a Romanticist reaction against it. The Romanticist tendency at the present time is felt strongly in terms of the rise of tribalism and the desire to swathe oneself in the protective bonds of the emotional community (Maffesoli, 1996). It can also be found in the return of social theory to a philosophical basis of Nietzscheanism, with its flight from modernity and emphasis on the irrational. Nor can we simply return to an earlier age of grotesquerie and carnival, and it must be remembered anyway that carnival was only ever a momentary release from the power structures and repression of ecclesiastical authorities in the Middle Ages. While there has been a reactionary tendency in modernity, with its bureaucratic structures of control and discipline, there has also been alongside this the tendency to open more spaces of resistance and greatly increase the scope for democratic participation. The counter or anti-modern tendencies, then, can also take on a reactionary political stance, as they tend not to discriminate between different aspects of modernity and can therefore oppose the liberating potentials of modernity as well as its oppressive features.

The move towards a relational understanding of the social world has political implications, for we strive to seek wholeness in the face of fragmentation and division, a wholeness from which new patterns of embodied activity may emerge. As Bohm says, '[if we] can include everything coherently and harmoniously in an overall whole that is undivided, unbroken, and without a border, then . . . from this will flow orderly action within the whole' (quoted in Gergen, 1991: 239). All politics, then, is life politics, where we recognize our connections to other life forms and to things, seeking not the eradication of difference but the necessity of relatedness across boundaries or borders. It is from this sense of relatedness that ethics grow and flourish. However, in this study I have suggested that the current relations between people are based on normative forms of control rather than ethical considerations. That is, through the application of norms to the behaviour of others and to ourselves, we seek to control and police activity rather than to realize it in an ethical form. In this sense, the modern subject is still in a state of immaturity, tending to look to external authorities for the validation of behaviour and applying norms created by hegemonic powers. Capabilities for autonomous action need to be disconnected from the intensification of power relations. However, to be free and autonomous agents is a state that must be realized relationally, as we are always formed as agents in relation to one another and with nature. Thus the freedom of the agent is only possible in social and political conditions that encourage autonomy and these can only be created collectively.

Ethical relations can be traced back to embodiment, which gives us a sense of our own physical strengths and weaknesses and how these are similar to those of the others who populate our world. The sense of powerfulness and vulnerability forms a connection between humans that can be elaborated into ethical concern. This is spun through the human need to co-operate in order to achieve physical or intellectual tasks and in dealing with the body's vulnerability in terms of the need to bring up the young, to deal with sickness, injury and death. All societies have dealt with these things in different ways and have elaborated a variety of ethical codes around them. The vulnerability and openness to one another which we experience is based upon our embodiment as human beings, but this in itself does not dictate the particular form of ethical codes. These depend upon the way we develop such codes through communicative interactions in various social and historical contexts. Yet, in the West, our moral codes have become focused more on a concern for control than for care, for regulating one another rather than for caring for each other. The powers of the body to transform the socio-natural world are also kept in check through normative control and institutional regulation, as opposed to the ethical consideration of what changes the powerful body may effect and how those powers should be directed.

The effects of normative control on the body are ones of armouring, where vulnerability and openness become dangers that need to be closed off behind layers of defensiveness. Thus the modern communicative body becomes one that hides as much as it reveals. In attempting to overcome some of this concealment, the ethical relation forged between modern people would have to focus more on care and concern for the other than the attempt to bring behaviour into line with normative regulations. In this way, an embodied rationality and ethical forms of practice may emerge out of daily living. For O'Neill (1985), such rationality would lead to a strengthening of the family and all the social relations based around it. However, we need to be careful about such an idea, for nowhere does O'Neill define exactly what he means by the family: if this refers to the human family, then fine, for such a notion can be inclusive, emphasizing the necessary relatedness of all human beings at various different levels. Other definitions of the family could prove exclusionary and would need to be avoided. However, having said this, the idea is similar to what I am advocating here: that embodiment within a network of relations to others, and the sense of openness and vulnerability this can bring, should lead to an emphasis upon our necessary interconnectedness as humans and to an ethics of care and responsibility.

In terms of our relations to the non-human, I have already suggested that we are always in some way related to the other creatures and things of the world, so that ethical considerations should once more be an issue. This does not arise from any demands to confront them as 'original nature', but to consider what our relationship to them should be and how we should conduct ourselves in that relationship. The attitude of modern Western people towards the non-human world has often been one of mastery and manipulation, taking control of the world and seeing it only as a resource to be exploited. The issue is not one of our intervention in nature, or particularly of our manipulation of it; rather, it is a question of what our relation to nature should be? What constitutes good and bad intervention? For example, with reference to the growing possibilities for the genetic engineering of human beings, what would constitute good or bad intervention? While it is not my aim to address such questions here, I offer a brief if tentative suggestion: that it would be ethical to consider gene therapy which might prevent the development of certain medical conditions, but not therapy that would select or eradicate certain human attributes. This would, of course, depend on what was defined as a medical condition, and a new round of the ethical debate would begin. However, in many ways this only serves to illustrate my point: that ethical and political considerations are very much based on our current social and historical relations with nature and cannot be divorced from that context. As these relations change, so do our ethical dilemmas.

I have sought in this book to show how we must begin to understand bodies, persons and objects as located and interrelated within socio-ecological contexts, including the artifacts that mediate these relations. The emphasis on embodied relatedness means we can no longer rest happy with the division of humans into body and mind, the material and the mental, the emotions and rationality, nor with the private self cast against others in the public domain. It is in this sense that I seek to understand modern individuals as bodies of thought – as theoretical, aesthetic, symbolic and bodily beings, whose existence is multi-dimensional and fundamentally related to other people and objects in the world.

References

Althusser, Louis (1971) *Lenin and Philosophy and Other Essays*. London: New Left Books.

Ardrey, R. (1966) *The Territorial Imperative*. New York: Atheneum.

Armon-Jones, Claire (1986) 'The thesis of constructionism', in Rom Harré (ed.), *The Social Construction of Emotions*. Oxford: Blackwell.

Averill, James R. (1986) 'The acquisition of emotions during adulthood', in Rom Harré (ed.), *The Social Construction of Emotions*. Oxford: Blackwell.

Badcock, Christopher (1991) *Evolution and Individual Behaviour: an Introduction to Human Sociobiology*. Oxford: Blackwell.

Bakhtin, Mikhail M. (1984) *Rabelais and his World,* trans. Hélène Iswolsky. Bloomington, IN: Indiana University Press.

Bakhtin, Mikhail M. (1986) *Speech Genres and Other Late Essays*, trans. V.W. McGee. Austin: Texas University Press.

Bakhurst, David (1991) *Consciousness and Revolution in Soviet Philosophy: from the Bolsheviks to Evald Ilyenkov*. Cambridge: Cambridge University Press.

Barker, Francis (1995) *The Tremulous Private Body: Essays on Subjection*. Ann Arbor: University of Michigan Press.

Bateson, Gregory (1973) *Steps to an Ecology of Mind: Collected Essays in Anthropology, Psychiatry, Evolution and Epistemology*. St Albans: Paladin.

Baudrillard, Jean (1983) *Simulations*. New York: Semiotext(e).

Baudrillard, Jean (1988) *Selected Writings*, ed. Mark Poster. Cambridge: Polity Press.

Bauman, Zygmunt (1991) *Modernity and Ambivalence*. Cambridge: Polity Press.

Beck, U., Giddens, A. and Lash, S. (1994) *Reflexive Modernization: Politics, Tradition and Aesthetics in the Modern Social Order*. Cambridge: Polity Press.

Benjamin, Jessica (1990) *The Bonds of Love: Psychoanalysis, Feminism and the Problem of Domination*. London: Virago.

Benjamin, Jessica (1995) *Like Subjects, Love Objects: Essays on Recognition and Sexual Difference*. New Haven, CT: Yale University Press.

Benton, Ted (1991) 'Biology and social science: why the return of the repressed should be given a (cautious) welcome', *Sociology*, 25 (1): 1–29.

Berman, Marshall (1982) *All That is Solid Melts into Air*. London: Verso.

Bhaskar, Roy (1989) *Reclaiming Reality: a Critical Introduction to Contemporary Philosophy*. London: Verso.

Bhaskar, Roy (1991) *Philosophy and the Idea of Freedom*. Oxford: Blackwell.

Billig, M., Condor, S., Edwards, D., Gane, M., Middleton, D. and Radley, A. (1988) *Ideological Dilemmas: a Social Psychology of Everyday Thinking*. London: Sage.

Borchert, Catherine M. and Zihlman, Adrienne L. (1990) 'The ontogeny and phylogeny of symbolizing', in M. LeCron Foster and L.J. Botscharow (eds), *The Life of Symbols*. Boulder, CO: Westview Press.

Bourdieu, Pierre (1977) *Outline of a Theory of Practice,* trans. R. Nice. Cambridge: Cambridge University Press.

Bourdieu, Pierre (1984) *Distinction: a Social Critique of the Judgment of Taste*, trans. R. Nice. London: Routledge.

Bourdieu, Pierre (1990) *The Logic of Practice*, trans. R. Nice. Cambridge: Polity Press.

Bourdieu, Pierre (1991) *Language and Symbolic Power*, trans. G. Raymond and M. Adamson. Cambridge: Polity Press.

Braudel, Fernand (1973) *The Mediterranean and the Mediterranean World in the Age of Philip II*, 2 vols, trans. S. Reynolds. London: Collins.

Braudel, Fernand (1977) *Afterthoughts on Material Civilization and Capitalism*. London: Johns Hopkins University Press.

Burkitt, Ian (1991) *Social Selves: Theories of the Social Formation of Personality*. London: Sage.

Burkitt, Ian (1993) 'Overcoming metaphysics: Elias and Foucault on power and freedom', *Philosophy of the Social Sciences*, 23 (1): 50–72.

Burkitt, Ian (1996) 'Civilization and ambivalence', *British Journal of Sociology*, 47 (1): 135–50.

Burkitt, Ian (1998) 'Sexuality and gender identity: from a discursive to a relational analysis', *Sociological Review*, 46 (3): 483–504.

Butler, Judith (1990) *Gender Trouble: Feminism and the Subversion of Identity*. New York: Routledge.

Butler, Judith (1993) *Bodies that Matter: on the Discursive Limits of 'Sex'*. New York: Routledge.

Butler, Judith (1997) *Excitable Speech: a Politics of the Performative*. New York: Routledge.

Buytendijk, F.J.J. (1974) *Prolegomena to an Anthropological Physiology*. Pittsburgh: Duquesne University Press.

Classen, Constance (1993) *Worlds of Sense: Exploring the Senses in History and across Cultures*. London: Routledge.

Collins, Randall (1990) 'Stratification, emotional energy, and the transient emotions', in T.D. Kemper (ed.), *Research Agendas in the Sociology of Emotions*. Albany: SUNY Press.

Costall, Alan (1995) 'Socializing affordances', *Theory and Psychology*, 5 (4): 467–81.

Craib, Ian (1995) 'Some comments on the sociology of the emotions', *Sociology*, 29 (1): 151–8.

Craib, Ian (1997) 'Social constructionism as a social psychosis', *Sociology*, 31 (1): 1–15.

Danziger, K. (1997) 'The varieties of social construction', *Theory and Psychology*, 7 (3): 399–416.

Davidson, Arnold I. (1986) 'Archaeology, genealogy, ethics', in David Couzens Hoy (ed.), *Foucault: a Critical Reader*. Oxford: Blackwell.

Davis, Kathy (1997) 'Embody-ing theory: beyond modernist and postmodernist readings of the body', in Kathy Davis (ed.), *Embodied Practices: Feminist Perspectives on the Body*. London: Sage.

Dawkins, Richard (1986) *The Blind Watchmaker*. London: Longman.

Dawkins, Richard (1989) *The Selfish Gene*. Oxford: Oxford University Press.

Deleuze, Gilles and Guattari, Félix (1984) *Anti-Oedipus: Capitalism and Schizophrenia*, trans. R. Hurley, M. Seem and H.R. Lane. London: Athlone.

Deleuze, Gilles and Guattari, Félix (1988) *A Thousand Plateaux: Capitalism and Schizophrenia*, trans. B. Massumi. London: Athlone.

Denzin, Norman K. (1984) *On Understanding Emotion*. San Francisco: Jossey-Bass.

Denzin, Norman K. (1991) *Images of Postmodern Society: Social Theory and Contemporary Cinema*. London: Sage.

Descartes, René (1640/1968) *Discourse on Method and The Meditations*, trans. F.E. Sutcliffe. London: Penguin.

Douglas, Mary (1966) *Purity and Danger: an Analysis of the Concepts of Pollution and Taboo.* London: Routledge.

Duncombe, J. and Marsden, D. (1993) 'Love and intimacy: the gender division of emotion and "emotion work" ', *Sociology*, 27 (2): 221–41.

Edwards, D., Ashmore, M. and Potter, J. (1995) 'Death and furniture: the rhetoric, politics and theology of bottom line arguments against relativism', *History of The Human Sciences*, 8 (2): 25–49.

Elias, Norbert (1978) *The Civilizing Process*, vol. I: *The History of Manners,* trans. E. Jephcott. Oxford: Blackwell.

Elias, Norbert (1982) *The Civilizing Process*, vol. II: *State Formation and Civilization*, trans. E. Jephcott. Oxford: Blackwell.

Elias, Norbert (1983) *The Court Society*, trans. E. Jephcott. Oxford: Blackwell.

Elias, Norbert (1985) *The Loneliness of the Dying*, trans. E. Jephcott. Oxford: Blackwell.

Elias, Norbert (1987a) *Involvement and Detachment*, trans. E. Jephcott. Oxford: Blackwell.

Elias, Norbert (1987b) 'On human beings and their emotions: a process-sociological essay', *Theory, Culture and Society*, 4 (2–3): 339–61.

Elias, Norbert (1988) 'Violence and civilization: the state monopoly of physical violence and its infringement', in J. Keane (ed.), *Civil Society and the State: New European Perspectives.* London: Verso.

Elias, Norbert (1991a) *The Society of Individuals*, trans. E. Jephcott. Oxford: Blackwell.

Elias, Norbert (1991b) *The Symbol Theory*, ed. R. Kilminster. London: Sage.

Falk, Pasi (1994) *The Consuming Body*. London: Sage.

Foucault, Michel (1967) *Madness and Civilization*, trans. R. Howard. London: Tavistock.

Foucault, Michel (1977) *Discipline and Punish: the Birth of the Prison*, trans. Alan Sheridan. London: Penguin.

Foucault, Michel (1979) *The History of Sexuality*, vol. I, trans. R. Hurley. London: Penguin.

Foucault, Michel (1982) 'Afterword: the subject and power', in H.L. Dreyfus and P. Rabinow, *Michel Foucault: Beyond Structuralism and Hermeneutics*. Brighton: Harvester.

Foucault, Michel (1986a) *The History of Sexuality*, vol. II: *The Use of Pleasure*, trans. R. Hurley. London: Penguin.

Foucault, Michel (1986b) 'Nietzsche/genealogy/history', in P. Rabinow (ed.), *The Foucault Reader*. London: Penguin.

Foucault, Michel (1986c) 'What is Enlightenment?', in P. Rabinow (ed.), *The Foucault Reader*. London: Penguin.

Foucault, Michel (1988) *The History of Sexuality*, vol. III: *The Care of the Self*, trans. R. Hurley. London: Penguin.

Freud, Sigmund (1930) *Civilization and its Discontents*. London: The Hogarth Press.

Futuyama, Douglas J. (1995) *Science on Trial: the Case for Evolution*. Sunderland, MA: Sinaver Associates.

Gardiner, Michael (1996) 'Alterity and ethics: a dialogical perspective', *Theory, Culture and Society*, 13 (2): 121–43.

Gatens, Moira (1996) *Imaginary Bodies: Ethics, Power and Corporeality*. London: Routledge.

Geras, Norman (1983) *Marx and Human Nature: Refutation of a Legend*. London: Verso.

Gergen, Kenneth J. (1991) *The Saturated Self: Dilemmas of Identity in Contemporary Life*. New York: Basic Books.

Gergen, Kenneth J. (1994a) *Realities and Relationships: Soundings in Social Construction*. Cambridge, MA: Harvard University Press.

Gergen, Kenneth J. (1994b) 'The limits of pure critique', in H.W. Simons and M. Billig (eds), *After Postmodernism*. London: Sage.

Gergen, Kenneth J. (1995) 'Metaphor and monophony in 20th-century psychology of emotions', *History of the Human Sciences*, 8 (2): 1–23.

Gergen, Kenneth J. (1997) 'The place of the psyche in a constructed world', *Theory and Psychology*, 7 (6): 723–46.

Gibson, J.J. (1979) *The Ecological Approach to Visual Perception*. Boston, MA: Houghton Mifflin.

Giddens, Anthony (1984) *The Constitution of Society: Outline of the Theory of Structuration*. Cambridge: Polity Press.

Giddens, Anthony (1987) *Social Theory and Modern Sociology*. Cambridge: Polity Press.

Giddens, Anthony (1990) *The Consequences of Modernity*. Cambridge: Polity Press.

Giddens, Anthony (1991) *Modernity and Self-Identity: Self and Society in the Late Modern Age*. Cambridge: Polity Press.

Gilligan, Carol (1982) *In a Different Voice: Psychological Theory and Women's Development*. Cambridge, MA: Harvard University Press.

Grosz, Elizabeth (1994) *Volatile Bodies: Towards a Corporeal Feminism*. Bloomington, Ind.: Indiana University Press.

Hammond, M., Howarth, J. and Keat, R. (1991) *Understanding Phenomenology*. Oxford: Blackwell.

Hampshire, Stuart (1987) *Spinoza: an Introduction to his Philosophical Thought*. Harmondsworth: Penguin.

Haraway, Donna J. (1991) *Simians, Cyborgs and Women: the Reinvention of Nature*. London: Free Association Press.

Haraway, Donna J. (1992) *Primate Visions: Gender, Race, and Nature in the World of Modern Science*. London: Verso.

Harré, Rom (ed.) (1986) *The Social Construction of Emotions*. Oxford: Blackwell.

Harré, Rom (1990) 'Exploring the human *Umwelt*', in R. Bhaskar (ed.), *Harré and his Critics: Essays in Honour of Rom Harré with his Commentary on Them*. Oxford: Blackwell.

Harré, Rom (1991a) *Physical Being: a Theory for a Corporeal Psychology*. Oxford: Blackwell.

Harré, Rom (1991b) 'The discursive production of selves', *Theory and Psychology*, 1 (1): 51–63.

Harré, Rom (1993) *Social Being*, 2nd edn. Oxford: Blackwell.

Harré, Rom and Gillett, Grant (1994) *The Discursive Mind*. Thousand Oaks, CA: Sage.

Hartsock, Nancy C.M. (1983) 'The feminist standpoint: developing the ground for a specifically feminist historical materialism', in Sandra Harding and Merrill B. Hintikka (eds), *Discovering Reality*. Dordrecht: D. Reidel.

Harvey, David (1990) *The Condition of Postmodernity: an Enquiry into the Origins of Cultural Change*. Oxford: Blackwell.

Harvey, David (1993) 'The nature of environment: the dialectics of social and environmental change'. Paper delivered at the Detraditionalization Conference, Lancaster University.

Heidegger, Martin (1977) 'The age of the world picture', in M. Heidegger, *The Question Concerning Technology and Other Essays*, trans. W. Lovitt. New York: Harper Colophon Books.

Hirst, P. and Woolley, P. (1982) *Social Relations and Human Attributes*. London: Tavistock.

Hochschild, Arlie R. (1983) *The Managed Heart: Commercialization of Human Feeling*. Berkeley, CA: University of California Press.

Hollingdale, R.J. (1965) *Nietzsche: the Man and his Philosophy*. London: Routledge and Kegan Paul.

Hood-Williams, John (1996) 'Goodbye to sex and gender', *Sociological Review*, 44 (1): 1–16.

Hood-Williams, John (1997) 'Real sex/fake gender: a reply to Robert Willmott', *Sociological Review*, 45 (1): 42–58.

Ilyenkov, Evald V. (1977) *Dialectical Logic: Essays in its History and Theory*, trans. H. Campbell Creighton. Moscow: Progress Publishers.

Jackson, Stevi (1993) 'Even sociologists fall in love: an exploration in the sociology of emotions', *Sociology*, 27 (2): 201–20.

Jameson, Fredric (1991) *Postmodernism, or the Cultural Logic of Late Capitalism*. London: Verso.

Jay, Martin (1986) 'In the empire of the gaze: Foucault and the denigration of vision in twentieth-century French thought', in David Couzens Hoy (ed.), *Foucault: a Critical Reader*. Oxford: Blackwell.

Johnson, Mark (1987) *The Body in the Mind: the Bodily Basis of Meaning, Imagination, and Reason*. Chicago: Chicago University Press.

Keat, Russell (1986) 'The human body in social theory: Reich, Foucault and the repressive hypothesis', *Radical Philosophy*, 42: 24–32.

Kemper, Theodore D. (1981) 'Social constructionist and positivist approaches to the sociology of emotions', *American Journal of Sociology*, 87: 336–62.

Kemper, Theodore D. (ed.) (1990a) *Research Agendas in the Sociology of Emotions*. Albany: SUNY Press.

Kemper, Theodore D. (1990b) 'Social relations and emotions: a structural approach', in T.D. Kemper (ed.), *Research Agendas in the Sociology of Emotions*. Albany: SUNY Press.

Kögler, Hans-Herbert (1997) 'Alienation as epistemological source: reflexivity and social background after Mannheim and Bourdieu', *Social Epistemology*, 11 (2): 141–64.

Latour, Bruno (1993) *We Have Never Been Modern*, trans. C. Porter. London: Harvester Wheatsheaf.

Leakey, Richard E. (1981) *The Making of Mankind*. London: Michael Joseph.

Leakey, Richard E. and Lewin, Roger (1977) *Origins: What New Discoveries Reveal about the Emergence of our Species and its Possible Future*. London: Macdonald and Jones.

Lefebvre, H. (1971) *The Critique of Everyday Life*. Harmondsworth: Penguin.

Leontyev, A.A. (1981) 'Sign and activity', in James V. Wertsch (ed.), *The Concept of Activity in Soviet Psychology*. Armonk: M. E. Sharpe.

Leontyev, A.N. (1978) *Activity, Consciousness and Personality*. Englewood Cliffs, NJ: Prentice-Hall.

Leontyev, A.N. (1981) *Problems of the Development of the Mind*. Moscow: Progress Publishers.

Levins, Richard and Lewontin, Richard (1985) *The Dialectical Biologist*. Cambridge, MA: Harvard University Press.

Livesay, Jeff (1989) 'Structuration theory and the unacknowledged conditions of action', *Theory, Culture and Society*, 6 (2): 263–92.

Lorenz, Konrad (1963) *On Aggression*, trans. M. Latzke. London: Methuen.

McNamee, Shelia and Gergen, K.J. (1999) *Relational Responsibility*. Thousand Oaks: Sage.

Maffesoli, Michel (1996) *The Time of the Tribes: the Decline of Individualism in Mass Society*. London: Sage.

Martin, Emily (1989) *The Woman in the Body: a Cultural Analysis of Reproduction*. Buckingham: Open University Press.

Marx, Karl (1845/1977) 'Theses on Feuerbach', in David McLellan (ed.), *Karl Marx: Selected Writings*. Oxford: Oxford University Press.

Marx, K. and Engels, F. (1970) *The German Ideology*. London: Lawrence and Wishart.

Mauss, Marcel (1979) *Sociology and Psychology*. London: Routledge.

Mead, George Herbert (1934) *Mind, Self and Society from the Standpoint of a Social Behaviourist*, ed. C.W. Morris. Chicago: Chicago University Press.

Mead, George Herbert (1964) *On Social Psychology: Selected Papers*, ed. A.L. Strauss. Chicago: Chicago University Press.

Mellor, Philip A. and Shilling, Chris (1997) *Re-forming the Body: Religion, Community and Modernity*. London: Sage.

Merleau-Ponty, Maurice (1962) *Phenomenology of Perception*, trans. C. Smith. London: Routledge.

Murphy, R. (1994) 'The sociological construction of science without nature', *Sociology*, 28 (4): 957–74.

Nietzsche, Friedrich (1973) *Beyond Good and Evil*, trans. R.J. Hollingdale. Harmondsworth: Penguin.

Nietzsche, Friedrich (1977) *The Nietzsche Reader*, trans. and ed. R.J. Hollingdale. Harmondsworth: Penguin.

Northrop, F.S.C. (1946/1979) *The Meeting of East and West: an Inquiry Concerning World Understanding*. Woodbridge, Conn.: Oxbow Press.

O'Neill, John (1985) *Five Bodies: the Human Shape of Modern Society*. Ithaca: Cornell University Press.

Pateman, Carole (1988) *The Sexual Contract*. Cambridge: Polity Press.

Pinker, Steven (1998) *How the Mind Works*. London: Allen Lane/Penguin.

Plumwood, Val (1993) *Feminism and the Mastery of Nature*. London: Routledge.

Reich, Wilhelm (1950) *Character Analysis*, trans. T.P. Wolfe. London: Vision Press.

Rorty, Richard (1980) *Philosophy and the Mirror of Nature*. Oxford: Blackwell.

Schatzki, Theodore R. (1993) 'Wittgenstein: mind, body, and society', *Journal for the Theory of Social Behaviour*, 23 (3): 285–313.

Scheff, Thomas J. (1990a) *Microsociology: Discourse, Emotion, and Social Structure*. Chicago: Chicago University Press.

Scheff, Thomas J. (1990b) 'Socialization of emotions: pride and shame as causal agents', in T.D. Kemper (ed.), *Research Agendas in the Sociology of Emotions*. Albany: SUNY Press.

Scott, Ann (1998) '(Productively) caught in the middle: the homoeopathic body in the borderlands'. Paper presented at the British Sociological Association Annual Conference, Edinburgh.

Sève, Lucien (1978) *Man in Marxist Theory and the Psychology of Personality*, trans. John McGreal. Brighton: Harvester.

Shilling, Chris (1993) *The Body and Social Theory*. London: Sage.

Shotter, John (1992) 'Is Bhaskar's critical realism only a theoretical realism?', *History of the Human Sciences*, 5 (3): 157–73.

Shotter, John (1993a) *Conversational Realities: Constructing Life through Language*. London: Sage.

Shotter, J. (1993b) *Cultural Politics of Everyday Life: Social Constructionism, Rhetoric and Knowing of the Third Kind*. Buckingham: Open University Press.

Simmel, Georg (1903/1971) 'The metropolis and mental life', in *On Individuality and Social Forms*, ed. Donald N. Levine. Chicago: Chicago University Press.

Smart, Barry (1993) *Postmodernity*. London: Routledge.

Smith, Adam T. (1994) 'Fictions of emergence: Foucault/genealogy/Nietzsche', *Philosophy of the Social Sciences*, 24 (1): 41–54.

Stone, Allucquere R. (1991) 'Will the real body please stand up? Boundary stories about virtual cultures', in Micheal Benedikt (ed.), *Cyberspace: First Steps*. Cambridge, MA: MIT Press.

Taylor, Timothy (1997) *The Prehistory of Sex: Four Million Years of Human Sexual Culture*. London: Fourth Estate.

Thompson, John B. (1991) 'Editor's introduction', in Pierre Bourdieu, *Language and Symbolic Power*. Cambridge: Polity Press.

Tseëlon, Efrat (1992) 'Is the presented self sincere? Goffman, impression management and the postmodern self', *Theory, Culture and Society*, 9 (2): 115–28.

Turner, Bryan S. (1984) *The Body and Society: Explorations in Social Theory*. Oxford: Basil Blackwell.

Turner, Bryan S. (1992) *Regulating Bodies: Essays in Medical Sociology*. London: Routledge.

Varela, F.J., Thompson, E. and Rosch, E. (1991) *The Embodied Mind: Cognitive Science and Human Experience*. Cambridge, MA: MIT Press.

Vološinov, V.N. (1986) *Marxism and the Philosophy of Language*, trans. L. Matejka and I.R. Titunik. Cambridge, MA: Harvard University Press.

Vygotsky, L.S. (1987) 'Thinking and speech', in R.W. Rieber and A.S. Carton (eds), *The Collected Works of L.S. Vygotsky*, vol. I: *Problems of General Psychology*, trans. N. Minick. New York: Plenum Press.

Washburn, Sherwood L. (1960) 'Tools and human evolution', *Scientific American*, 203 (3): 63–75.

Weber, Max (1930) *The Protestant Ethic and the Spirit of Capitalism*, trans. Talcott Parsons. London: George Allen and Unwin.

Weber, Max (1947) *The Theory of Social and Economic Organization*, trans. A.M. Henderson and T. Parsons. New York: Oxford University Press.

Willmott, Robert (1996) 'Resisting sex/gender conflation: a rejoinder to John Hood-Williams', *Sociological Review*, 44 (4): 728–45.

Wittgenstein, Ludwig (1953) *Philosophical Investigations*, trans. G.E.M. Anscombe. Oxford: Blackwell.

Wittgenstein, Ludwig (1967) *Zettel*, ed. and trans. G.E.M. Anscombe. Oxford: Blackwell.

Young, Iris Marion (1990) *Throwing Like a Girl and Other Essays in Feminist Philosophy and Social Theory*. Bloomington, Ind.: Indiana University Press.

Index